# The Blue Guides

D1642995

# Malta & Gozo

Geoffrey Aquilina Ross

A&C Black • London
WW Norton • New York

5th edition © Geoffrey Aquilina Ross, September 2000
Published by A & C Black (Publishers) Limited
35 Bedford Row, London WC1R 4JH

Maps and plans drawn by RJS Associates, © A&C Black
Plans of Tarxien, Hagar Qim, and Mnajdra are reproduced courtesy of Mr D.H. Trump

Illustrations © Peter Spells

A CIP catalogue record of this book is available from the British Library.

ISBN  0–7136–5282–9

Published in the United States of America by
WW Norton and Company Inc.
500 Fifth Avenue, New York, NY 10110

Published simultaneously in Canada by
Penguin Books Canada Limited
10 Alcorn Avenue, Toronto
Ontario M4V 3B2

ISBN  0–393–32136–3 USA

The author and the publishers have done their best to ensure the accuracy of all the information in Blue Guide Malta and Gozo; however, they can accept no responsibility for any
loss, injury or inconvenience sustained by any traveller as a result of information or advice
contained in the guide.

**Geoffrey Aquilina Ross** is currently a Malta-based journalist and writer. For many years
a London magazine journalist and a columnist on London's *Evening Standard*, he also edited
national magazines and was the concept editor of *FHM*, one of today's most successful
men's magazines. He has written a number of travel books and an amusing study, *How to
Survive the Male Menopause*, that was translated into many languages.

**Ann Monsarrat**, a member of the Maltese Archaeological Society, widow of novelist
Nicholas Monsarrat, is a journalist and writer living on Gozo. For this edition of the Blue
Guide, Ms Monsarrat has very kindly compiled the sections on 'Ancient Malta' and
'Medieval times'.

**Cover photograph**: Detail of a traditional Maltese fishing boat. © Phil Robinson.

Printed and bound in Great Britain by Butler & Tanner Ltd., Frome and London.

# Contents

## Maps and plans

# Introduction to the Maltese Islands

The Maltese Islands lie midway between Gibraltar to the west and Port Said in Egypt to the east. To the north is Sicily and to the south the North African coast of Libya.

The archipelago is made up of three populated islands, Malta, Gozo and tiny Comino (with just one resort hotel and a population of five), and three uninhabited rocks, the largest of which, Filfla, is a bird sanctuary. The total area is 400sq km of which Malta, the largest island, takes up 320sq km. There are no mountains or rivers, just low hills to give the countryside definition. The coastline to the west is edged with sheer cliffs while, to the east, it is indented with bays and creeks. There are only a few sandy beaches but the numerous stretches of smooth white rock on the coastline with many a lido and watersport facility, more than make up for this.

The capital is Valletta, sitting elegantly above the Grand Harbour, the Islands' deep harbour that was once the base for ships of war but is now the port of call of cruise liners whose passengers are armed with nothing more sinister than credit cards and a camera.

In the days when the known world centred on the Mediterranean Sea, the Islands stood at the very crossroads of activity. For centuries, as the tides of war swept the region, so Fortress Malta with its sheltered deepwater harbours played a key role. The Islands retain traces of most episodes of a history that was often dramatically turbulent and brutal, but today, as we see them bathed in sunshine and surrounded by clear deep waters, it is easy to forget that they were once more than just holiday destinations. In fact, they are a splendid mixture of historical importance and sunshine resort.

The history embraces Neolithic temples older than the Pyramids; grand palaces built by the Knights of St John; great fortresses where history was made; a medieval walled city, lined with patrician houses, that is still alive and thriving; and, everywhere, signs of religious devotion, not least of which are the Baroque parish churches with their painted ceilings and faux marble columns. Some of these churches are so dressed up that visitors unfamiliar with Roman Catholic Baroque tradition in the Mediterranean often think they have walked into a cathedral rather than a simple village's centre of devotion.

For visitors there are excellent hotels to choose from and restaurants where the finest fresh fish is a speciality, together with a relaxed way of life and beach facilities that are ever improving.

There has probably never been a better time to visit the Islands than now. In recent years hotels have increased in number and quality, and many long established hotels have been upgraded to bring them into line with recognised international grades.

New restaurants have opened too, bringing much higher standards to a section of Maltese life that was once notoriously lacking in quality. Although there are inevitable exceptions and bad days, it is now possible to eat well at all levels.

To meet these changes, more information on Where to stay and Where to eat has been included in the guide. Indications of what they might cost are correct at time of writing, but bear in mind that prices in Malta and Gozo, as elsewhere, are subject to change.

Museums too are being upgraded and reorganised, and certain items and objets d'art have been moved between museums in an attempt to rationalise the way historical artefacts found on the Islands are displayed. With the financial help of international agencies like UNESCO and international companies like American Express, many sites of special interest are being restored to former glory. Malta's most important painting, *The Beheading of St John* by Caravaggio (the painter's only signed work), was restored in Florence thanks to funds made available by the Italian government. The magnificent painting hangs in the Oratory of Valletta's St John's Co-Cathedral.

Although the Islands have welcomed overseas investment, particularly in setting up light industry (for which the government has established a wide range of inducements and tax benefits), they depend on the tourist industry for the major portion of their revenue. Current figures put the number of travellers passing through Malta International Airport and arriving by sea on cruise liners at more than one million per annum. With the ever-increasing popularity of Mediterranean cruises and the enormous size of today's international liners, numbers of visitors arriving by sea are set to grow considerably. Although these passengers may not be on the Islands for more than a few hours—and on some days as many as 3000 may step ashore—their spending power while they tour Valletta and the important sites injects welcome money into the economy. A new sea terminal is being built in the Grand Harbour to greet them.

Malta may be small but there is a lot to see and do. If you are driving—and it is worth renting a car for a day or two as this is really the only way to explore or get around—it is easy to get lost, as even the locals do, in the winding country roads where dry rubble walls edge every field and where every village with its dominating parish church seems to be identical to its neighbour.

The Islands generously repay anyone exploring, whether looking for a page of history or a secluded place to swim. There is more than first greets the eye.

# Highlights

### *Principal sights*

#### Valletta
The Grand Master's Palace
St John's Co-Cathedral with its treasures and Caravaggio's masterpiece the
*Beheading of St John the Baptist*
The superb Grand Harbour
The remarkable Church of St Paul Shipwreck

#### Mdina
The rich Cathedral dedicated to St Paul
The charming medieval walled city itself

#### The Neolithic temples
Ħaġar Qim and Mnajdra near Wied iż-Żurrieq

## Gozo

In Victoria, the walled Citadel with its Cathedral
The Inland Sea with Fungus Rock
Xlendi Bay
Ta' Pinu Sanctuary
Ġgantija Neolithic temples

## *Boat cruises*

See Malta and Gozo from the sea.

In Malta, a company called **Captain Morgan** offers a variety of cruises that set off from Sliema's Strand. They range from a leisurely tour of the Grand Harbour to a day out on a gracious twin-masted yacht complete with gourmet food. Sail around Malta if you wish.

In Gozo, **Xlendi Pleasure Cruises** set out from Xlendi or Marsalforn with tours of the Gozo and Comino coastlines. Many stops for swimming and snorkeling.The company's *Gozo Princess* also does night cruises that come complete with buffet and live music.

All hotels and travel agencies have details.

## *Beaches*

**Ghadira (Mellieħa Bay)**: Malta's longest and most popular sandy beach. Many cafés and beach establishments. Full hire facilities. Paragliding too. Parking on road along length of beach.
*Bus: 44 45 48 441 645*

**Għajn Tuffieħa**: down a steep track or endless steps. Superb setting with beach rarely crowded due to difficult access. Small beach concession on the sands in summer months sells cold drinks and hires out umbrellas, etc.
*Bus: 47 51 52 652*

**Ġnejna**: Small picturesque bay with gritty sand. Popular with families and children. Concession offers full catering facilities, umbrellas and beds and boats, canoes. Parking beach level.
*Bus: 47 as far as Mġarr. Long walk, steep hill*

**Golden Bay**: Popular family beach with small concession selling cold drinks and snacks and renting out canoes, pedalos, jet skis etc. Below Golden Bay hotel. Cars park on hill down to beach.
*Bus: 47 51 52 652*

**Ramla** in Gozo: the Islands' most popular beach and the only sandy one. Selection of cafés but only simple hire facilities. No boats. Crowded parking.
*Bus: 42 43*

**Comino**: nowhere is finer than the Blue Lagoon but it can be crowded in high summer. No facilities at all, so take picnics or catered boat trip. Hotel has its own private beach with full facilities.
*Ferry from Ċirkewwa or Mġarr, Gozo.*

# PRACTICAL INFORMATION

## Fact file

**Airport**  Malta International Airport: at Gudja, 9km from the capital.
**Capital**  Valletta.
**Climate**  Mediterranean (for details see *Climate and geology* below).
**Electricity**  240 volts/single phase/50 cycles.
**Geology**  The Islands are composed of various limestone strata with deposits of clay. There are no rivers as such and the rivulets of water that trickle down the rocky valleys in periods of heavy rain dry up in summer. But the Islands' patches of rich soil make it fertile. The small terraced fields protected by dry stone walls produce excellent crops for local consumption and for export. Maltese vegetables and fruit, especially oranges, are highly flavoursome. Gozo, with greater stretches of farming land, is more fertile than the sister island of Malta where towns, factory estates and ribbon-development have encroached on fertile ground.
**International dialling code**  356.
**Language**  *Malti* (Maltese) and English are both official languages of the Islands although English is spoken less (and less well) than formerly. Many Maltese speak Italian. See also p 34.
**Nationality**  The nation is Maltese, but the people from Gozo are Gozitan.
**Population**  375,000. Of these 345,000 live in Malta. The urban areas of Malta are densely populated. It is estimated that there are more than this number of Maltese living abroad, the majority in Canada and Australia as a result of mass emigration after World War Two.
**Religion**  Roman Catholicism.
**Time zone**  Central European Time (CET), i.e. GMT + 1 hour. Between the last Sunday of March and the last Sunday of October, Malta moves with central Europe to Summer Time. Clocks are then a further hour ahead of GMT.
**Water**  All tap water is drinkable although sometimes it is oddly flavoured. Many Maltese families drink only locally bottled mineral water. Rainfall is insufficient to supply fresh water for consumption and crop irrigation, but the shortage is rectified by a number of reverse osmosis water establishments that convert sea water into drinking water (at great expense).
**Weights and measures**  Metric.

 ## Planning your trip

### Climate

In winter the temperatures rarely fall below 12°C (54°F) and snow and frost are unknown. Rain is only likely between November and March, creating an average rainfall of 500mm. Sudden storms, winds and brief periods of hailstones the size of golf balls can sweep over the Islands during February and March, but these never last long.

Apart from a short-lived shower between April and September there is virtually non-stop sunshine.

During August temperatures hover at or above 37°C (100°F). In 1999 a record 43.8°C (111°F) was set on 10 August—appropriate perhaps, since this date is the feast day of St Lawrence, who met his martyrdom being grilled.

In common with Europe, temperatures in Malta are registered as Celsius grades, not Fahrenheit. For quick reference:

| | |
|---|---|
| 0°C = 32°F | 20°C=68°F |
| 10°C =50°F | 25°C=75°F |
| 15°C=60°F | 30°C=86°F |

April, May, early June and then October and November are generally considered the best months for a visit if you dislike the heat. The hottest months, July and August, are best suited to visitors who simply want to swim and laze in the sun. September may be humid. Watersports at this time are, of course, excellent.

## Passports and formalities

Visitors from the EU require a valid passport or identity card. Visitors from the Commonwealth, Japan and the USA require a valid passport. Other nationals will also need a visa.

Entry is granted for a maximum of three months as a tourist. To work in the Maltese Islands a work permit is necessary.

If you wish to stay longer than three months, or to take up residence, you should apply to the Immigration Police at Police Headquarters, Calcedonius Street, Floriana. ☎ 224002.

## Customs regulations

Items for personal use are not liable to duty. Each adult is permitted a duty-free allowance of 200 cigarettes, or their equivalent in cigars or tobacco, together with one litre of spirits and one litre of wine, and a reasonable quantity of perfume or toilet water.

These allowances are not normally checked. Customs officers are more concerned with checking for electronic equipment, televisions and videos. Being found with any amount of banned substances (drugs) or pornography will mean arrest, an appearance in court and a sentence that will include deportation.

Malta International Airport has tax-free shopping for both arriving and departing passengers. When the new cruise ship terminal opens in the Grand Harbour it will offer similar tax-free incentives.

## Maltese tourist offices

The **Malta Tourism Authority** constantly prepares and updates brochures and fact sheets for visitors. These are available free from their various offices and cover all subject areas, from hotel and accommodation guides to recommendations about skydiving and pilgrimages. They are suitable for independent travellers as well as for organisers of conferences and incentive tours.

The Malta Tourism Authority has nine overseas offices and, currently, 14 representative offices.

**Overseas offices:**

**Austria**: Fremdenverkehrsamt Malta, Opernring 1/R/5/517, A-1010 Wien. ☎ (43) 1 5853770.
**Benelux**: Verkeersbureau Malta, 4th Floor, Singel 540, 1017 AZ Amsterdam. ☎ (31) 20 6207223.
**France**: Office du Tourisme de Malte, 9 Cité de Trevise, 75009 Paris. ☎ (33) 1 4800 0379.
**Germany**: Fremdenverkehrsamt Malta, Schillerstrasse 30-40, D-60313, Frankfurt am Main. ☎ (49) 069 285890.
**Italy**: Ente per il Turismo di Malta, Via M.Gonzaga 7, 20123 Milan. ☎ (39) 0286 7376.
**Russia, Ukraine & CIS States**: Malta TourismOffice, Office 219, 7 Korovy Val Street, Moscow 117049. ☎ (7) 095 232 6413.
**Scandinavia**: Malta Turistbyra, Tegnergatan 35, 11161 Stockholm, Sweden. ☎ (48) 84112490.
**United Kingdom**: Malta Tourist Office, Malta House, 36-38 Piccadilly, London W1V 0PP. ☎ (44) 0207 292 4900
**United States (& Canada)**: Malta Tourist Office, Empire State Building, 350 Fifth Avenue, Suite 4412, New York 10118. ☎ (1) 212 695 9520.

Representative offices:

Australia ☎ (61) 2 9321 9154
Czech Republic ☎ (420) 2 232 7213
Eire ☎ (353) 1 405 8200
Finland ☎ (358) 9 6820565
Hungary ☎ (48) 22 6241 1931
Israel ☎ (972) 3 5165182/3
Japan ☎ (81) 45 823-5488
Kuwait ☎ (965) 2450937
Poland ☎ (36) 1 2689830
Sicily ☎ (39) 932 654999
Spain ☎ (34) 913192341
Turkey ☎ (90) 2122372420

In Malta: Head Office, Malta Tourism Authority, 280 Republic Street, Valletta CMR 02, Malta. ☎ (356) 22 44 44/5 🖺 (356) 22 04 01; e-mail: info@visit-malta.com; web site: www.visitmalta.com

## Inoculations

Under normal circumstances no inoculations are required by visitors coming from Europe, Australia, Canada and the US. Travellers from other countries would do well to check current regulations.

## Currency

Malta's currency is decimal. Each Maltese Lira (written as Lm) is equal to 100 cents. There are notes to the value of Lm20, Lm10, Lm5 and Lm2. The coins are Lm1, 50c, 25c, 10c, 5c, 2c and 1c.

Visitors are permitted to bring any amount of foreign currency into Malta, but if it is more than you might spend on holiday or business, the amount must be declared on arrival. The maximum amount of Maltese currency that may be brought in is Lm50.

Visitors can take out any foreign currency that remains unspent and a maximum of Lm25.

Most international **credit cards** are accepted in banks, shops, hotels and restaurants. If you are drawing money at a counter in a bank you will need to present you passport or ID card for identification. ATMs are in most major towns and accept all major credit cards. The local representative of **American Express** is at 14 Zachary Street, Valletta. ☎ 232141.

## Disabled travellers

It has to be said that Malta and Gozo are not ideal for anyone with walking or seeing difficulties, or with a wheelchair or pram. The surfaces of both streets and pavements are generally in poor condition. Many pavements in newly developing areas might even be considered dangerous, especially where access to an underground garage is considered more important than the needs of a pedestrian.

That said, hotels are well aware of the problems and many go to great lengths to ensure that people with walking disabilities have the kinds of access or aids they need. If you are planning a summer visit, it is recommended that you check how easy it is to getting in or out of the pool. Some hotel pools do not have low-rising steps.

Many museums and sites do not yet have facilities for wheelchairs or people with walking disabilities, but efforts are being made to rectify this.

Malta International Airport offers help to disabled travellers but needs to be informed of passenger/flight details in advance in order to prepare the correct assistance.

• For further information about facilities for disabled travellers, contact the **National Commission for the Handicapped** (☎ 487789) or the **Health Education Unit** (☎ 224071).

## Getting to Malta

### By air

The national airline, **Air Malta**, operates scheduled flights from the major cities in Europe, their frequency depending on seasonal requirements. The airline has offices in these European cities as well as New York and Middle Eastern centres such as Tripoli (Libya), Cairo, Damascus, Istanbul, Tel Aviv and Dubai.

All scheduled and charter airline flights operated by Air Malta and other leading carriers arrive at Malta International Airport, Gudja. Although a regular bus service links the Terminal with Valletta, it is primarily a service for airport workers. Passengers travelling independently or not being met by tour company representatives usually use taxis to get to their final destination. To save visitors from haggling with taxi drivers, many of whom are belligerent, travellers can pre-pay the government fixed rate for the journey at a desk in the terminal. The taxi driver is then presented with a voucher, not money.

Among other airlines operating scheduled services to Malta are **Aeroflot**, **Alitalia**, **Austrian Airlines**, **Balkan Bulgarian Airlines**, **British Airways** (operated by GB Airways), **CSE** (from the Czech Republic), **Egypt Air**, **Emirates**, **Interflug**, **jat**, **klm**, **Lufthansa**, **Monarch**, **Swissair**, **Tunisavia** and **uta**.

Malta is rapidly developing as a hub for passengers linking Sicily, North and South Africa, Libya, the Middle East and further afield to Europe. Air Malta schedules are designed to make Malta an excellent transfer point.

## From Britain

Air Malta operates regular flights from Heathrow Terminal 4, Gatwick, Stansted, Birmingham, Manchester and Glasgow, while charter flights operate from the regional airports during peak seasons. Flying time from London to Malta International Airport is 3hrs and 20mins.

## To Gozo

There is only one airport to service the Maltese Islands, but a small heliport on Gozo links the two islands with a 20-seater helicopter service. Its timetable connects with most incoming and departing international flights. It is advisable to pre-book the helicopter links.

Private planes can also use Gozo's heliport.

## Air Malta

Malta International Airport: ☎ 223596. Telephone Sales: ☎ 245694. Reservations: ☎ 662211. Valletta office: Freedom Square ☎ 240686-8. Gozo office: 13 Pjazza Independenza, Victoria: ☎ 559341-2. E-mail: info@airmalta. com. The Air Malta sales office at Malta International Airport is open 24 hours. Other offices open Mon–Fri: 08.00–18.00 Sat: 08.00–13.00.

## *By sea*

Although many international cruise liners make an impressive entry into the spectacular Grand Harbour carrying thousands of tourists each day for a few hours sightseeing, if you are an independent traveller, the only means of getting to the Islands by sea is by taking one of the more mundane car ferries or the fast catamaran from Sicily.

In the height of summer there is usually a service from Pozzallo, the southernmost tip of Sicily, or further north from Catania on the eastern coast. At other times, there are larger more comfortable ferries (complete with cabins, restaurant, cinema, nightclub). One of these, for example, does a round trip: Genoa—Palermo—Valletta—Tunis—Genoa. It takes two days to reach Malta from Genoa.

The car ferry services change each year, their regularity and schedules determined as much by the domestic demands of the Italian shipping companies running the routes as by the seasonal needs of the travellers trying to get to and from Malta. Most constant are **Grimaldi Ferries** with a weekly link from Salerno, near Naples, and **Ma.Re.Si.** with a twice a week ferry from Catania. Passages can be booked through any travel agent. The ferry journey takes 8 to 12 hours depending on the route (from Pozzallo is shortest, Syracuse or Catania longest).

In summer months the Maltese company **Virtu Ferries** runs a speedy catamaran car ferry to and from Pozzallo. This carries 80 cars and takes around 90 minutes. There is also a passenger only catamaran. (The catamaran services runs from about May to September and shuts down when the sea is rough.)

To make direct reservations on the catamaran with **Virtu Ferries**, ☎ 318854 or 🖹 345221.

Since the spread of computer links in Italy and elsewhere, most travel agents can now book a passage for car and passengers to Malta. Or you could use Malta-based travel agents like **S. Mifsud & Sons** (☎ 232211) and **A&V von Brockdorff** (☎ 322600).

## Arriving with a car

No visitor may keep a car on the Islands for longer than three months without either paying Customs Duty, which is punitive, or having special Police permission (for example, being a member of the Diplomatic Corps).

Arriving with a car does not require a permit, but the car must have current international Green Card insurance that specifically mentions Malta. The driver must have a valid driving licence.

On arrival in the Grand Harbour all documents are closely examined by Police and Customs and the car's engine and chassis numbers are checked and logged. Apparently this is to ensure that the same items are on the car when it is taken off the island again and that parts of the car have not been exchanged or sold for profit on the local market.

The Customs officials also check the car for goods on which duty is payable.

As Malta has applied to join the European Union these laws will be amended as and when the Islands are granted membership.

## Arriving with a yacht

When a boat enters Malta, the skipper must fly the Q flag and a courtesy flag. He must also contact Valletta Port Control on VHF Channel 9 or go to the **Yacht Centre** on **Manoel Island** in Marsamxett Harbour: 35° 54'.35 N, 14° 30'.6 E.

The visitors berths are in **Lazzaretto Creek**. If they are occupied, take all relevant papers, crew list and passports to the Customs & Immigration office on Manoel Island. Anchoring in the creek is only permitted until a berth has been allocated.

On Malta, the Malta Maritime Authority has two principal marinas: **Msida Marina** and the **Lazzaretto** and **Ta'Xbiex** quays. Other marinas are being developed around Senglea and Kalkara in the Grand Harbour. To date there is only one on Gozo, in **Mġarr Harbour**.

Water and electricity are available at every berth; showers, toilets, overseas telephone facilities, *poste restante* and cafeteria are all found at the Yacht Centres on Manoel Island and on the Msida Marina.

The Malta marinas are close to banks, shops, inexpensive hotels, restaurants, chandlery shops and yacht agencies. Msida will accommodate 700 yachts up to 18m on serviced pontoons. Larger yachts use Lazzaretto and Ta'Xbiex quays with stern-to moorings. Repair facilities are available and the charges for hauling out and storing are reasonable. See also Manoel Island Yacht Yard page 136.

In Gozo at Mġarr there are 120 berths for boats up to 16m. Berths on its pontoons are in demand in summer months when Malta-based yachts use them for weekending.

All services come under the *Malta Maritime Authority*:
Yacht Centre, Ta'Xbiex: ☎ 332800
Berthing Master Ta'Xbiex: ☎ 330975
Manoel Island Yacht Marina: ☎ 338589
Msida Yacht Marina: ☎ 235711
Gozo Office, Mġarr Harbour: ☎ 558856-7

> ### Winds
> The prevailing wind is the northwesterly *majjistral* (the mistral). In September the southerly *xlokk* (sirocco) takes over, bringing humidity. The most unpleasant wind is the *grigal*, the northeasterly, that sweeps down from the Adriatic bringing rough seas and high winds and a drop in temperature in a blast that usually lasts three days. Boats never leave harbour in a *grigal* and cruise liners rarely attempt to enter the Grand Harbour. The north wind, the *tramuntana*, blows only rarely.

 # Where to stay

The Islands have a wide range of accommodation with considerable expansion and regrading taking place in the five-star and five-star de luxe sector. In order to meet the conditions set by the World Tourism Organization, many hotels have raised their standards considerably.

The Hotels and Catering Establishments Board authorises official maximum prices for each category, but many hotels offer substantial reductions out of season. Off peak is late January to early March and November to early December. If booking direct, it is worth asking 'What is your best price?' This can bring considerable savings even in the top hotels.

Most of the hotels listed below can be found in travel brochures.

All hotels are now classified from 5-star to 1-star.

✩✩✩✩✩ and ✩✩✩✩✩ **de luxe**. These are the Islands' premier hotels. Fully air-conditioned of course, all rooms with private bath and shower, terrace, television, telephone and 24-hour room service. There is usually a choice of restaurants as well as a bar, coffee shop, pool and sport facilities. Laundry, pressing, dry cleaning, hairdresser. Good conference facilities. ££££

✩✩✩✩ **High standard**. All rooms air-conditioned with private bath or shower, television, telephone and, often, balcony. Room service available breakfast to midnight. Restaurant, bar, pool or beach facility. Laundry, pressing, dry cleaning, hairdresser. Conference facilities. £££

✩✩✩ **Good accommodation**. All air-conditioned rooms have private bath or shower. Most with bar and restaurant. Lounge. Arrangements for laundry, pressing and dry cleaning. ££

✩✩ **Modest accommodation**. Only some rooms with private bath or shower, telephone or service bell in rooms. Breakfast only. Front office open during day; porter at night. £

✩ **Small hotel**. All rooms with wash-hand basin but share common bath or shower. Office open during day; porter at night. £

## Malta hotels

✩✩✩✩✩ *Corinthia Palace*, de Paule Avenue, Attard. ☎ 440301. 🖹 465713. Decorated in manner of modern grand hotel, it is at island's centre, near official residence of the President at San Anton Palace. Well appointed, with (heated) indoor and outdoor pools, health spa, restaurants. Courtesy transport to Valletta and San Gorg Lido, the Corinthia Group's beach resort at St George's Bay.

The Corinthia Group is a Maltese chain with more than 30 hotels spread across the Czech Republic, Gambia, Hungary, Portugal, Turkey and Tunisia.

☆☆☆☆☆ *Corinthia San Gorg*, St George's Bay, St Julians. ☎ 374114-6. ▤ 234219. Opened in 1995, on water's edge location with excellent views. Facilities include choice of restaurants, pools and beach lido known for its watersports. Executive suites. Business centre. Facilities for disabled.

☆☆☆☆☆ *Crowne Plaza*, Tigne Street, Sliema SLM 11. ☎ 343400. ▤ 311292. In easy walking distance of shops and waterfront cafés of this resort town. Excellent family hotel with pool (heated), tennis, sauna and gym. Selection of restaurants, nightclub disco. Facilities for physically disabled.

☆☆☆☆☆ *Hilton Malta*, Portomaso, St Julians STJ 02. ☎ 336201. ▤ 341539. Newly built in a Portomaso waterside development that includes business and conference centres and apartments plus yacht marina creek hewn out of the rocky peninsular. Hotel replaces old colonial Hilton that stood here. Doors opened late 1999. Hotel has 75 executive rooms, 201 deluxe rooms and one presidential suite. All with electronic facilities and PC and fax modem. Excellent pool and selection of restaurants.

☆☆☆☆☆ *Le Meridien Phoenicia*, The Mall, Floriana. ☎ 225241. ▤ 235254. In its prime this was Malta's prestige hotel, ideally situated outside the gates of the capital. As the hotel changed hands, so it lost its gloss. Now under Meridien banner it is endeavoring, with some success, to recapture original status and international business travellers. Refurbished, with choice of restaurants and outdoor pool. Ideal for visitors hoping to walk into Valletta.

☆☆☆☆☆ *Radisson SAS Bay Point*, St George's Bay, St Julians. ☎ 374894. ▤ 374895. At entrance of bay, the hotel faces both open sea and sheltered bay. Excellently appointed family hotel. Two restaurants, bar, pools, tennis, gym. All rooms with views.

☆☆☆☆☆ *Westin Dragonara Resort*, Dragonara Road, St Julian's STJ 02. ☎ 381000. ▤ 378877. Opened spring 1997, hotel is attractively presented and stylish with 311 comfortable and modern rooms with sea views. Set in landscaped gardens with The Dragonara Palace Casino and The Reef Club beach lido where Malta's smart set gather to swim, sunbathe and be seen. Good conference facilities, choice of restaurants, shops, pools. Dive school.

☆☆☆☆☆ *Xara Palace*, Mdina MDN 02. ☎ 450560. ▤ 52612. An old hotel reborn (summer 1999). New management has turned derelict hotel that was a converted late 17C *palazzo* in the medieval walled city of Mdina into an exclusive, beautifully furnished and restored luxury hotel. There are 17 suites, each one individually designed with antiques, paintings and computer and modem facilities. Elegant roof top restaurant with spectacular views. Ground floor pizzeria.

☆☆☆☆ *Best Western Les Lapins*, Ta'Xbiex Sea Front, Ta'Xbiex. ☎ 342551. ▤ 343902. Not by the sea but overlooking the Msida yacht marina and its promenade. Restaurant, café, disco, pool, children's pool, tennis.

☆☆☆☆ *Coastline*, Salina Bay. ☎ 573781. ▤ 581104. On attractive stretch of coastline outside Qawra and Bugibba, a well-appointed hotel belonging to go-ahead hotel group. With pools, watersports facilities, tennis, gym and sauna. Facilities for physically disabled.

✮✮✮✮ *Corinthia Jerma Palace*, Dawret it-Torri, Marsascala. ☎ 633222. ▤ 639485.The only major hotel on the south of the island, though others are planned. Managed by the Corinthia Group. Pools, good watersports facilities, tennis, gym and sauna.

✮✮✮✮ *Corinthia Marina*, St George's Bay. ☎ 380039. ▤ 381708. Attractive new hotel, all rooms overlooking the bay. Well appointed, friendly service, choice of restaurants, cafés and bars. Shares beach lido with elegant Corinthia San Gorg Hotel.

✮✮✮✮ *Fortina*, Tigne Sea Front, Sliema.☎ 343380. ▤ 332004. Nicely situated on the waterfront of Marsamxett Harbour facing Valletta and a minute's stroll from town's shopping streets. An all-inclusive hotel, comfortable with attractive landscaped gardens, pools, gym and tennis.

✮✮✮✮ *Forum*, St Andrew's Road, St Andrew's.☎ 370493. ▤ 370324. On busy road, with 10-minute walk to St Julians and Paceville resort areas or the nearest rock beach. Comfortable and friendly, family hotel with pool, sauna, gym and tennis.

✮✮✮✮ *Golden Tulip*, Dragonara Road, St Julians.☎ 378100. ▤ 378101. Part of the Vivaldi Hotels group, opened 1999 in the heart of Paceville entertainment area, by the sea and Casino. Comfortable rooms most with sea view, business and conference facilities, rooftop terrace and bar, restaurant, bar and grill, indoor pool, rooftop pool, fitness centre.

✮✮✮✮ *Grand Hotel Mercure Selmun Palace*, Selmun, Mellieħa. ☎ 521040. ▤ 521060. On hill in countryside, a modern hotel attached to one of the superb watchtowers built by the Knights. Pools, watersports available, gym, tennis. Beach nearby.

✮✮✮✮ *Howard Johnson Diplomat*, 173 Tower Road, Sliema. ☎ 345361 ▤ 345351. On Sliema's popular promenade with its smooth rock beaches. Discreet hotel with swimming pool, sauna and coffee shop. Stroll the promenade to town centre.

✮✮✮✮ *Mellieħa Bay*, Għadira, Mellieħa. ☎ 573844. ▤ 576399. Tucked in on side of Mellieħa Bay, alongside Malta's most popular and crowded sandy beach, hotel is popular with groups who enjoy being together and the nightly entertainment. Pools, watersports, tennis and gym.

✮✮✮✮ *New Dolmen*, Qawra. ☎ 581510. ▤ 581081. Popular, large family hotel (387 rooms) on the coast road between developing Qawra and bustling Buġibba. Facing the bay, it has pools, watersports, tennis and gym. Its Oracle Casino has a slot machine hall as well as traditional gaming tables (dress code: anything goes until 18.00. After that, 'smart casual').

✮✮✮✮ *Paradise Bay*, Ċirkewwa. ☎ 573981. ▤ 573115. On northern tip of Malta, close to Gozo ferry quay and Paradise Bay. Heated indoor and outdoor pools. Tennis, squash, pools. Facilities for physically disabled.

✮✮✮✮ *Preluna Hotel & Towers*, 124 Tower Road, Sliema. ☎ 334001. ▤ 337281. On Sliema's main promenade close to shops and cafés. High-rise, well-appointed hotel. Small heated pool but with good beach facilities during summer season. Watersports, gym, tennis, sauna. Nightclub.

✮✮✮✮ *Suncrest*, Qawra Promenade, Qawra. ☎ 577101. ▤ 575478. With 413 rooms, this is Malta's largest hotel. There's a wide variety of accommodation including self-catering. Go-ahead management team. On waterfront road with own Sun & Surf lido, pools, children's play area, watersports and restaurants. Conference facilities.

✮✮✮✮ *Victoria*, Ġorġ Borg Olivier Street, Sliema. ☎ 334711. ▤ 334771. Charming, small hotel in centre of residential Sliema. Popular with businessmen.

Restaurant (goes alfresco on the roof in summer), rooftop pool. Minute's walk to Sliema's amenities and beaches.

There is a rapidly growing number of hotels in the ☆☆☆ category. Among them:
☆☆☆ *Castille*, Castille Square, Valletta. ☎ 243677. 🗎 243679. Alongside Auberge de Castille, the prime minister's offices, the hotel is a perfect location for visitors wanting to be in Valletta. 38 simple rooms. Rooftop restaurant with views, pizzeria in basement.

☆☆☆ *Golden Sands*, Golden Bay, Ghajn Tuffieha. ☎ 573961. 🗎 580875. Perched above one of Malta's best loved sandy beaches, it is ideal for families with young children. Attractive location. Pools, tennis, disco, watersports facilities.

☆☆☆ *Milano Due*, 113 The Strand, Gżira. ☎ 345040. 🗎 345045. On waterfront where boat cruises set out. Minute's walk to Sliema's cafés and shops. Rooftop restaurant with views of harbour and Valletta. Facilities for physically disabled.

☆☆☆ *Plevna*, 2 Thornton Street, Qui-Si-Sana, Sliema. ☎ 331031. 🗎 336496. Family hotel in quiet residential location on a slight hill. Close to shops and cafés. Own beach facilities on rock foreshore a short walk away.

☆☆☆ *Rafael Spinola*, Upper Ross Street, St Julians. ☎ 374488. 🗎 366266. This claims to be a boutique-hotel, which means it is charmingly decorated. 32 comfortable rooms. In quiet street off the busy resort district's major thoroughfare.

☆☆☆ *Sliema Chalet*, 117 Tower Road, Sliema. ☎ 335575. 🗎 333249. Recently refurbished family hotel complete with name change (it used to be Eden Beach). 47 rooms, coffee shop. On promenade with all Sliema's shops, cafés and beaches in easy walking distance.

☆☆☆ *Tigne Court*, Qui-Si-Sana, Sliema. ☎ 332001. 🗎 332004. Quiet family hotel in residential quarter. Faithful clientele. Some of the 87 rooms have sea view. Own beach concession. Within easy reach of Sliema's centre.

☆☆☆ *Tower Palace*, Tower Road, Sliema. ☎ 337271. 🗎 311235. Reopened mid-1999 after considerable refurbishment, it has 45 pleasant rooms, most with views over seafront promenade. Roof restaurant and bar. Smooth rock beach across the road is popular with Sliema residents.

## Gozo hotels

☆☆☆☆☆ *L'Imġarr*, Triq Sant'Antnin, Għajnsielem. ☎ 560455. 🗎 557589. Excellently positioned overlooking Mġarr Harbour with its yacht marina, fish restaurants and ferry quay. Majority of rooms with sitting rooms. All with balconies or large terraces. Good restaurant, two pools, sauna, gym and conference facilities. Rooftop dining in summer. Facilities for physically disabled.

☆☆☆☆☆ *Ta' Ċenċ*, Sannat. ☎ 556830. 🗎 558199. Regularly featured as one of world's top hotels. Elegantly understated and single-storey so barely visible in the peaceful countryside. All rooms have terrace or private garden. Italian restaurant, two pools, one heated and reserved for adults, Transport to rock beach nearby.

☆☆☆☆☆ *San Lawrenz*, Triq ir-Rokon, San Lawrenz. ☎ 558639, 558640. 🗎 562977. Opened summer 1999 and peacefully located. Built around large pool in spacious landscaped gardens not far from Inland Sea. Impressive stonework, restaurants, conference facilities, floodlit tennis, billiards, squash, pools and Thalgo centre with exclusive marine algae therapy.

☆☆☆☆ *Cornucopia*: Triq Ġnien Imrek, Xagħra. ☎ 556486. 🗎 552910. Charming family hotel with five suites, 48 rooms, on outskirts of village. Several pools.

Worth visiting in Xaghra is *Oleander* restaurant. Not far away is resort area of Marsalforn with beaches.

☆☆☆☆ *The Grand*, Triq Sant Antnin, Ghajnsielem. ☎ 556183. 📠 559744. Attractive, newly built hotel with spacious rooms and views towards Malta and Comino over Mġarr Harbour. Pool on roof, sauna, fitness and games room. Roof garden restaurant and conference hall.

☆☆☆☆ *St Patrick's*, Xlendi. ☎ 562951. 📠 556598. Decorative seafront hotel in pretty but over-built bay that bustles with summer life. Some of 49 rooms have sea views, jacuzzi and large balconies. More rooms in extension not overlooking sea. Restaurant and terrace café. Plunge pool on roof.

☆☆☆ *Calypso*, Marsalforn. ☎ 562000. 📠 562012. On busy waterfront dotted with busy restaurants. Just paces away from the beaches. It has 84 rooms and 12 apartments. Simple restaurant, floodlit tennis, squash courts and dive centre.

## Farmhouses on Gozo

The plain architecture of these square stone buildings, many built hundreds of years ago, gives Gozo's villages and countryside their distinctive look. Many have been rescued from collapse and renovated with great style to make them suitable for the popular holiday lets they have become, ideal for families. Car rental is essential as they are often some distance from village or town amenities.

There are three main agents:

*Gozo Farmhouses*: 3 Triq l-Imġarr, Ghajnsielem. ☎ 561280. 📠 558794. These combine charming rustic simplicity with the modern facilities. Most have pools, jacuzzi and hairdryers. Some have television, washing machine and telephone. A cook is available. ££

*Gozo Village Holidays*, 11 Triq il-Kapuċċini, Victoria. ☎ 557255. 📠 558397. Attractively decorated, these are probably best seen as simple hideaways: no television, no telephone. But most have pools. ££

*Gozo Holidays*, Dunny Lane, Chipperfield, Hertfordshire WD4 9DQ, UK. ☎ (44) 01923 260919/260059. 📠 (44) 01923 263482. This group has a wide selection of farmhouses (and villas). Some share the facilities of the *Cornucopia Hotel*. ££

## Comino

☆☆☆☆ *Comino Hotel*, Island of Comino. ☎ 529821-9. 📠 529826. Simple hotel with own private sandy beach. Also has 45 apartments grouped just a short walk along the rocky coastline. Peaceful and a honeymooners' favourite. Excellent watersports facilities, dive school, tennis (with tennis pro in residence) and sauna. Hotel's small boat ferries guests to Ċirkewwa (Malta) and Mġarr (Gozo). There is nothing on this small island apart from hotel and one small homestead. Island's Blue Lagoon is crowded with day trippers on a variety of boats.

The hotel welcomes guests for the day, offering them full facilities. For this book by telephone.

## Tourist village on Malta

*Corinthia Mistra Village Clubhotel*, Xemxija Hill, St Paul's Bay. ☎ 580481. 📠 582941. Part of successful Corinthia Hotel group. The Village is a purpose-built centre with hotel and apartments, some self-catering, around pools and restaurants. Very popular. 255 rooms. On high ground above St Paul's Bay, its amenities are excellent, summer and winter, and a team is constantly at hand to keep children amused. Pools, restaurants, kids club, tennis and a dive school.

### Holiday complexes on Malta

☆☆☆☆ **Sunny Coast**, Qawra Road, Qawra. ☎ 572964. 📄 576820. Well-maintained complex facing into bay. 60 rooms. Good facilities, watersports, tennis, squash, gym.

☆☆☆ **Buġibba Holiday Complex**, Triq it-Turisti, Buġibba. ☎ 580861, 580867. In hectic Buġibba close to shops, cinemas, restaurants and nightlife. Hotel and self-catering units of studios and apartments. Total of 340 rooms. Summer rates are competitive; winter rates even lower. Facilities for physically disabled.

☆☆☆ **Ramla Bay**, Ramla Bay, Marfa. ☎ 573522. 📄 575931. Faces island of Comino on northern tip of Malta. Good watersports facilities, waterskiing, canoeing, etc. Tennis. Timeshare.

# Food and drink

### Food

True Maltese cooking, the kind you find in homes, is, like Maltese bread, distinctive. It takes its influences from Italy and North Africa and yet remains steadfastly Maltese. Much of it has a kind of peasant simplicity, and much of it is oven cooked.

Until quite recently it was not unusual on Sunday mornings to have streets around the village bakery filled with the delicious aromas of baked meats and macaroni pies and to see members of families armed with the cleanest of dishcloths collecting the cooked dishes from the bakery. In those days, after the bread was baked, for a few pence the baker would use his ovens to cook the village lunches.

Many restaurants claim to offer Maltese dishes and although they may not be quite like mamma would make, they do give a visitor an idea of what is enjoyed behind family doors.

First, however, try *ħobż*, Maltese bread. It is truly praiseworthy—delicious, crusty and flavoursome. If you enjoy Italian *bruschetta* try the Maltese version called *ħobż biż-żejt* (bread dribbled with oil, rubbed with halved tomatoes and sprinkled with salt, pepper and herbs; capers are optional): there's nothing finer.

Look out for **timpana**, a macaroni pie made with minced meat, aubergines, eggs and ricotta cheese wrapped in a case of flaky pastry. Or **ros-fil-forn**, which is much the same as *timpana* except rice is used instead of pasta.

Then there's **bragioli** which are rolled slices of beef that have been stuffed and **torta tal-lampuka**, a fish pie. This is a great Maltese favourite in September when *lampuki* (dolphin fish—not to be mistaken for the mammal dolphin) are in season. *Lampuki* are caught in a centuries-old traditional way. Floats made of palm fronds are placed on the water; when the fish gather underneath in their shade, the fishermen encircle them with nets. *Lampuki* are often fried, but the local speciality and family treat is a pie with fillets of *lampuki*, tomatoes, cauliflower, spinach, onions, olives and parsley.

Then there are *ġbejniet*. (Pronouncing this is easier than it looks: Jib-bay-nee-it.)

This is a popular local cheese made from sheep or goat's milk and is enjoyed either soft and new with a salad or allowed to harden and enjoyed with *galletti*, Malta's delightful plain, crunchy biscuit. *Ġbejniet* made, and served, in Gozo are reputed to be the best.

### Drink

Maltese **wines** for a while had a doubtful reputation and even now some 'farmer's' wines can have unfortunate side effects. But the wines from the two major wineries, *Marsovin* and *Delicata*, are justifiably popular—particularly their Chardonnay and Cabernet Sauvignon selections. A new house, *Meridiana*, produces very high quality—and highly priced—wines from vines recently planted. Wine buffs go for their *Isis* (Chardonnay) and *Melqart* (Cabernet Sauvignon and Merlot).

**Beer** has been brewed with great success locally for many decades. Best local brews are *Cisk lager*, *Hop Leaf* and *Blue Label*, all produced by the *Farsons Brewery*. They also make *Kinnie*, a distinctive bitter-sweet fizzy soft drink.

As for **water**, most homes and restaurants will serve only bottled water, most of it locally produced. Although domestic drinking water is safe—much of it the product of reverse osmosis plants that convert sea water into acceptable drinking water—it is not to everyone's taste, hence the popularity of bottled water.

# Where to eat

Eating out in Malta and Gozo is more rewarding now than ever before. The days when the restaurants seemed to cater exclusively for the tastes of British service-men or travellers on a tight budget have gone. In those days the Maltese them-selves rarely ate in restaurants as the food, they knew, was always better at home. There is a wide selection of restaurants to choose from, whether you want to try Maltese cooking, *la cucina Italiana*, French cuisine or, quite simply, local fresh fish.

However, even the most constant of the Islands' restaurants can have 'off' days: crops have short seasons here, and good chefs are lured into or out of new businesses, or set up on their own.

Some restaurants seem to have weathered the storms of change and remained popular. In Valletta, for example, there are *The Carriage* and *Rubino*; in St Julians *La Dolce Vita* and *San Giuliano;* in Marsascala *Grabiel*. In Gozo, the restaurant at the *Ta' Ċenċ Hotel* has its fans as does *Il-Panzier* in Victoria.

Authentic Maltese cooking is hard to find outside the family home, but dishes that are part-Maltese, part-Italian, are on most menus. Perhaps it is best to say that most cooking is Italian in style but Maltese in delivery.

Fresh fish is often delicious and there are many restaurants whose reputations hinge on serving it well. During the winter months much of the fish served may be frozen as fishermen rarely venture out. Fish farms supply silver bream (*qawrata*) most of the year.

It is worth remembering that standards can dip considerably at weekends, when local people eat out and restaurants struggle to cope with extra clientele. For the best food and service, visit restaurants Tuesday to Friday. Most close on Mondays.

Rabbit (*fenek*) is the national favourite, served when families get together. It rarely appears on menus. If you are invited to a *fenkata*, it will be an inexpensive noisy evening at a village bar where fried or stewed rabbit is served with chips and lots of red wine to crowds of friends. But go with a Maltese host, as the success of the evening can depend on knowing the bar's owner. All Maltese have their favourite places.

## Malta restaurants

### Valletta

On weekdays the city slows down and sleeps early. Sometimes, it can appear to be deserted as soon as shops close at 19.00. Sundays are even quieter, unless it is Carnival weekend or there is a festa (see p 36). But there are plans to revitalise the capital and bring life back to its ancient streets. A new cinema complex is seen as a step in the right direction. Meanwhile most restaurants are open only for lunch.

**British Hotel**, 276 St Ursula Street. ☎ 224730. This 2-star hotel is not famed for its cooking, but it has a prime position on the bastions, perched above the Grand Harbour, and the six tables on the balcony have a fabulous view. Cooking, like the hotel, is friendly and unassuming. Lunch. Casual and inexpensive. Book balcony table. £

**Blue Room**, 58 Republic Street. ☎ 238014. A few steps from the Palace on the main thoroughfare leading to Fort St Elmo, this Cantonese restaurant is popular with the smart set, especially after performances at the Manoel Theatre. Lunch and dinner. Book. ££

**The Carriage**, Valletta Buildings, South Street. ☎ 247828. Hidden in an unattractive office building, this rooftop restaurant with open terrace is known for elegance and imaginative cooking. Smart clientele, businessmen and politicians come because standards are consistently high. Known for excellent vegetarian dishes too. Lunch Monday–Friday. Dinner Friday and Saturday only. Booking essential. £££

**Giannini**, St Michael's Bastion (off Windmill Street). ☎ 237121/236575. One of the island's favourite restaurants, this is on bastion walls overlooking Marsamxett Harbour towards Sliema; a gracious house with bar on the ground floor and restaurant on top, reached by an elevator. Sweeping views. Cooking is a mix of Maltese and Italian influences. In winter, lunch served daily (except Sunday); dinner Friday and Saturday. In summer, dinner only. Booking essential. £££

**Malata**, Palace Square. ☎ 233967. Below ground and boisterous, it's popular with politicians and businesmen as well as the smart crowd. Cooking is to a high standard, with Italian influence; good *antipasto* and fresh fish. Late nights often turn into parties. Closed Sundays. Book. £££

**Le Meridien Phoenicia**, The Mall, Floriana. ☎ 225241/221211. Outside the city's main gate, the hotel is striving to recapture its glory before internal strife and changing ownership affected quality. Restaurant with a fine summer terrace. Also a bistro. Lunch and dinner. ££

**De Robertis**, Castille Hotel, Castille Square. ☎ 243677. Hotel's rooftop restaurant overlooks Grand Harbour. Eat alfresco in summer. In the basement is *La Cave* pizzeria. £

**Rubino**, 54 Old Bakery Street. ☎ 224656. Regarded as one of the best restaurants in Malta. Cooking is distinctly Mediterranean in style with two or three typically Maltese dishes daily. Fashionable because standards remain high, with unusual dishes and welcoming service. Lunch Monday to Saturday. Dinner, Tuesday and Friday only. Booking essential. £££

*Sicilia*, 1 St John Street. ☎ 240569. Inside, there's room for no more than 14. Outside, on a small piazza with fine views of Grand Harbour, tables seat many more when weather allows. Popular with locals who come for the inexpensive pasta. Lunch weekdays only. £

*Trattoria Palazz*, 43 Old Theatre Street. ☎ 226611. Charming, air-conditioned basement (steep staircase) set in the ancient stone foundations of the National Library, *Bibliotheca*, that was established late 18C. Popular trattoria serving excellent pasta, fish. Crowded after events at nearby Manoel Theatre. Lunch and dinner. Closed Sunday. Book. ££

*Trattoria da Pippo*, 136 Melita Street. ☎ 241975. Truly popular, especially with the business crowd in the city. Traditional Maltese dishes are served in over-generous portions. Very casual, friendly and welcoming atmosphere. Lunch only. Booking essential. ££

## Marsascala

*Grabiel*, Marsascala Bay. ☎ 634194. If you enjoy fish, this is the place to come. Dedicated to diners who want sea-dates and clams as starters as well as superb grilled fish, octopus stew or a prawn platter. High standards. Lunch and dinner. Book. £££

*La Favorita*, Gardiel Street. ☎ 634113. Casual, popular restaurant with fish served unpretentiously in Maltese manner. Crowded at weekends. £

*Il re del pesce*, Triq id-Dahla ta'San Tumas. ☎ 634178. More fish—some would say the best, at a price. ££

## Marsaxlokk

*Rizzu*, The Waterfront. ☎ 871569. Fresh fish served alfresco in summer months. Popular. £

## Mdina

*Medina*, 7 Holy Cross Street. ☎ 454981. Long-time favourite of British residents and visitors. Pretty alfresco summer dining in coutyard sheltered by tall oleander tree. International cuisine with local dishes and speciality nights. Dinner. £££

*Il-Veduta*, is-Saqqijja, Rabat. ☎ 454666. On edge of massive car park just outside Mdina's gate, this casual pizza and pasta place is popular because its terrace overlooks inland Malta. Go for pizza. Lunch and dinner. £

## Mellieħa

*The Arches*, 113 Main Street. ☎ 523460. In central Mellieha, a large and brightly lit place, with bustling service and large portions. Roof dining in summer. Crowded by regulars who enjoy the exuberant quantities on each plate. Varied menu. Book. £££

*Giuseppi's*, 8 St Helen's Street. ☎ 574882. On two floors, this is considered a good example of a truly Maltese restaurant, both in decor and cooking. Menu changes daily depending on what is available in local market. Popular and moderately priced. Dinner. Book. ££

*Il Mithna*, 45 Main Street. ☎ 520404. Eat in a windmill; regulars praise the baked dishes. ££

## Mosta

*Lord Nelson*, Main Street. ☎ 432590. Close to Mosta Dome, old village bar transformed by owners into easygoing restaurant for the smart crowd. Excellent home cooking with both Maltese and British influences. Impeccable, friendly service. Casual. Booking essential. ££

## Qawra

The coastline of Qawra and Buġibba is burgeoning with new hotels, cafés and restaurants catering for the package holidaymaker. There are many inexpensive places to choose from as well as the following:

*Gran Laguna*, Ta' Xtut Street. ☎ 571146. Ignore the scruffy location. The restaurant is patronised by Italians and Sicilians who care about pasta and fresh fish being prepared properly—in the Italian manner. Dinner. Book. ££

*Luzzu*, Qawra Road. ☎ 573925. Long-established, relaxed atmosphere with friendly service. £

*Savini*, Qawra Road. ☎ 576927. On outskirts of Bugibba, old farmhouse with terraces for alfresco summer dining. Italian dishes served with a flourish. £££

## Sliema

*Barracuda*, 195 Main Street. ☎ 331817. Smart restaurant overlooking Balluta Bay and Portomaso complex. Businessmen regularly entertain important visitors here. Popular venue for visiting Hollywood stars. Dinner. £££

*Chez Philippe Bistrot*, 181 The Strand, Gzira. ☎ 330755. Behind the frontage of a bread shop called *Bon Pain* is a very French bistro directed by Philippe. Some excellent dishes. Always very crowded. Lunch only. Book. ££

*Christopher's*, Ta'Xbiex Seafront, Ta'Xbiex. ☎ 337101. With an excellent reputation, but pricey. Faithful clientele not discouraged by the time each dish takes to prepare. Beside Msida's yacht marina with fine view of Valletta. Lunch and dinner. Book. £££

*Galeone*, 35 Tigne Sea Front. ☎ 316420. Popular, casual and long established, with owner-chef Victor Bezzina presiding. Known for pasta and meat dishes. Book. ££

*Maroya*, Qui-si-sana. ☎ 346920. Its odd location on first floor of apartment block with only a few alfresco tables on outside pavement does not affect the success of this gregarious restaurant. Friendly, with truly loyal clientele. Closed Mondays. Book. ££

*Piccolo Padre*, 195 Main Street. ☎ 344875. Easygoing pizzeria beneath the *Barracuda* restaurant (see above). A rowdy place crammed with families and children. Some tables hover over sea. Excellent pizza. No booking. Queueing at weekends. £

*Ponte Vecchio*, Tower Road. ☎ 314591. Elegant Maltese restaurant with international menu. Tables on terrace during summer months. Dinner. Book. ££

## St Julians

The resort area that stretches from St Julians Bay to Paceville and St George's Bay is packed with restaurants, bars, pizza-and-pasta houses, discos and eveything you might imagine associated with nightlife. Here too are top hotels, the Dragonara Palace Casino and the new Portomaso complex with its purpose-built marina and Hilton. There are also severe parking restrictions and tow zones.

The following are the neighbourhood restaurants favoured by the Maltese:

*Caffè Raffael*, Spinola Road, St Julians Bay. ☎ 319988. Traditional open-air café with large terrace (under same management as *San Giuliano* restaurant, see below). Pretty location. £

*La Dolce Vita*, 155 St George's Road. ☎ 337836. Much loved by the young crowd for its fish, and always busy. Some tables overlook Bay. Eat on the roof in summer. Dinner. Book (specify if you want table with a view). ££

*Peppino's*, 30 St George's Road. ☎ 373200. Terrace and air-conditioned restaurant. Ground-floor bar serves good light lunches and suppers. First floor offers diners interesting à la carte menus. On Fridays it's a crowded late-night meeting place. Cooking to a consistently high standard. Alfresco roof dining for hot August nights. ££

*Pizza Hut*, St George's Road. ☎ 376600. Every child's favourite. Take-away available. £

*San Giuliano*, Spinola Road. ☎ 332000. Often considered Malta's smartest eating place; international stars come here for star treatment when filming in Malta. Good atmosphere, good cooking. Good view too, over St Julians waterfront. Book. £££

*Sumatra*, 139 Spinola Road. ☎ 31099. Locals seeking a change come here for Malaysian, Singaporean and Indonesian cooking. £

## St Paul's Bay

*Gillieru*, Church Street. ☎ 573480. Fish restaurant that for decades has taken pride in the variety of fish available. Today the restaurant jutting out into the sea—plus an open terrace—is very big indeed, perhaps too big for its kitchen. Crowded at weekends and public holidays. Unsophisticated cooking. Family orientated and casual. Lunch and dinner. ££

*Da Rosi*, 44 Church Street. ☎ 571411. Small family-run restaurant with fine home cooking. Dinner. Book. ££

## *Gozo restaurants*

### Gharb

*Jeffrey's*, 10 Gharb Road. ☎ 561006. Highly regarded little trattoria. Closes Sundays and usually mid-January to mid-March. Charming courtyard for alfresco dining in summer. Most ingredients from the cook's own farm. Dinner only. Book. ££

*Salvina's*, 21 Triq il-Blata. ☎ 552505. Pretty restaurant in village house. Local and international cuisine served with relaxed charm. Closed Sundays. ££

### Marsalforn

*Il-Kartell*, Bakery Street. ☎ 556918. On water's edge. Downstairs is a friendly, reasonably priced trattoria with good fish and local dishes, as well as pasta and pizzas. £. Upstairs, grills and flambés. ££

*Auberge Ta' Frenċ*, Marsalforn Road. ☎ 553888. Stylish old farmhouse with wide range of international dishes. Peaceful atmosphere. Dinner only. £££

*Otters*, Triq Santa Marija. ☎ 562473. Old waterpolo club now an alfresco restaurant at water's edge. Excellent fish, pasta, salad. Pizza in evenings. Umbrellas and sunbeds for anyone who wants to swim. £

*The Republic*, 18 Triq ix-Xatt. ☎ 556800. Popular trattoria with pleasant open terrace facing bay and beach. Closed Mondays. £

## Mġarr

*Manoel's* 27 Triq Manoel de Vilhena. ☎ 563588. Crowded outside terrace with view of bay in summer, closed in winter. Maintains good standard. Go for fish and pasta. Book. ££

*Il-Kċina tal-Barrakka*, 28 Triq Manoel de Vilhena. ☎ 556543. Known to regulars as Sammy's (after the owner). Alongside Manoel's, also always crowded. Regulars praise quality of fish and reasonable prices. Own wine. Summer only. Book. ££

*Park Lin*, Triq Manoel de Vilhena. ☎ 561967. In same street as previous two. Known also as Park Lane. Simple food served unpretentiously. £

## Victoria

*Café Jubilee*, it-Tokk. On the main square, French café recreated with some style. Popular and tiny, and always crowded. Some tables on square when weather is fine. Café snacks.

*Il-Panzier*, Triq il-Karita. ☎ 559979. Highly considered, with small menu presented to consistently high standards. Closed Monday. £££

*Riccardo's*, 4 Triq il-Fossos. ☎: 555953. After a visit to the cathedral, stop off for local wine, cheese and light snacks in part of an old house in the Citadel. £

## Xagħra

*Oleander*, Victory Square. ☎ 557230. Bustling, noisy restaurant. Excellent local dishes, fish and steaks. Tables outside in the square under the oleander trees in summer months when booking is advisable. Closed Monday. ££

## Xlendi

*Paradise*, Trejqet il-Madonna tal-Karmnu. ☎ 556878. Known to everyone as 'the Elvis place' because only pictures of 'the King' hang on its walls. Charming but simple. Excellent cooking, especially fresh fish, jumbo prawns, calamari and, occasionally, lobster. Tables outside in good weather. Good value. £

*Stone Crab*, Triq il-Port, Xlendi. ☎ 556490. Unpretentious with tables outside at the water's edge. In the cool of the evening with the sea only feet away, pasta, fresh fish and a bottle of wine can seem just perfect. Often they are. £

## Café life

The Maltese and Gozitans enjoy café, or *caffè*, life, especially during office hours or in the evening while shops are still open, sitting outside and gossiping over a drink or a coffee. (*Caffè*, the Italian spelling, is often used.)

Traditionally in the mornings cafés serve hot *pastizzi*, a savoury delight of flaky pastry stuffed with ricotta cheese or a dried pea mixture. And there are many other hot savoury pastry versions stuffed with cheese or meat mixtures too. These are considered an ideal mid-morning snack, but for many they would, and do, make an excellent lunch. Of course all cafés also serve cakes and ice cream.

Naturally some cafés are better than others, and catching the waiter's attention can be a serious problem in most.

The best known café in Valletta is *Caffè Cordina* on Republic Street, with tables inside and on the square outside. It is the daytime haunt of Valletta businessmen, lawyers and the fashionable set.

In Sliema look for the *Caffè Oasis* and *Giorgio's* on the waterfront road where the ferry sails to Valletta. In St Julian's there is *Caffè Rafael*. In Victoria, try *Café Jubilee* on the main square. (See above.)

They are all great meeting places.

# Getting around

## By bus

In **Malta** the central **bus terminus** is outside the gates of Valletta with buses setting out to all points of the Islands. As the system is updated so additional numbers of services also run from Sliema and Buġibba. Passengers on certain routes no longer have to change buses in Valletta to reach their final destination.

The Maltese buses are distinctive. Painted bright yellow with a broad orange stripe, they are known to all as bone-shakers because most were at their newest in the 1950s. Old and lumbering now, they are all privately owned and have a certain charm along with, more often than not, ill-tempered drivers. The Maltese are looking forward to the days when better buses service the routes with, it is hoped, air conditioning or, at least, windows that open.

There are some slightly newer buses, c 1960, which were purchased second-hand from Britain. The Government has plans to change all the buses in the near future to match up to today's international standards, but no date has been fixed.

Bus travel is inexpensive, if slow. **Tickets** are purchased from the driver. Prices set in 2000 make the fare on most routes 15cents. The maximum fare is 40 cents for direct, long distance routes.

It is always advisable to check the time of the last bus as many routes shut down early.

In **Gozo** the central bus terminus is in **Victoria** (known as **Rabat** to many locals). The system operates in the same manner as in Malta, but with fewer buses. All buses return to Victoria approximately 10 minutes after reaching their furthest destination. Gozo buses are painted grey with a single dark red stripe.

Ferry passengers arriving in Gozo find the Victoria connection on the quay.

## Bus routes on Malta
**From Valletta City Gate Terminus (☎ 224001)**

Armier  50
Attard  40
Bahar iċ-Ċaghaq  68
Balzan  40
Birkirkara  71, 74, 78
Birżebbuġa  11
Buġibba  48  58  449
Buskett  80  81
Ċirkewwa  45
Cospicua  1  2  4  6
Dingli 80  81
Fgura 18  19  21  22
Floriana  all buses
Ghadira  44  48  50  441  645
Ghajn Tuffieha  47  51  52  652
Ghar Lapsi  94 (Thur & Sat via
Siggewi)

Gharghur  55
Ghaxaq  8
Golden Bay  47  51  52  652
Gudja  8
Gzira  62  64  67  68  667  671
Hamrun  71  80  81
Kalafrana  12
Kalkara  4
Kirkop  34
Lija  40
Luqa  32  34
Malta International Airport  8
Marfa  45
Tarxien  8  11
Marsa 1  2  4  6  27  28  29  30
Marsascala  19  22
Marsaxlokk  27  30

Mdina  80  81
Mellieħa  43  44  45  50  441
Msida  all Sliema buses
Mtarfa  84
Naxxar  55  56
Paola  1  2  4  6
Paceville  62  67  671  68
Qawra  49  449  499
Qormi  91
Qrendi  35
Rabat  80  81
Safi  34
St Andrew's  67  681
St Julians  62  64  667  671
St Luke's Hospital  75
St Paul's Bay  43  44  45  50  441
St Thomas Bay  30
San Anton Gardens  80  81

San Ġwann  41  42
Santa Lucia  15
Santa Venera  80  81
Senglea  3
Siġġiewi  89
Sliema Ferries  62  64  67  68  667
652  671
Sliema Savoy  60  63  163
Sliema Spinola  62  67  68  671
Ta'Giorni  42
Tarxien  8  11  27  29  30
University of Malta, Tal'Qroqq  41
42
Vittoriosa  1  2  4
Wied iż-Żurrieq  38  138
Xemxija  43  44  45  50
Xgħajra  21

**From Sliema**
Buġibba  70  652
Ċirkewwa  645
Għajn Tuffiieħa  652
Golden Bay  652

Mdina  65
Qawra  652
Rabat  65

**From Buġibba**
Ċirekwwa  48
Għajn Tuffieħa  51  652
Golden Bay  51  652
Marsaxlokk  427  627

Mdina  86
Rabat  86
Sliema  627
Vittoriosa  627

**Bus routes on Gozo**
**From Victoria (Rabat) and back again**
Dwejra  1  2
Għajnsielem  42  43
Għarb  1  2
Għasri  91
Kerċem  14
Marsalforn  21
Mġarr (ferry quay)  25
Munxar  50  51
Nadur  42  43

Ramla  42  43 (not all buses)
San Lawrenz  1  2
Sannat  50  51
Santa Lucia  14
Ta' Pinu  91 (not all buses)
Xagħra  64  65
Xewkija  42  53
Xlendi  87
Zebbuġ  91

## By car

Driving in Malta is an experience—many find it a terrifying one.

Although officially the rules of the road are on British rather than European lines (you drive on the left side of the road), you must not expect any other rules or courtesies to apply. Anticipate poor driving. Slow cars drive in the outside lane (often, it must be said, to avoid potholes), faster cars overtake on the inside. Cars pull out on to main roads even if traffic is approaching at speed. Many reverse into traffic on a main road, and it is not unknown for cars to go the wrong way around a roundabout simply because the route is shorter.

If a road narrows, expect the oncoming car to accelerate into the narrow space before you can. The driver will not slow down or allow you right of way, even if it is yours. Do not expect signals indicating turning left or right.

Weekend driving is worse. And when the roads are wet it can be worse still. Roads become slippery and in heavy storms many flood.

Since the recent introduction of traffic lights some crossings are safer, but still be wary as not all drivers respect them. The state of the roads is generally poor but plans are in hand to upgrade the whole system.

Currently, the newly introduced Vehicle Road Test ignores faults that might have been caused to vehicles by the poor state of the roads. This applies to the state of tyres. The test so far only covers lights, brakes and whether the engine and chassis numbers match those in the log book. Many do not.

Driving could well improve with the introduction of provisional driving licences (after passing the driving test, a driver is on a three-year trial before being given a full licence). Road signs are already greatly improved although it is still easy to get lost. The locals do anyway.

---

A leader in the [Malta] *Times* on 13 August 1999, calling for tougher action by the government and police, summed up the situation. *'Malta,'* said the newspaper, *'has one of the highest rates of road accidents in Europe. Many of us, drivers or not, are worried about this ... Apart from the excessive numbers of vehicles on the road, an appreciable number of them fit for the scrap-heap, we have few parking facilities in urban areas, our roads are the shame of the country and the scandal of Europe, and, above all, our drivers suffer from the impatience, poor discipline and hot temper that seem to be endemic in the Mediterranean region.'*
The solution: be alert and wary.

---

**Speed limits**  The speed limit is 64kph (40mph) on highways, 40kph (25mph) in towns and villages. Random breath testing at night has been introduced in the hope of reducing alcohol-related accidents.

**Accidents**  If you are involved in an accident do *not* move the car but wait until police have been called. Police notification is essential in any insurance claim.

In an emergency or if you have an accident:
**Police**: ☎ 191, **Ambulance**: ☎ 196

**Petrol stations**  Petrol stations open Mon–Sat from about 07.00 to 18.00. All have automatic machines (which take paper money only, not coins or credit cards) to supply petrol after hours or on Sundays.

## Car hire

There is a large number of car rental companies in Malta and Gozo, many with excellent modern cars in good condition. At Malta International Airport international names like *Hertz* and *Avis* have car rental desks, and it is possible to pick up and leave a hire car at the airport. There is no great advantage in pre-booking a hire car, except possibly in high season to ensure you get one.

Charges vary, with the well-known international names charging the highest rates but offering the best cars and insurance cover. Many smaller companies working from towns and villages offer more competitive rates. All cars are rented with unlimited mileage.

A valid driver's licence is required and drivers must be aged 25 or over. It is advisable to take out full insurance.

Leaders in the car rental field are:

### Malta
*Alamo*: John's Garage, 38 Triq Villambrosa, Ħamrun. ☎ 238745, 238580.
*Avis*: 50 Msida Sea Front, Msida. ☎ 225986.
*Europcar*: Alpine House, Naxxar Road, San Ġwann. ☎ 387361.
*Hertz*: United House, 66 Gżira Road, Gżira. ☎ 314636.
*Percius*: Triq Annibale Preca, Lija. ☎ 442530.
*Wembley's*: 50 St George's Road, St Julians. ☎ 374141, 332074.

### Gozo
*Gozo Garage*: 5 Triq Luigi Camilleri, Victoria. ☎ 555908.
*Mayjo*: Triq Fortunato Mizzi, Victoria. ☎ 556678.

### Car hire with a chauffeur
Many car hire companies like *Percius* and *Wembley* (see above) have a fleet of cars, usually shiny black Mercedes, complete with chauffeurs. These can be used simply as taxis or they can be taken for a day or half-day for sightseeing or touring the Islands. If you are visiting for a short time this is a very comfortable and easy way of getting around.

Agree a price first and discuss the sights and places you want to see. The drivers are not guides but may have picked up interesting information anyway. Of course the restaurants and shops they recommend may be the ones owned by relatives or where they collect a percentage. (See *Where to eat*, pp 23–28 for recommendations.)

## By taxi
Taxis are white, often diesel Mercedes, and carry the recognised Taxi sign on the roof. They are all fitted with meters but many drivers refuse to use them even though use of them is mandatory. So if you decide to take a cab, bargain *before* you enter. Maltese taxi drivers are inclined to be aggressive.

Taxis are only available from ranks and keep to their own hours of work. If you need a cab to collect you late at night, use a chauffeur-driven car.

## By motorcycle or bicycle
Motorcycles and scooters are readily available and inexpensive. A valid driving licence is required. All drivers and passengers on motorcycles must wear a helmet (available with the bike) when travelling.
*Albert's Scooter Shop*, 216 Rue d'Argens, Gżira. ☎ 340149.
*Peter's Scooter Shop*, 175A Rue d'Argens, Msida. ☎ 335244.

Although **cycling** is gaining popularity on the Islands it is not to be recommended in the summer months unless you are accustomed to the intense heat and sunshine. It is worth bearing in mind that the state of Maltese roads leaves much to be desired and Maltese car driving is remarkably short on courtesy. Cycles can be rented for the day.

*Cycle Store*, 135 Eucharistic Congress Street, Mosta. ☎ 432890.

*Victor Sultana*, Main Gate Street, Victoria. ☎ 556414.

## The karrozzin

The charming horse-drawn gharry, the Maltese *karrozzin*, has been in use since about 1850. For many years, particularly during the world wars, it was the only means of transport available. Today however the *karrozzin* numbers have dwindled and the carriage is now used only for short trip sightseeing. Many believe the horses should not be put to work on hot summer's days.

If you do take one for a short ride, negotiate the price before setting off.

## Getting from Malta to Gozo and Comino

The small heliport outside the village of Xewkija is used by **helicopter services** that connect with arriving and departing international flights at Malta International Airport.

If your final destination is Gozo or the hotel on Comino, the Tourist Information office at the airport can advise you on the best ways of getting there.

Independent travellers planning to use the helicopter can make seat reservations by telephone.The flight time is 20 minutes.

*Gozo Heliport:* ☎ 557905.

Malta helicopter reservations desk: ☎ 882920.

If you are not taking the helicopter, you need to get to Ċirkewwa on Malta's northern tip to catch the regular **car ferry** to Mġarr (Gozo) or the small craft that belongs to the *Comino Hotel.* The Gozo ferry timetable changes according to the season. The crossing takes about 20 minutes.

There is also an express passenger-only catamaran that races to Gozo and back, weather permitting, twice a day. It sails, somewhat inconveniently, from Sa Maison, outside Valletta, but makes a brief stop for passengers on Sliema's waterfront too. The journey time is about 30 minutes; the timetable is subject to changes.

There are two ways of getting to Ċirkewwa from the airport: by taxi or—and this is less advisable—by taxi to the Valletta central bus terminus where you catch the regular bus service to the ferry quay. This bus is often crowded and has no space for luggage. The service only runs in daylight hours.

If you take a taxi to the ferry quay, pre-pay at the official desk in the airport.

Should your destination be the Comino hotel, confirm arrangements with the hotel by telephone: ☎ 529821. The Hotel's own ferry runs from Ċirkewwa and takes about 15 minutes.

If you are renting a car for your visit to Gozo, this can be collected at the airport. However, to get to Gozo you will still have to drive to Ċirkewwa for the ferry. There are no cars, or roads, on Comino.

• **Tickets** for the Gozo ferry are not purchased in Malta, but on the quay at Mġarr in Gozo when you are returning. The trip *to* Gozo is 'free'; travellers purchase a ticket in Gozo having already travelled in one direction. The theory is that everyone has to return from Gozo unless you are Gozitan—in which case you qualify for a special rate anyway.

### Sightseeing tours

There are countless numbers of sighting tours on offer that come complete with a knowledgeable guide and air-conditioned coach. Hotels have most brochures and will make recommendations. So will most travel agents.

### A day trip to Sicily

In good weather a day-trip to **Catania** is a great favourite with Maltese who use the catamaran and coach link to get to the hectic city for a day's shopping. On such days the return to Malta can mean considerable delays at Customs while duty is levied on fellow nationals in a particularly severe manner.

A good, if long, day-tour of **southern Sicily** from Valletta is available on the *Virtu Ferries* catamaran (☎ 318854 ). The trip includes a 90-minute catamaran ride to Pozzallo, luxury coach trip through the lush countryside to the slopes of **Mount Etna** and then on further to the charming hillside resort of **Taormina.** There is time for lunch (extra) on the volcano and light refreshments (extra) in Sicily's most famous and elegant destination. As a day out it is to be recommended although it lasts in the region of 10 hours. Bookings can be made through all local travel agents.

# Language

While all officials, doctors and professionals speak English, Maltese and some Italian, bus and taxi drivers may be fluent only in Maltese. But, in all instances, there is almost certainly someone close by who will step in as willing translator—so a visitor need never worry. The Maltese are renowned for being a friendly nation and they take pride in welcoming visitors to the Islands.

*Malti* is a Semitic language, supposedly Phoenician in origin and modified later by Arabic accretions before AD 1000. Many words in daily use today however have been taken from more recent rulers and protectors of the Islands. The Knights of St John introduced Italian and French in the 16C when they arrived, and for many years Italian was considered the language of elegant society. English, of course, became the prominent language after the Islands came under the protection of Britain in 1800.

*Malti* is written in Roman characters, with additional adapted letters in the alphabet reputed to have been created by the Knights to accommodate the pronunciation of Arabic sounding words when written in Roman script. As a result the Maltese alphabet has 29 letters.

Three letters are dotted like an **i** to give additional characters and different pronunciation. A dotted **ċ**, for example, becomes the English *ch*—as in church. A dotted **ġ** takes the sound as in gem and dotted **ż** sounds like zebra. (Without the dot, *z* is pronounced *ts*.)

In addition an **h** (which is silent) can be crossed like a *t and so be pronounced as in hat* **while an** *x is always pronounced* sh. *So the town of Naxxar is pronounced* nash-ar.

You will also see **gh** in many words. This is regarded as a single letter and sometimes not pronounced at all. Often, when it is the final letter of word, it is pronounced as an *h*—but there are exceptions.

And there is a **q** that is an Arabic glottal stop, faintly like a *k*.

A great Maltese pleasure is asking visitors to pronounce *triq* (street), *sqaq* (alley) and *tqiq* (flour). Ask for a lesson.

The Maltese word for 'Yes' is *iva* (eeva). 'No' *is le* (as in *let*). 'Please' is derived from the Italian *grazzie* and becomes *grazzi* (grat-see).

*Tpejjepx*, when you see it, means No Smoking. It's easy to pronounce after you have heard it once.

---

### Street names

There was a time when all street names were both in English and Maltese but as local councils improve their districts, so all street name plaques are being changed to Maltese only. However, if you are having a problem saying Triq tat-Teatru l-Antik, Old Theatre Street will do. The Maltese and Gozitans know their streets by both names.

---

# Museums and monuments

The Government-run museums and places of historic importance are open to government approved schedules. Summer and winter hours are different. Opening hours are given with the descriptions in the main text. Government museums and national monuments include:

## Malta

**Valletta**
National Museum of Archaeology
National Museum of Fine Arts
War Museum
The Palace Armoury

**Birżebbuġa**
Ghar Dalam Cave and Museum

**Burmarad**
San Pawl Milqi

**Mdina**
National Museum of Natural History
(currently closed)

**Paola**
Ħal Saflieni Hypogeum

**Qrendi**
Ħagar Qim and Mnajdra Temples

**Rabat**
St Paul's Catacombs
Museum of Roman Antiquities

**Tarxien**
Tarxien Temples

**Vittoriosa**
Inquisitor's Palace
Maritime Museum

**Entrance fees** Lm1 per person, Lm4 for a Week Ticket. The fee also covers entrance to the Palace of the Grand Masters, Valletta. Entrance is free for anyone younger than 19 or over 65.

## Gozo

**In the Citadel, Victoria**
Folklore Museum
Museum of Archaeology
Natural History Museum
Cathedral Museum

**Xaghra**
Ġgantija Temples
Ta'Kola Windmill Museum

**Entrance fees**  To museums within the Citadel: LM1 per person per site; LM1.50 per person for first 3 sites (same day only). In Xaghra: Lm1 per person for both sites.

# Festivals and public holidays

## National holidays

There was a time when national holidays seemed to change with each political party as it took up office after an election. The greatest exponent of calendar change was the all-powerful Dom Mintoff who, when he came into power in the 1970s, decided there were far too many holy days in honour of saints. The Church, he believed, was too powerful and, as factories and offices would come to a halt during a *festa* in honour of a saint at least twice each month and many more times in the summer, he tidied the calendar. St Joseph the Worker's day became May Day, while the rest of the saints' days disappeared. The following is the present standard calendar of holidays:

New Year's Day: 1 January
Feast of St Paul's Shipwreck: 10 February
Feast of St Joseph: 19 March
Good Friday
Freedom Day: 31 March
May Day: 1 May
Sette Giugno: 7 June
Feast of the Assumption: 15 August
Victory Day: 8 September
Independence Day: 21 September
Feast of the Immaculate Conception: 8 December
Republic Day: 13 December
Christmas Day: 25 December

Of these, two public holidays are exclusive to Malta.

**Sette Giugno**: commemorates the bread riots of 1919 when starving Maltese took to the streets and a number were shot by the British forces.

**Victory Day**: (also the Feast day of Our Lady of Victories) was the day the Great Siege was lifted in 1565, when the islanders and the Order of St John defeated the Ottoman Turks. The day commemorates the islanders' bravery over the centuries with wreath-laying ceremonies in Valletta's Great Siege Square as well as Fort St Angelo and Adolorata Cemetery.

## The Festa

While a number of national holidays commemorate historical events or a religious occasion like Christmas Day or Good Friday, as far as most Maltese and Gozitans are concerned, the most important event is a local *festa*. This is especially true in smaller villages and rural communities.

Each town and village on the Islands has a parish church dedicated to a saint and this saint has his or her special day when the parish celebrates. (So as not to affect the working week, this day has generally become by custom a Saturday, and the *festa*, therefore, a weekend event.)

For the *festa*, the church's exterior is elaborately lit with coloured lights and its interior decked out with all the finery it can muster, with silver on display, candles, banks of flowers and draped columns. To alert the neighbourhood, petards shatter the sky above, exploding as they might in times of war—thus telling everyone for miles around whose *festa* it is.

The *festa* is a Mr and Mrs Average event. The whole family dresses up in their best, and usually the fronts of their houses are given a fresh coating of paint. In the evenings preceding the big weekend, bands march through the decorated streets; when the celebrations really start, they march in front, as a life-size effigy of the saint is paraded shoulder high at a snail's pace through the streets. Some statues, complete with elaborate stages, are so heavy it takes ten or more (willing) volunteers to carry them just a few steps at a time.

From Friday evening, the *festa* is a weekend of music, rowdy gatherings, loud bangs that frighten dogs and children, people strolling up and down eating hamburgers and chips, and a lengthy church service extolling the saint's virtues. Each night there is either a static display of fireworks on the parish square or an aerial display that costs the village a small fortune. (This money, even in the poorest community, is raised by door-to-door collections that take place every two weeks or so throughout the year.)

The *festa* season lasts from May to September.

## Other religious customs

These are not unique to the Maltese Islands but they are important to the local way of life.

**Carnival**  The weekend before Lent begins. As in all other Christian countries, carnival is only a part of religious practice in the sense that it is the last jollification before the abstinences of Lent. The first carnival in Malta, it is believed, was introduced to the Islands by the Knights of the Order of St John in about 1530.

The major parades of giant floats, grotesques and children in fancy dress are in Valletta where carnival groups also dance in Freedom Square. There is bizarre version in Gozo too, in Nadur. Here the custom is for men to dress as ugly women or figures of death.

**Easter**  A particularly favoured Maltese custom of this important Christian celebration is the ritual visiting of seven churches on the eve of Good Friday to pray at the Altars of Repose that have been solemnly draped for the occasion. It is not unusual to see families winding their way from church to church praying together or just chatting quietly. Groups may even visit the same church seven times, using different doors to enter and exit.

Good Friday itself is a public holiday with all shops closed and the local and Italian television stations broadcasting 'holy' movies like **Song of Bernadette** or **The Robe**. Cinemas remain open.

In many villages it is the custom for a solemn procession to start at about 17.00 and progress with all due gravity through the streets. Villagers dressed as figures from the time of Christ, from peasants to Roman centurions, lead the way as life-size statues depicting Christ's suffering and crucifixion follow, carried with all due solemnity by white hooded and robed figures reminiscent of the Ku Klux Klan. In some towns, such as Mosta and Żejtun, anonymous penitents often walk shrouded or barefoot in the procession. Many local travel agencies put these processions on their tour programmes.

Easter Sunday itself is a day for rejoicing, and in Vittoriosa, Żebbug and Qormi traditional early morning processions centre on a statue of the Risen Christ. In these towns, groups of young men, surrounded by cheering crowds, run through the streets carrying the statue in a show of natural exuberance. To restore dignity, the ecclesiastical hierarchy, the Curia, is attempting to put a stop to the tradition. Their words have yet to meet with success.

In Valletta this procession is held in the evening.

Easter Sunday is a family occasion and it is customary to visit relatives carrying Easter eggs for Granny and the grandchildren and later to have a lavish lunch together that will include roast baby lamb as one of the courses.

Another traditional—and delightful—Easter gift is a *figolla* made with sweet pastry filled with marzipan. Shaped like a fish, mermaid or lamb, the *figolla* is decorated with coloured icing and, probably, half a small chocolate Easter egg. Many families make their own but confectioners make excellent versions.

**Mnarja** 29 June, the Feast of St Peter and St Paul. By tradition a folk festival is held on this day in the leafy Buskett Gardens, below Verdala Castle, outside Rabat. The word *Mnarja* derives from *Luminarja* (illumination), going back to the centuries-old way of celebrating the feast by lighting the bastions of Mdina with flaming torches on the eve and feast day itself. It is a sort of harvest festival with the pride of Maltese fruit and vegetables on display; families arrive early with picnics ready to see the produce and, as dusk approaches, they gather together for folk music and song. The entertainment lasts into the early hours.

In the past *Mnarja* was so popular that it was not unusual for a groom to promise to take his bride to Buskett for *Mnarja* every year. Best finery was worn.

 # Entertainment

## Cinema and theatre

As in many countries, cinema attendance is booming in Malta. This may be because new releases reach the cinemas sooner or, more likely, because today's cinemas are better appointed and more comfortable than before. Be warned, the sound systems are very loud indeed.

There are 30 screens in Malta, two in Gozo. The biggest complex, **Eden Century**, has 16 screens at St Julians and four at Fgura. Other complexes are at Buġibba, Ħamrun, Marsascala, Valletta and Victoria, Gozo.

Malta's national theatre is **Teatru Manoel**, known to all as 'The Manoel'. A gem of a theatre (there are tours of the building and it has a charming café and shop), its programme is varied, from Verdi opera with visiting Italian singers to Shakespeare in Maltese. It is essential to pre-book for opera and concerts and for plays presented by national theatre companies visiting the island (☎ 222618). The season runs from October to June. At Christmas a traditional English-speaking panto is presented for two weeks. (Performances often last three hours.)

Large productions are often presented in the theatre at the **Mediterranean Conference Centre** (☎ 243840-6).

## Nightlife

Malta's late night area, albeit with a questionable reputation, is Paceville, the northerly neighbour of St Julians. It stays open until the early hours and the streets teem with young and very young people, a mixture of locals, brash youth in from the villages, and foreign students in Malta to learn English. Drugs are alleged to be part of the culture and many bars serve lethal cocktails. The average age would seem to be 16.

Every bar keeps it doors open and its music on full blast to attract attention although legislation limits this cacophony to 02.00. There is no obvious police presence and it is not unknown for a fight or two to break out in the early hours or a young tourist to claim she has been raped.

However, if you're young and with a gang of friends, this could be the place to be. Inexpensive bars jostle with cafés and hamburger joints. The best discos are here. Parking is almost impossible and there are many tow zones.

Sharing the district are St Julians, St George's Bay and Dragonara with smart hotels that have a choice of bars and restaurants. Just 100 metres from St George's Bay there is a giant air-conditioned cinema complex (20 screens) showing latest releases and a large bowling alley next to it. At Dragonara is the Islands' original casino (see below) and The Reef Club, the island's smartest beach club (see **Westin Dragonara Resort**, p 142).

To date there is little to do in the capital at night unless the season has begun at the Manoel Theatre (see above). There are, however, some excellent restaurants and a new cinema complex is regarded as part of broader plans for regenerating life in Valletta.

Resort areas like Buġibba and Qawra have their late-nights bars and discos. The island's second casino, The Oracle (see below), in Qawra, is open daily until 04.00.

## Gambling

The Maltese as a nation enjoy gambling, and the government runs three well-subscribed numbers competitions during the week from local Lotto Offices. There is also a National Lottery drawn four times a year.

There are two casinos, the **Dragonara Palace Casino** at St Julians and the **Oracle** at the New Dolmen Hotel. Both are run on strictly supervised international rules with roulette, Black Jack and *chemin de fer* and halls with a variety of slot machines. Minimum age of entry is 18 and all foreign nationals must produce a passport or ID card on a first visit. Both casinos have restaurants. Check dress code before going.

**Dragonara Palace Casino**, St Julians STJ 02. ☎ 382362-4.
**The Oracle Casino**, New Dolmen Hotel, Buġibba. ☎ 570057.

## Gay Life

There is an ever-changing number of bars and cafés popular with the gay and lesbian community. While most go out of fashion or close after a short life, in Paceville there is always a new one to take its place. There is no helpline for the homosexual community. The age of consent is 18. Cases of AIDS have been reported.

# Sport and leisure

The excellent climate from May to October makes Malta, Gozo and Comino ideal locations for anyone interested in watersports. Even in the winter months, when temperatures drop, they fall only to a modest 14°C and there is still an average 6 hours a day of sunshine.

## International sporting events in Malta

The following events have taken place, or may take place annually, in the Maltese Islands:

International Games of the Small States of Europe
Malta Spring Marathon
World Paralympics Swimming Championships
European Waterpolo League
FIFA and EUFA Football Competitions
Cycling Tour of Malta
Malta Spring International Triathlon
Association of Tennis Professionals Challenger Tournament
Malta Open Judo Championships

## Swimming

Although the Islands are in some of the cleanest and clearest blue waters of the Mediterranean, beaches in the traditional sense are fairly limited, especially if you are looking for sand.

The best sand beaches are **Għajn Tuffieħa** and **Golden Bay** on Malta and **Ramla** with its red sand on Gozo. On the rare day the red flag is flying on the promontory that separates the two Maltese bays, do not swim far from the shore-line—there can be a treacherous undercurrent.

The largest stretch of sand, and certainly the most popular and most crowded because of its facilities like cafés and beach establishments, is **Ghadira** just below Mellieha. Easy parking too.

Then, worth checking out, there is **Ġnejna** with gritty sand (much less crowded as a result) and the smaller places like **Paradise Bay**, **Armier** and **Little Armier**, and even **Slug Bay** where there is room for little more than a dozen sunbathers. On Comino there are two sandy beaches.

Because of the pounding rough seas in winter, the sandy beaches have more sand some years than others. But they are excellent for young children.

The Maltese enjoy swimming off the stretches of smooth white rock that run down the easterly sides of the Islands just as much as they do on sand. And there are plenty of sheltered coves and good spots around the resort areas of **St Julians**, **Sliema** and **St George's** as well as on the south of the island at **Delimara**, **Xrobb il-Għaġin** and **Peter's Pool**.

On Gozo, the best swimming spots are around **Marsalforn** and **Xlendi**.

By and large, if you are exploring and see a group of Maltese or Gozitans swimming, then it's a good spot.

If you like things to be more sedate and more fashion conscious, there are also popular beach clubs and lidos. These have beds, umbrellas, showers, cafés, snack bars, service and good swimming facilities as well as dive schools.

The *Reef Club* at Dragonara just off St Julians is considered the most elegant beach resort (it is not unknown for bikinis and sarongs to be changed many times during the day). The *Corinthia Resort* at St George's Bay with its wide assortment of cafés, bars and restaurants is a family favourite.

Remember: topless or nude sunbathing and swimming are not permitted. There are, however, secluded spots where both take place.

## Diving

There are a number of professional and well-accredited dive schools in Malta and Gozo and a wide selection of excellent dives dotted around the Islands for both beginners and experienced divers. The tourist offices have a list of licensed diving schools.

If you plan to take a diving course you must possess a medical certificate confirming your good health. It is best to bring this to Malta with you.

• For diving contacts there are:

*Professional Association of Diving Instructors* (PADI), Msida Court, 61/2 Msida Seafront, Msida.

*Federation of Underwater Activities–Malta* (FUAM), PO Box 29, Gżira.

There is a decompression chamber at St Luke's Hospital in case of accidents and there is an excellent air and sea rescue service.

## Football

Soccer is a Maltese passion with fans following both Italian and British leagues. The Maltese supporters club for Manchester United is reputed to be the largest outside Britain. If a match is screened on television with either Manchester United or Juventus playing, the streets are empty. When a local team wins a game in the local cup, however, they are crowded as supporters take to their cars and the roads with horns blaring and flags waving.

The local season starts in September and runs until May. Top matches are played at the modern **National Stadium** at **Ta'Qali**, just outside Mdina.

## Shooting

Many Maltese and Gozitans, like their neighbours the Sicilians, shoot or trap any bird as it migrates across their territory. Although open seasons are regulated, the rules are flouted. To avoid contentious discussion with the Maltese, avoid this subject.

The **Bidnija Shooting Range** in the countryside outside Mosta is run by the *Malta Shooting Federation*, who acted as hosts to the fifth International Games of the Small States of Europe. The range offers clay pigeon shooting as well as Olympic trench and sheet.

Courses and training camps are organised. The shooting range follows the regulations required by the Union Internationale de Tir.

Contact: Secretary, Malta Shooting Federation, PO Box 340, GPO Valletta. 415715.

## Skydiving

This is *the* new Malta experience.

Skydiving is considered to be one of the most exhilarating sports of modern times—and you can do it in Gozo. There are parachuting courses where after two days of ground-training you jump from 1200m from a helicopter attached to a static line. Tandem jumping, where you jump safely attached by harness to your instructor, is also available. There is an AFF (Accelerated Freefall) course aimed at those whose ambition is to become skydivers. None are for the timid.
Contact: *Sport Parachuting Association of Malta*, 8 Buckingham Court, Fisherman Street, Buġibba. ☎ 582153 ▤ 585766.

## Sports and Country Club

Tennis, squash, cricket and golf can be played at the **Marsa Sports Club** just a short distance from Valletta. It has landscaped gardens set alongside a golf course. Polo is also played. The club welcomes temporary members. There is a pool, choice of restaurants and, as the base of the Royal Malta Golf Club, it offers golfing visitors full facilities including hire of equipment, coaching fees and golf clinics.
Contact: The Executive Secretary, Marsa Sports Club. ☎ 233851. ▤ 231908.

## Waterpolo

This may not be as popular a sport as football, but in the summer months you would be forgiven for thinking it is. The supporters of various Maltese waterpolo clubs are as vociferous as as any football fans when the season is in full swing. The three big names to support, or beat, are Sirens, Sliema and Neptunes whose own pitch at Balluta, Sliema, is the great outdoor venue on Saturday evenings.

The **National Swimming Pool** that forms part of the University Sports Complex, Tal-Qroqq, is where the top games take place.

 # Health

Malta follows the World Health Organisation's recommendations on health safety. There are two government-run hospitals, the main one being **St Luke's** which has an exemplary ITU emergency service department. Under construction is a large new hospital close to the University which will take some of the load off St Luke's. There are three small private hospitals.

Also run by the Government are a number of health centres and polyclinics in the towns and villages. These are well staffed and able to offer first aid.

The health service in Malta has a reciprocal agreement for medical treatment with Britain that provides for immediate medical care for British citizens for up to one month. More health agreements are being reached with member states of the EU.

All hotels have the services of a local doctor available. Doctors in Malta and Gozo speak English and Maltese and, often, Italian.

● **Emergency Service/Ambulance**
Malta ☎ 196     Gozo ☎ 561600
● **Hospitals**
*St Luke's Hospital*, Gwardamanga, Msida, ☎: 241251 or 234101.
*Gozo General Hospital*, Triq l'Arċisqof Pietru Pace, Victoria, ☎ 561600.

## Pharmacies

Pharmacists have wide prescribing powers and most well-known prescribed medicaments are available. Occasionally they will accept the medical prescriptions of overseas doctors but, if in doubt or the drug is protected by a Government list, they will refer the patient to a local doctor. Many chemists have doctors' clinics on their premises.Visitors with specific medical requirements should ensure they have an adequate supply of drugs etc to meet their needs.

 # Telephone and postal services

## Telephones

Direct dialling is possible to every country already accessible on the international system.

The communications system is operated by **Maltacom** who have a monopoly until Malta becomes a member state of the EU. Unless you find an old style phone box, call boxes only take phonecards. These are generally available at stationers and some bars and supermarkets to values of Lm2, Lm3, Lm4 and Lm5.

Although many distinctive red British call boxes are still in use, new call boxes are aluminum and glass.

### Useful telephone numbers

**Directory Enquiries**: 190    **Overseas Operator**: 194    **Time check**: 195

As Maltacom's Directory Enquiries service can often seem permanently engaged, it is quicker for local enquiries to call the service offered by Vodaphone, the original mobile telephone provider on the Islands: ☎ 09190.

Maltacom's main branch, at Mercury House, Triq San Ġorg, St George's, is open 24 hours a day. ☎ 310980.

Branch offices in Birkirkara, Ħamrun, Malta International Airport, Mosta, Naxxar, Paola, Qawra, The Plaza Shopping Mall in Sliema, Vittoriosa and Victoria, Gozo, are open during office hours.

Vodaphone will arrange a short term GSM mobile telephone if requested: ☎ 493073.

### Emergency telephone numbers

**Ambulance** 196          **Fire** 199                    **Police** 191

## Postal services

At the hub of the Mediterranean, the Maltese Islands are linked to Europe and further afield by air, so today's mail is speedily delivered.

Many towns and some villages have post offices or a sub-post office. Stamps are available from most stationers and hotels.

The **General Post Office** is in the Auberge d'Italie, Merchants Street, Valletta. Post office hours in Valletta are:

1 October–15 June: Mon–Sat 08.00–18.00 (open all day)
16 June–30 September: Mon–Sat 07.30–18.00

Branch post offices in Malta and Gozo open year round, Monday to Saturday 07.30–12.45.

All offices are closed on public holidays.

> ### Philately
> The Maltese Post Office prides itself on the quantity and quality of its output of stamps. It has efficient arrangements for 'first day' franking. Its *Philatelic Bureau* offers a comprehensive service to stamp collectors worldwide, including standing accounts for new stamp issues.

 # Additional information

## Banking services

Banking hours are usually Mon–Fri 08.30–12.45, Sat 08.00–12.00, but they sometimes vary slightly between summer and winter.

The main banks are *HSBC Bank* (Malta), the *Bank of Valletta*, *Lombard Bank* and *APS*. All have branches across Malta and Gozo.

The best exchange rates are available through banks because the Central Bank of Malta issues the official rates. Malta International Airport has round-the-clock foreign exchange facilities.

## Embassies in Malta

**Australian High Commission**: Ta'Xbiex Terrace, Ta'Xbiex. ☎ 338201-5. ▤ 344059.

**British High Commission**: 7 St Anne Street, Floriana. ☎ 233134-7. ▤ 292001.

**French Embassy**: Villa Seminia, 12 Sir Temi Zammit Street, Ta'Xbiex. ☎ 331107/335856.

**German Embassy**: Il-Piazzetta, Entrance B, Tower Road, Sliema. ☎ 336531. ▤ 333976.

**Italian Embassy**: 1 Vilhena Street, Floriana. ☎ 233157-8.

**Indian High Commission**: Regional Road, St Julians SGN 02. ☎ 344302-3.

**Libyan Embassy**: Dar il-Jamaharija, Notabile Road, Balzan. ☎ 436347-8. ▤ 483939.

**Palestinian Embassy**: Villa Kasana, Triq il-Verdun, Kappara. ☎ 382355. ▤ 370605.

**Tunisian Embassy**: Dar Carthage, Qormi Road, Attard BZN 02. ☎ 498853. ▤ 499973.

**United States Embassy**: Development House, St Anne Street, Floriana. ☎ 235960-5. ▤ 246917.

## Shopping hours

Shops generally open between 09.00 and 09.30, Monday to Saturday. They close for lunch generally, between 12.30 and 16.00, and close for the day at about 19.00. The hours are fluid because many shops stay open longer to service tourists; others close earlier because life here is relaxed. Most jewellers close on Saturday afternoons as do village grocers.

If you are self-catering check the times of neighbourhood food shops. All grocers and butchers close on Wednesday afternoons and many close on Saturday afternoons too.

● The best fruit and vegetables are sold from vans. Produce is invariably fresh as the van's owner buys his stock from the *pitkali*, the wholesale market, and buys just enough for his regular clientele. The freshest produce is available Monday and Thursday evenings, the days he stocks up. They do not work on Saturdays, Sundays or Monday mornings.

## Personal security

Although nothing should be taken for granted, the Islands are comparatively safe and there is little violent crime. In summer months there have been instances of bag-snatching, and many hire cars (easily identified by their coded number plates) become prey when interesting objects like cameras or bags are left in sight. Women need not feel threatened out alone at night, but common sense should always prevail.

### Police

If you do become the victim of a crime, notify the police immediately. If necessary, seek assistance from your embassy. If you are detained by the police, you must contact your embassy.

There is a police station in each town or village but it may not be open after office hours. The crime rate in Malta does not seem to merit extended hours.

**In Malta**: Police General Headquarters, Calcedonius Street, Floriana. ☎ 224 001. Open 24 hours.

**In Gozo**: Police General Headquarters, 113 Republic Street, Victoria. ☎ 552 040.

## Newspapers

There are two local English-language newspapers, the long established, pro-establishment *Times* and its challenger, the equally pro-establishment *Malta Independent*. The *Times* sells nearly three times as many copies as the *Independent*.

There are a number of Maltese-language dailies too, the two leaders being *In-Nazzjon*, the voice of the Nationalist party, and *L-Orizzont*, the voice of the Labour party. All newspapers have their Sunday editions.

Most British national newspapers and a number of the leading dailies from Italy and Germany are available in Malta in the evening of the day of publication or early the following morning. Their arrival depends on flight schedules. In Gozo they are on the bookstands the following morning.

British Sunday newspapers are available the same morning in Malta and Gozo.

Most major English and Italian monthly magazines and periodicals are available within a day of their publication.

## Television and radio

There are eight local **television** stations fighting for the same audience and besieging the same sources of advertising for the revenues they need in order to survive. Some, therefore, are doomed.

The government-run and financially supported station is *TVM*, while the two main political parties have their own stations, *Net TV* (Nationalists) and ***Super One***

(Labour Party), each with its own loyal viewers. Although the stations broadcast in Maltese, regular fare is provided in the form of old and new British and US comedy shows, series and soaps broadcast in English. *Super One* has the largest audience.

There is also a monopoly cable TV service which relays the local stations plus CNN, BBC World and BBC Prime, Discovery, National Geographic, all the Italian stations and some others. In all, more than 50 channels.

There are also 18 licensed **radio** stations broadcasting daily, mostly in Maltese. Some broadcast for just a few hours, others offer a 24-hour service. One station is backed by the Church and offers religious programmes. Chart music is the common denominator of the others.

## Religious services

Services in **Roman Catholic** churches in Malta and Gozo are in Maltese. Special Sunday Masses are held in other languages.

**In English**
Valletta: Santa Barbara, Republic Street, noon
Birżebbuġa: St George's Chapel, 10.00
Buġibba: St Maximilian Kolbe church, 10.30, summer months
Marsascala: St Anne's, 11.00
Mellieha: Our Lady's Sanctuary, 10.00
Rabat: St Dominic's, 11.15
Sliema: St Patrick's, 08.00, 09.00, 10.00, 18.30, 19.30
**In Italian**
Valletta: St Catherine of Italy, Sunday 11.15
**In French**
Valletta: Santa Barbara, 10.00
**In German**
Valletta: Santa Barbara, 11.00
**In Greek**
Valletta: Our Lady of Damascus, 09.00

## Other denominations

**Anglican**
Valletta: St Paul's Anglican Pro-Cathedral. ☎ 225714
Sliema: Holy Trinity Church, Rudolph Street. ☎ 330575
**Bible Baptist Church**
Msida. ☎ 322752
**Church of Scotland, Methodist and Free Churches**
Valletta: South Street. ☎ 222643
**Protestant Church of Germany**
Valletta: South Street. ☎ 454145
**Greek Orthodox**
Valletta: Church of St George, 83 Merchants Street. ☎ 221600
**Jewish Community**
Secretary. ☎ 445924

## Etiquette

• **In church** When visiting a church 'decency' in dress is called for as they are, above all, sacred places of worship. This means women should cover bare shoulders or deep plunging necklines. A scarf or shawl will do.

Short shorts worn by men or women may also cause problems. At the Ta' Pinu Sanctuary in Gozo wrap-around skirts with Velcro fastening are given to both men and women to wear, the ecclesiastical authorities preferring to see a man in a skirt rather than with thighs exposed.

• **Swimming and sunbathing** Although there are certain stretches of beach where people swim and sunbathe nude, this is illegal and a punishable offence. So is topless bathing even though it is occasionally condoned by hotels in the privacy of their pool areas. Peeping Toms with binoculars haunt the more secluded beaches in the hope of finding cavorting nude tourists.

## Tipping

As a rough guide, the following is acceptable appreciation for service rendered:

**Airport** for baggage: 50 cents (total)
**Hairdresser** 10 per cent
**Hotel chambermaid** Lm1 per week
**Waiter** 10 per cent
**Taxi driver** no tip
**Chauffeur** 50 cents to Lm1, depending on length of journey

## Urgent despatch

Large international carriers like *FedEx* and *TNT* have offices in Malta. But unless a package is deemed urgent it may only be delivered during normal office hours on work days. It is worth checking delivery times with the office concerned if you are expecting a package.

### Local offices

*DHL International*, Triq Ġanni Vassallo, Luqa LQA 02. ☎ 800148. 🖺 691295
*Federal Express*, Seaspeed House, Ninu Cremona Street, Paola PLA 01. ☎ 693715. 🖺 804130.
*TNT Express Worldwide*, Aircargo House, Dawret Ħal-Luqa, Luqa. ☎ 666999. 🖺 665044.

# BACKGROUND INFORMATION

## History of Malta

### The making of history: key dates

**BC**

**5000–4100**  *Neolithic Age* The first settlers arrive.

**4100–2500**  *Temple Period* New settlers arrive from Sicily. Their experimentation in building leads to the construction, from 3600, of unique megalithic temples notably those at Ġgantija in Gozo and Ħaġar Qim and Mnajdra in Malta. They are the oldest, free-standing stone edifices in the world.

**2500–700**  *Bronze Age* Villages (like Borġ in-Nadur) take shape.

**700–550**  *Phoenician* Phoenician merchants use Malta as a commercial base.

**550–218**  *Carthaginian* Carthaginians conquer Malta to take control of sea routes.

**264–241**  First Punic War between Rome and Carthage.

**218**  Roman forces capture Malta in Second Punic War. Islands incorporated into Republic of Rome.

**AD**

**60**  St Paul shipwrecked on his way to stand trial in Rome. Introduces Christianity to the Maltese.

**117–138**  During Hadrian's reign the Islands become a Roman municipality.

**535–870**  *Byzantine* Malta is part of the Eastern Roman Empire and an important naval base.

**870–1127**  *Arab* Invasion of Aghlabid Arabs. They introduce their religion, Islam, and crops like cotton, figs and citrus fruit.

**1090**  Count Roger the Norman invades from Sicily but fails to secure the Islands.

**1127–1194**  *Norman* Count Roger II occupies Malta and makes it part of Kingdom of Sicily.

**1194–1266**  *Swabian* (German) The Queen of Sicily marries the ruling Duke of Swabia and the Islands come under German rule.

**1266–1282**  *Angevins* (French) Charles of Anjou, brother of Louis IX, conquers the Kingdom of Naples and Sicily. Malta becomes part of his empire.

**1282–1530**  *Aragonese* (Spanish) Peter the Great, King of Aragon, helps the Sicilians massacre the Angevins, and the Maltese Islands come under Spanish rule.

**1530–1798**  *Order of St John* Enter the Knights who have been given the Islands as their base by Emperor Charles V (King Charles I of Spain). A force of more than 4000 settles around Birgu (Vittoriosa).

| | |
|---|---|
| **1551** | Corsairs from the Barbary Coast (North Africa) attack Gozo. They seize population as slaves. |
| **1565** | *The Great Siege of Malta* Ottoman Turks besiege this Christian outpost. For three months Suleiman the Magnificent's land force lays siege. Help finally comes from Sicily. |
| **1566** | The fortified city of Valletta is founded. |
| **1574** | The Inquisition is established in Malta. |
| **1683** | Ottoman Turk force is defeated outside Vienna. As peace returns so, for the next century, many of the Islands' finest Baroque buildings are erected. |
| **1798–1800** | *French* Napoleon Bonaparte arrives. French force takes Malta without a shot fired. The Order of St John is despatched. |
| **1800–1964** | *British* The Maltese rise against the French. Britain offers help in the name of the King of the Two Sicilies. Malta comes under protection of British Crown. |
| **1802** | Peace of Amiens declares Malta should be returned to Order of St John but Maltese people object and vote to remain under British protection. |
| **1814** | Treaty of Paris awards Malta to Britain. Islands become a British Crown Colony. |
| **1835** | First Council of Government. |
| **1914–1918** | *World War One* Malta becomes known as 'Nurse of the Mediterranean' as it provides care for the wounded. |
| **1919** | *Sette Giugno* riots. Unemployment and poverty as economy fails after the Great War. Troops called in to control crowds in Bread Riot. Four Maltese shot. |
| **1921** | Self-government is granted. Opening of Malta's first parliament. |
| **1930** | Constitution suspended by Britain after Church tells people to vote Nationalist. |
| **1932** | Constitution restored. |
| **1933** | Britain withdraws Constitution. Malta reverts to Crown Colony government status of 1814. |
| **1936** | Constitution again restored. Members of Executive Council are nominated. |
| **1939–1945** | *World War Two*. |
| **1940** | 11 June, first air raids from Italy. |
| **1942** | Islands enter Second Great Siege. More than 1500 civilians are killed. Supply lines are cut causing severe famine. People of Malta awarded George Cross for Gallantry by George VI. |
| **1943** | Italy surrenders. Blockade of Malta ends. |
| **1947** | Restoration of self-government with Governor as head of state. |
| **1964** | *Independence* Malta becomes independent state within British Commonwealth. Reduction of British forces and garrison leads to unemployment and emigration. |
| **1971** | First Maltese Governor General is appointed. |
| **1974** | *Republic* Malta becomes a Republic with a ceremonial President. The Islands remain in Commonwealth. |
| **1979** | After 180 years, as military agreements terminate, last of the British force sail out of the Grand Harbour. |

| | |
|---|---|
| **1987** | Malta declares itself a neutral and non-aligned state. |
| **1989** | The Malta Summit: 1–3 December. US President George Bush and Soviet leader Mikhail Gorbachev meet at Marsaxlokk to mark end of Cold War. |
| **1990** | Malta applies for membership of European Community. |
| **1990** | 25–27 May. Pope John Paul II visits. |
| **1992** | 28–30 May, Queen Elizabeth II unveils Siege Bell during George Cross 50th anniversary celebrations. |
| **1996** | Labour party in power freezes application for European Union membership. |
| **1998** | Nationalist government resubmits EU membership application. |
| **2000** | European Union in discussion with Malta about future membership. |

# Ancient Malta

*by Ann Monsarrat*

There is no known area in the world the size of Malta that packs in so many and such a variety of ancient relics. These three small islands, with a total land area of little more than 300sq km, have been prey to almost every empire builder in the Mediterranean and have played a role in the history of Europe out of all proportion to their size. At the very dawn of civilisation, however, it was the Maltese who led the way, building massive, megalithic temples, which are now regarded as the oldest, free-standing stone buildings in the world.

### Old bones

The first signs of life on Malta were discovered at the beginning of the 20C in a long, snaking cavern called **Ghar Dalam** (the Cave of Darkness). During the great ice ages, sea levels were so low that what are now the Maltese Islands were merely the highest peaks of a triangular land mass that spread southwards from Sicily. A strange menagerie of hippopotamuses, elephants and red deer roamed across this fertile peninsula and were trapped when the seas rose again. From around 250,000 to 10,000 years ago their skeletons were washed into this vast repository.

The larger species had adapted to diminishing space and food supplies, and to a lack of natural predators, by decreasing in size, while many of the smaller birds and beasts grew larger. Remains have been found of a swan with a 2.5m wingspan, a dormouse the size of a rabbit and an adult elephant no larger than a St Bernard dog. There is now a charming little museum on the site and many more fossilised bones still protruding from the cave floor between the stalagmites and stalactites.

The first evidence of human activity was also discovered here, though some of it proved misleading. What appeared to be two Neanderthal teeth caused considerable excitement for a while, seeming to indicate a very early human presence. But the flurry ebbed when the same kind of teeth were found in the Islands' Neolithic population and evaporated completely when a modern Maltese dentist extracted one from the mouth of one of his patients.

## The first settlers

It is now thought unlikely that the Islands were inhabited before 5000 BC. Indeed, they are thought to have been uninhabitable until man learned to farm and to build boats sturdy enough to transport livestock. On a clear day, the archipelago can be seen from the southern foothills of Sicily, 80 or so kilometres away, and there are many indications that the first settlers sailed from this direction. They brought with them cattle, goats, pigs and enough wheat, barley and lentils for their first harvest.

For a while these Stone Age families lived in caves and then constructed small villages. One of them, at **Skorba** (western Malta), flourished for well over 1000 years. Their dwellings were simple, with walls of mudbrick set on an oval foundation of rough stone. The contents of two of them indicate some form of religious activity: goat skulls, explicitly female figurines and cows' toe bones, levelled off so that they could stand upright.

There appears to have been a flourishing trade in goods not available locally. Flint, obsidian, lava grinding stones and ochre were all imported. Some of them came from the Lipari Islands and Pantelleria, though they were all probably routed through Sicily.

About 1000 years after the first settlers arrived there was either an influx of new people or a sudden change in local customs. Instead of single burials in shallow pits, the dead began to be buried in fine chambers carved deep into the soft limestone. The lobed shape of one of these graves at **Xemxija** (above St Paul's Bay) appears to have influenced the design of the great stone temples.

## Temple builders

The French artist, Jean Houel, who visited Malta and Gozo in 1777, said he had seen the remains of huge, megalithic monuments wherever he went and suspected that many more had been pulled down to make way for new buildings. Since then, many others have disappeared into field walls and house foundations, but there are still 23 known temple sites and another 25 scatterings of huge stones that have yet to be investigated. They were all built between 3600 and 2500 BC.

Many are complexes, with two or three temples protected by one massive stone overcoat and the remains of smaller temples dotted around them, as at **Ħaġar Qim**, **Mnajdra** and **Tarxien**. There is even a subterranean re-creation of a temple in a labyrinthine burial area called the **Hypogeum**.

At **Ġgantija** (the Giantess), in Gozo, the massive walls of hard, grey limestone encircling two early temples still, after 5000 years, rise to a height of 6m and contain one block the size of a small cottage. The last of the temple complexes to be built, **Tarxien**, shows an astonishing advance in the masons' craft. The great blocks of its walls, though they no longer rise to the same height as at Ġgantija, were cut with such precision that they still look like a crack army unit on parade. The soft limestone interior carvings, of spirals and animal friezes, were not to be rivalled anywhere in the world for at least 1000 years.

All this was achieved by a people with no written language or knowledge of any kind of metal. Their tools were stone axes, flint, the volcanic glass obsidian, and levers of wood and antlers. They rolled the great blocks around on stones shaped like cannon balls, which can still be seen on many of the sites.

Before radiocarbon dating, these ancient marvels were thought to be latecomers, inspired by Mycenae and Knossos. The new dating techniques changed all that. They proved that the Maltese temples are not only far older than these early

Greek civilisations, but that they were already being built 1000 years before the Egyptians set to work on their first pyramid c 2500 BC. As one unique phenomenon, they are now a UNESCO World Heritage Site. (For temple sites, see also *The Neolithic Temples*, pp 193–200.)

## Religious rituals

The temple builders left too many clues behind to doubt that these monuments were places of worship with rituals linked to birth, death and rebirth. Hoards of charred animal bones in intricately carved niches, a flint knife in a secret drawer, tethering holes, hearths and piles of broken pots, are a pretty good indication that animals were sacrificed and the cooked flesh or liquid offerings distributed to the congregation.

The carved friezes of cattle, goats, fish and pigs (now on display at the Museum of Archaeology, Valletta) are doubtless a tribute to the sacrificed beasts. There are oracle and libation holes and an inner sanctum with carved spirals on its threshold, which glare out like a pair of guardian eyes.

## Fat ladies

Elegantly posed, carved stone statues, with massive hips, arms and thighs, and neat little hands and feet, were found in abundance in several of the temples. With unusual candour they were called 'fat ladies' until it was noticed that they had either no breasts or ones so meagre they would shame a sumo wrestler. Some of them wear pleated skirts, but these too are no indication of gender: patently male figurines wear them too.

The terms now used are obese or fat figures and the discovery of a monumental example, in a prime position at **Tarxien**, leaves little doubt that this was the chief deity. The corpulence is now taken to represent fertility in its widest sense of general prosperity. The carvings of bulls and snakes and some fine stone phalluses, two of them handsomely encased in their own little shrine, may indicate that minor cults operated too.

These temple carvings have notched up some impressive records of their own dating from between 3600 and 2500 BC. They include what is probably the first portrayal of a deity, the first representation of ritual garments and the first decorative spirals. Before radiocarbon dating, carved spirals were thought to have been a Greek invention.

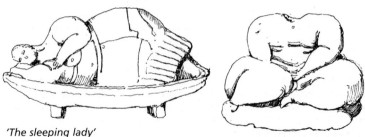

'The sleeping lady'

Another 'fat figure', this one found at Ħagar Qim

If the worshippers dressed half as well as their cult statues they must have been an elegant sight, with their pleated skirts (long and mini), tiny turban hats and hooded jerkins, smartly bobbed hair, pigtails and rows of curls like a judge's wig. Their burial places have shown them to be in the main a fine-boned race with some sturdier people of a type still to be found on the Islands. Some of them had bunions and arthritis and one little girl was buried with a puppy. They also seem to have been remarkably peaceable people. The only weapons found for the entire period are a couple of sling-shots.

There is, however, no sign that these supreme workers in stone used their talent for domestic purposes. The few houses so far discovered only vary from the mudbrick huts of the first settlers in having better foundations. How this great era came to an end is still a tantalising mystery. Many theories have been put forward from drought or overpopulation, to too much effort going into temple-building at the expense of agriculture, priestly rivalry or religious mania.

## Bronze Age warriors

By the time a new group of settlers arrived around 2500 BC, the temples seem to have been abandoned, probably for a few hundred years, though this does not necessarily mean that the entire temple population had disappeared. The newcomers, for the first time, brought metal to the Islands, bronze axes and daggers, and the first indications of warfare. Even their obsidian arrowheads were a good deal more lethal than the temple builders' sling-shots.

They have been called the **Tarxien Cemetery People** because they turned **Tarxien** and a few other temples into crematoriums, burning the bodies in one part, storing the ashes in pottery urns in another and probably using the beams that had once roofed the temples for their funeral pyres.

They also erected menhirs (single standing stones) and dolmens, a very different form of disposing of the dead. There are still a few of both scattered around the Islands. On Gozo, a whole line of dolmens, only two of which are still complete, once stared across the valley from the **Ta'Ċenċ ridge**. The holes and grooves carved into some of their great capstones are identical to the markings on dolmens near Otranto, in the heel of Italy, and provide the only clue to where the newcomers had sprung from.

After about 500 years the Bronze Age people took to the hilltops and built massive defensive walls where necessary, though why they felt the need to do so remains a puzzle. Internal rivalry, hostile invasions or an increasing threat from pirates are the most likely solutions. Within these strongholds, they again lived in mudbrick huts or, where they happened to be conveniently to hand, domesticated temple ruins.

After another half-century or so, there was another small injection of new blood from Sicily. This group kept themselves very much to themselves on their own fortified promontory at **Baħrija**, in the west of Malta. They made pottery far superior to that of the older settlers and, judging by the amount of clay loom weights they left behind, set up a busy weaving industry.

This period coincided with the great flowering of Knossos and Mycenae, the expansion of mining for tin, copper, silver and gold and the extended trade routes needed to spread around these prestigious goods. There is little to show that the inhabitants of Malta, huddled on their hilltops, benefited much from any of this. A piece of Mycenean pottery found in one of the settlements, **Borġ in-Nadur**, and pots from the same settlement found in Sicilian graves are the only indications so far that they were not completely isolated.

## Cart tracks

Of all the enigmas in Malta's mysterious past its cart tracks are the most baffling. These pairs of deep grooves in the bare rock, always the same distance apart, can be seen in many places, careering over the landscape. They curve, branch off in different directions and disappear beneath fields, over cliffs and into the sea. In one area they criss-cross in such profusion that the place has been called **Clapham Junction**, after the busy railway station that filters traffic into London.

They were obviously made by some form of vehicle, but the depth of some of the tracks and the occasional sharp bends rule out carts with wheels or runners. What propulsion was used is another puzzle since there is no sign of wear on the rock between the tracks, as there should be if hoofed animals had been used.

The latest proposition is that it was man who did the donkeywork, with two crossed pieces of wood resting on his shoulders and the other end of the struts running along the tracks: what is known as a slide car.

Just what was transported in this manner is another problem. Salt or soil, for the terracing of fields, have been suggested. Building materials are also a possibility, since small piles of stone have been found at intervals alongside some of the tracks.

How old they are is another matter of lively debate. Phoenician tombs were cut through some of them, so they are presumed to pre-date the Phoenicians, though one distinguished Maltese archaeologist links them with Roman quarries. The jury is still out but, since none of them lead to temple sites while some head for Bronze Age settlements, they are currently placed in the Bronze Age.

## Phoenician traders

Malta's many fine harbours were used by the Phoenicians (the Canaanites of the Bible) as early as the 8C or early 7C BC. These master mariners, in their round merchant ships and armed galleys with two banks of oars, were the supreme traders of their age, more interested in safe havens and trade routes rather than conquest. But they were forced into harsher measures in the 6C BC, after the Abyssinians had overrun their homeland, in what is now Lebanon, and the Greeks were threatening their long-established ports in Sicily. It was then that the Phoenicians' great colony, Carthage, rose in power, took control of their other North African bases and occupied Malta.

## Carthaginian colonists

At the height of its power Carthage was the richest city in the Mediterranean. A million people inhabited its glorious, impregnable fortress in the Bay of Tunis, and many more farmed the fertile land beyond its towering walls. Malta soon reaped the benefit of being allied to such wealth. Greek chroniclers recorded its ambitiously constructed buildings, with their ornate, stucco cornices, and the skill of its workmen in every type of craft, especially in weaving the finest and softest linen. The chief survivor of this affluence, a monumental tower, over 5m high, still stands in the village of **Żurrieq** in southern Malta, where it now adorns the garden of the parish priest.

For the first time Malta and Gozo had towns as well as villages, a central administration, headed by a ruling magistrate, their own coinage and a garrison of up to 2000 men, no doubt made up of a typically Carthaginian assortment of mercenaries culled from all over the Mediterranean. The Carthaginians raised sanctuaries to their deities, Astarte and Melqart, and inscribed on marble slabs their gratitude to the local population for their help in building and restoring them.

They left behind two small, carved pillars, which proved to be Malta's equivalent of the Rosetta Stone. With their dedications to Melqart in both Phoenician and Greek, they helped to unlock the mysteries of the Phoenician alphabet, the foundation of all European written languages.

Luxury goods poured in: ivory, ostrich eggs and precious stones from Africa, gold amulets from Egypt, ceramics from Corinth and Rhodes, gold and silver jewellery and multicoloured glass vials. Pottery and cloth were exported and a small breed of local dog became popular in Greece.

The Carthaginians' power and riches inevitably caught the eye of the next great civilisation on the make. It took the Romans over 100 years and three major wars to bring them to their knees. Both sides could field over 300 quinqueremes (with five banks of oars) and over 150,000 men. Blood was shed all over the Mediterranean and doubtless many of these towering war galleys limped into Malta's harbours for repairs. During the First Punic War (264–241 BC, Romans v Carthaginians) Malta was thoroughly raided and pillaged but remained a Carthaginian colony. Thirteen years later, at the outset of the Second Punic War, the Islands appear to have sensed which way the political wind was blowing and offered little resistance.

One symbol common throughout the Phoenician world lives on in Malta today. Local fishermen may now have a Christian shrine amidships, but they still paint the Eye of Osiris on the bows of their boats as additional protection from peril on the sea.

## Roman rule

During its seven centuries of Roman rule Malta was annexed to Sicily and, to a large extent, shared the same fate as its nearest neighbour. The Islands were made municipalities with considerable control over their own affairs. They also had the right to send ambassadors to Rome, a privilege they made good use of, along with Sicily, when **Gaius Verres**, the most rapacious of all Rome's provincial governors, began a reign of despoliation.

They were well-informed enough to know that the great orator, **Cicero**, was the man to present their grievances at his impeachment. Verres fled after the first of Cicero's six prepared speeches, but enough had been said to show what were then Malta's most prized products and possessions. Without having stirred from Sicily, Verres had managed to amass two huge elephant tusks from a temple to Juno, sacred statuettes, 400 jars of Malta's famous honey, great quantities of cloth, 50 sofa cushions, numerous candelabra, and so many clothes that Cicero sneered: 'but what would you want with as many garments as if you were going to clothe the wives of all your friends.'

The Islands became famous and were praised by poets. Homer called them 'the navel of the sea' and stranded his hero, Odysseus, on Gozo (which he called Ogygia) for seven years, in thrall to the nymph Calypso. To prove the legend true, there are now signposts to the nymph's cave above Gozo's prime beach, **Ramla Bay**. Ovid mentioned 'the fruitful isle of Malta'.

Roman villas spread out across the countryside, presiding over vineyards and olive groves first planted by the Carthaginians. The harbours became bustling depots and repair centres for trading ships and war galleys from all over the Mediterranean. The suburbs outside Malta's **Mdina** and Gozo's **Citadel** were massively walled with typically Roman thoroughness.

Visitors in the 18C said that the streets of Mdina and the Citadel were still lined with fragments of marble pillars and statues once dedicated to Roman emperors and their wives. The **Roman Villa Museum**, in Rabat, Malta, with its fine mosaic floors, is the chief remnant of this prosperous period.

### Shipwrecked

It was during Roman rule that the Islands' most famous visitor made a dramatic entrance into Malta. In AD 60, a ship that had been dogged the length of the Mediterranean by contrary winds and tearing gales, made a dawn dash for shelter and was wrecked on Malta's northern shore. Among its 276 passengers were several prisoners on their way to be tried in Rome. One of them was St Paul. He was being held on a charge of causing riots in Palestine.

St Luke, his travelling companion, later vividly described in the Acts of the Apostles (Chapters 27 and 28) how the local inhabitants kindly lit a fire for the bedraggled survivors and sheltered them from the storm. He calls their rescuers 'barbarians', which, in those days, meant nothing more offensive than that they knew neither Latin nor Greek. After more than 200 years of Roman occupation, the rural populace was presumably still speaking a Phoenician dialect, as it does, with many amendments and additions, to this day.

According to St Luke, during their three months on Malta, St Paul cured the father of Publius, the 'headman of the island', of a fever and a bloody flux and performed several other miracles. Tradition adds that St Paul converted the Roman Publius to Christianity, made him the first bishop of Malta and that **Mdina cathedral** stands on the site of Publius' house. There is also a fondly held belief that St Paul went on to convert the entire population, making Malta one of the earliest Christian colonies.

There are many Christian **catacombs** around Mdina, and those of Jews and pagans too, but so far no Christian symbols have been found earlier than the 4C BC.

The traditional site of the shipwreck is now called **St Paul's Island** (at the entrance to St Paul's Bay). Not too far inland from here, in the village of Bur Marrad, a chapel rebuilt many times is known to have attracted pilgrims at least since the 7C. The chapel is called **San Pawl-Milqi** (St Paul Welcomed). St Luke wrote that Publius first received the two saints at one of his 'possessions', close to where they had been hurled ashore, and courteously lodged them there for three days. The remains nearby of a Roman house and olive oil factory may well indicate that the chapel is aptly named.

# Medieval times

*by Ann Monsarrat*

After conquering every nation that touched on the Mediterranean and many further afield, the Romans predictably had problems. In an attempt to stop the rot, they split their unwieldy empire into two but it was too late to save the old, western heartland. The wealthier Eastern Empire, Byzantium, with its magnificent new capital, Constantinople, survived it by 1000 years.

## The Byzantine Empire

It was an eastern, Byzantine general, not one from nearer home, who came to the rescue when the Vandals swept down from the north with their pirate fleets and captured many of the Islands in the western Mediterranean. Belisarius, the greatest soldier of his age, called in on Malta in AD 533 on his way to demolish the Vandals' bases in Africa, and was back in the area two years later to liberate Sicily and make it part of the Eastern Empire.

Malta again became a province of its northern neighbour and an important naval base, with an admiral as well as a military governor. It also began a less savoury role: that of a secure place to send troublemakers. The Byzantine emperor Hercalius seems to have started the trend by packing off a conspiring nephew, with an order that, on arrival, the governor should have one of his feet cut off. For several centuries the name Malta was used as a synonym for prison or jailer.

## Arab onslaught

The Arab nations, inspired by their new Islamic faith, had already conquered North Africa and much of southern Europe by the time they turned their minds to Malta. They arrived around AD 870 and took the Islands in what seems to have been a bloody and destructive battle. But these were no mindless barbarians. The Arabs were way ahead in the sciences and agriculture, and the Aghlabids, with their splendid walled city of Kairouan (in what is now Tunisia), outshone them all. They were to rule Malta for more than 250 years.

The Islands were administered by an emir based in Palermo (Sicily), as well as a local military governor with a harbour stronghold where Fort St Angelo now stands. Some of the Arabs' additions to the walls of Mdina and Gozo's Citadel can still be seen. They also introduced cotton and citrus fruits.

Apart from this, it is a tantalising era with many mysteries still to be solved, not least what happened to Christianity and the local population. Not one building or grave, Christian or Muslim, has been found for the entire period. It has even been suggested that the Islands were uninhabited for many years.

However, a plaque on a fort in the Aghlabid port of Sousse (Tunisia) may solve the puzzle of why Malta has so few Roman and Byzantine remains. It records that all its dressed stones and marble columns had been shipped over as booty after the conquest of Malta.

The Arabs' chief legacies lie in the design of later Maltese houses, with their austere façades, flat roofs, courtyards and covered passageways, and the many Arabic names of places and families. There are still families called Caruana living in Malta and Gozo; the name is spelt differently but is clearly that of the Aghlibids' chief city.

## Norman Conquest

In 1090 **Roger the Norman** sailed into Malta, rode off his ship on horseback at dawn, and caused such military mayhem that the island's Muslim governor sued for peace within three days. The only inhabitants thrilled to see him were Greek captives, probably used as slaves, who streamed out of Mdina carrying crosses and crying *Kyrie eleison*, Lord have mercy. They were also the only inhabitants to accept his offer of free passage off the Islands.

He demanded the surrender of all weapons, an annual tribute and an acknowledgment that the islanders were now his subjects, then sailed smartly off again to finish conquering Sicily where, as Count Roger, he had made himself the ruler. The romantic tale that he tore his chequered standard in two and gave half (red and white) to Malta for its national flag is sadly no longer believed, since national flags had not then been invented.

Count Roger's grip on the Islands seems to have been so light that 37 years later his son, **King Roger**, had to conquer them again. This time, he appears to have left a Christian garrison behind. By 1156 Malta had its own bishop, though resident in Palermo, but very little else seems have changed. The Islands were still regarded as being inhabited by Muslims.

King Roger's court at Palermo was the most magnificent in Europe, more Byzantine than north European, harnessing the talents of Sicily's Arab, Greek and Jewish population. There is little to show that Malta shared in this splendour but, tucked away behind Mdina's walls, there are still a few rooms built in Norman times, and the Sicilian-Norman style of architecture was to remain popular for many years.

Muslim gravestones also survive from this period. A particularly fine one, with a poignant inscription recording the death of a young girl, is now in Gozo's Archaeological Museum, in the Citadel.

### Holy Roman Empire

After King Roger's daughter, Constance, inherited the Sicilian throne and married the Swabian king of Germany, Malta again became rather isolated, at the end of a long chain of command whose chief aim was to levy taxes. Constance's husband and son both became Holy Roman Emperors with most of western Europe as their realm and a constant preoccupation with rival, papal power. It was this rivalry which, after a bloody battle, put the Pope's candidate, Charles of Anjou, brother of Louis IX of France, on the throne of the Two Sicilies (ruling Naples, Sicily and Malta). He moved his court to Naples and left such rapacious bureaucrats in charge in Sicily that the population turned on them. In an uprising in 1282, known as the Sicilian Vespers and partly plotted in Malta, 2000 of Palermo's French citizens were slaughtered in one night.

King **Peter III of Aragon** stepped in to aid the oppressed and then made them part of his domain. For more than three centuries the Islands remained under Spanish rule.

Malta for some time had been regarded as a Sicilian county, handed over to court favourites, who called themselves counts of Malta and then often handed over their duties to sons, nephews or mere tax gatherers. In 1421 it was pawned for 30,000 gold florins to a man so unpopular that a plaque above the gate of Mdina still commemorates Malta's ousting of him. But gradually the Islands gained some degree of self-government.

The Muslim population had already been encouraged, by particularly high taxation, to leave or to become at least nominally Christian; the last of those who held out were expelled in 1271. The vacated Arab lands were taken over by the crown and leased to noble families from Sicily, Italy and Spain. A few fine palaces in Mdina and a unique cluster of houses in Gozo's Citadel are medieval Malta's most visible legacy.

A thriving trade in cotton and cumin brought some prosperity. Town councils were set up, with local mayors, aldermen and magistrates, though they were still at the mercy of Palermo's tax demands. Gozo, most at risk from corsair and Arab raids, complained bitterly in 1439 that they were already doing more than enough by fighting the king's enemies. Malta's most prized privilege was that of being allowed to appeal directly to the king, over the heads of the middlemen.

The title of the mayor encapsulates Malta's rich roots: the Italian and Spanish *Capitano della Verga* (Captain of the Rod) and the Arabic/Maltese *Hakem* (Ruler) were both in use for many centuries.

It was the Spanish Holy Roman Emperor Charles V, grandson of their very Catholic majesties, Ferdinand of Aragon and Isabella of Castile, who handed the Islands over, in 1530, to the Knights of the Order of St John of Jerusalem. It was their fight against a new rising tide of Islam that was to make Malta the focus of all Europe.

# The Order of St John

The arrival in Malta of the Knights of the Order of St John of Jerusalem changed the course of the Islands' history. It also changed the Order. The Knights brought with them, to an impoverished people, incalculable wealth and an absolute dedication to Christianity. When they left, all they had to show for a 268-year tenure was just one memento, the sobriquet they would proudly wear for centuries to come: 'The Knights of Malta'.

The Order was established in Jerusalem in 1048 by merchants from Amalfi in southern Italy. In order to provide care for the poor and sick pilgrims visiting the Holy Sepulchre in Jerusalem, the merchants approached the Caliph of Egypt, asking his permission to set up a Christian hospital in his domain. He agreed, the hospital dedicated to St John the Baptist was founded, and the nursing brotherhood came into being.

In 1099, however, when the First Crusade ended with the recapture of Jerusalem in the name of Christianity by Godfrey de Bouillon, the Order began to take on a military role, bearing arms in the defence of the religion. Five years later, acknowledging their bravery and assistance, King Baldwin of Jerusalem offered them land as a permanent home, and in 1113, as a sign of their legitimacy, Pope Paschal II put the Order and its possessions under papal protection, formally recognising the constitution of Knights Hospitallers. (This Bull is in Malta's National Library, the Bibliotheca.)

It was now that transition from Hospitaller to soldier was made. The Knights of the Order had become military defenders of the faith and the faithful; nursing was secondary. European commanderies (that is, districts in Europe under a commander in a religious military order) raised money to support them and soon the Order's banners and tunics emblazoned with a white cross on a field of scarlet would spread terror among the infidel armies. The Order's emblem was aptly called: 'the white cross of peace on a bloodstained field of war'.

The Order fought in both the Second and Third Crusades and as a reward for their fighting courage, Richard Coeur de Lion presented to them the town and harbour of Acre on the shores of the Mediterranean (in present-day Israel) as a permanent base. Acre had been snatched from the enemy in 1191 during the ferocious Third Crusade. The Order would remain there for nearly 100 years.

In 1291 Islam rose again and this time the Order was defeated. Acre was taken by the Sultan Khalil and the Knights fled to seek refuge in Cyprus. Then, in 1310, they moved again. After a four-year struggle, Fulke de Villaret had seized the island of Rhodes and the Order re-established itself there.

Rhodes they considered an ideal base. It had excellent harbours and its countryside was verdantly rich. In no time they set about fortifying their territory and building a powerful fleet. From being soldiers and Hospitallers, they became sailors and Hospitallers. The Order's fleet patrolled the Mediterranean and any ship considered as belonging to the enemy or his allies would be regarded as legitimate prey. These sailors were also privateers.

For two centuries the Knights continued to harass the Turks and plunder their galleons, but when Mehmet II captured Byzantine Constantinople in 1453, the time was ripe for the Ottoman Turks to seek retribution and turn their attention again to the Order's base on Rhodes. In 1480 the Knights fought off an invasion with great skill but in 1522, the Turks returned and, after a fierce six-month siege, Grand Master L'Isle Adam realising the seriousness of the situation, surrendered. Fortunately his vanquisher was a chivalrous young Turkish Sultan, the son of Suleiman the Magnificent, the great Ottoman leader. L'Isle Adam was allowed to capitulate on honourable terms and on 1 January 1523, with 180 Knights and almost 4000 soldiers, the Order of St John set sail, their final destination unknown.

For eight years they would be homeless while Grand Master L'Isle Adam beseeched Europe's kings asking for help and a home. Britain's Henry VIII proffered the sum of 20,000 crowns. Pope Clement VIII gave their dwindling numbers temporary shelter in Viterbo, north of Rome.

Eventually Emperor Charles V answered their prayers. He gave them Malta.

By Act of Donation on 24 March 1530 the Islands of Malta became the home of the Order in perpetual sovereignty. (This Act of Donation is also preserved in the Bibliotheca.) Charles V had inherited Malta through marriage but did not care for the Islands. With his gift he made two demands. The first, because the Knights were famed for their falconry, was that on All Saints' Day each year the Grand Master would make a ceremonial presentation of a falcon to the emperor's viceroy in Sicily. The second was that the Order would also protect the Christian stronghold of Tripoli on the North African coast. Both demands they were quick to ignore.

### To be a Knight

The Order of St John had attained its developed form in Rhodes. When it arrived in Malta every Knight and soldier knew his status and duty.

To preside over the Order was a **Grand Master** elected by his brethren for life. Below him were three principal ranks: **Knights of Justice** (who dominated the Order), **Conventual Chaplains** and **Servants-at-arms**. Catholic Knights had to prove noble birth without taint of illegitimacy for four generations on both sides of the family. They were the most exclusive aristocratic body in Europe. The Conventual Chaplains, who were not necessarily noble born, served in a religious capacity in the hospital, galleys and church, while the Serving Brothers, who had only to prove legitimate birth, acted as servants but also had military duties. On them, and others, the Grand Master could bestow the honorary title **Knight of Grace**.

The Order was divided into **Langues**, or nationalities. There were eight: Aragon, Auvergne, Castile et Leon, England, France, Germany, Italy and

# Grand Masters of the Order of St John in Malta

**DE L'ISLE ADAM**
1530-34 (French)

**DE LA CASSIERE**
1572-82 (French)

**DE REDIN**
1657-60 (Spanish)

**ZONDADARI**
1720-22 (Italian)

**DEL PONTE**
1534-35 (Italian)

**DE VERDALLE**
1582-95 (French)

**DE CHATTES GESSAN**
1660 (French)

**DE VILHENA**
1722-36 (Portuguese)

**DE ST JAILLE**
1535-36 (French)

**GARZES**
1595-1601 (Spanish)

**RAFAEL COTONER**
1660-63 (Spanish)

**DESPUIG**
1736-41 (Spanish)

**DE HOMEDES**
1536-53 (Spanish)

**ALOF DE WIGNACOURT**
1601-22 (French)

**NICOLAS COTONER**
1663-80 (Spanish)

**PINTO DE FONSECA**
1741-73 (Portuguese)

**DE LA SENGLE**
1553-57 (French)

**DE VASCONCELLOS**
1622-23 (Portuguese)

**CARAFA**
1680-90 (Italian)

**XIMENES DE TEXADA**
1773-75 (Spanish)

**DE LA VALLETTE**
1557-68 (French)

**DE PAULE**
1623-36 (French)

**ADRIEN DE WIGNACOURT**
1690-97 (French)

**DE ROHAN DE POLDUC**
1775-97 (French)

**DEL MONTE**
1568-72 (Italian)

**DE LASCARIS CASTELLAR**
1636-57 (French)

**PERELLOS Y ROCCAFUL**
1697-1720 (Spanish)

**VON HOMPESCH**
1797-98 (German)

Provence. (With the Reformation in 1540, the English Langue was disbanded by Henry VIII, but it continued in Malta in the hope of a Counter-Reformation restoring their position.)

Each Knight was bound by **Oath of Statute** to leave four-fifths of his wealth to the Order. Each Langue had its own home base, an **Auberge,** with a **Pilier** at its head.

At the head of the Order was a **Supreme Council** which consisted of the Bishop, the Prior of the conventual church, eight Piliers, priors, conventual bailiffs (these last two were heads of commanderies) and the Knights Grand Cross (Knights of particular distinction). It was presided over by the Grand Master.

## Taking over Malta

Until the Order's arrival the islanders were poor, the victims of plague, famine and raids carried out by corsairs from the Barbary Coast of North Africa. They also lived under permanent threat of invasion by the Ottoman Turks, determined to conquer Christian soil.

It was autumn when the Order took possession of the fishing village of the Borgo in the great harbour (the Grand Harbour). The island, the Knights recorded, was barren and without a sufficient water supply. It was difficult to defend and had 12,000 miserable inhabitants.

But it had a deep sheltered harbour and rudimentary fortifications. It was preferable to Tripoli which they had also been offered. That stretch of the North African coast they found to be inhospitable and Tripoli itself was difficult to defend and lacked drinking water or a good harbour. Although they did not care much for the Islands, Malta could be turned into a fortress.

The Order ignored the local nobility living in the walled city of Mdina, and they for their part were content to ignore the Knights. But while the Mdina residents eyed the Knights warily, a tolerant relationship was established, brought on by the common need for defence against the Ottoman threat.

The galleys of the Knights began to prey on Muslim shipping again and, perhaps in retaliation, in the 1550s attacks on Malta and Gozo from the Barbary Coast became increasingly frequent.

For many years the Knights still prayed that they might return as conquerors to Rhodes and this may account for the small scale of the defences they erected in and around Borgo in the years preceding the Great Siege. Although military advisers had pressed for a new fortress to be built on Mount Sceberras (where Valletta now stands), work was never started. This was probably due to insufficient finances. An important source of revenue was lost in 1540 when Henry VIII confiscated the possessions of the 43 commanderies of the Langue in England.

## The Great Siege

In 1565 **Suleiman the Magnificent**, now past his 70th year and still the scourge of Christianity, decided to turn the might of his Ottoman force once again against his old enemy, the Order of St John. He divided his command. The fleet he placed under Admiral Piali, the army under **Mustapha Pasha**. With an armada of 181 ships they sailed from the Golden Horn carrying more than 30,000 fighting men. Also at sea near Tripoli with more ships was the great corsair **Dragut Rais**. He would join forces as soon as he could.

To face them Grand Master **Jean Parisot de la Valette** had about 600 knights and servants-at-arms, 1200 infantrymen, mostly Italian and Spanish, and a Maltese militia of about 4500 untrained men. In all (and slaves were counted as a part of the force) the defenders totaled between 8000 and 9000.

As the armada assembled off the coast of Malta on 18 May 1565 it was a sight none could forget. All crops had been harvested and the water in the wells outside the walls of the Borgo and Mdina had been poisoned, but no galley of the Order set sail, no cannon fired. With the gates of the defensive positions secured, the Order and the Maltese were as prepared as they could be. The Turkish landing at Marsaxlokk went unopposed. Initially there were just a few cavalry skirmishes. Admiral Piali favoured storming Fort St Elmo so that his fleet might safely shelter in Marsamxett Harbour, but as a first priority Mustapha Pasha favoured the sacking of Borgo and the capture of Mdina using his mighty land force. While Piali and Mustapha vociferously disagreed, Dragut Rais arrived bringing with him 1200 mercenaries. The famous corsair, already in his eighties but strategically alert, quickly appreciated the threat Fort St Elmo presented. He made his decision: Fort St Elmo would be taken. The next day the fort was besieged.

For 31 days there was a barrage of mortar and cannon fire as well as repeated land assaults. It was a brutal campaign. At one point the bodies of the dead lay so deep outside St Elmo they became bridges of rank and decomposing flesh. When Mustapha Pasha had four captured Knights brought before him, he ordered them beheaded and their heads floated on shields across the harbour to the Borgo. In retaliation, La Valette ordered the heads of captured Turkish soldiers to be fired as cannon balls.

On 23 June the fort fell, just five days after Dragut Rais himself had fallen when mortally struck by rocks thrown up by a cannon ball fired from St Elmo. Only four Maltese survived the siege of Fort St Elmo, they escaped in the mêlée and swam to Fort St Angelo. The Turks lost 8000 men. (See also Valletta, p 86.)

The Turks now turned their attention to Fort St Angelo, Borgo and L'Isla (Senglea). The Order's stronghold presented an impregnable face. Between the outposts, the Port of the Galleys had a chain drawn across its mouth to bar entrance and, behind that, a bridge of boats allowed soldiers to cross from one post to another when reinforcement was called for.

During the hot summer months each attack was repelled with conspicuous bravery, often with great cost to life. Until finally, on 7 September, the long-awaited relief force from the Viceroy of Sicily came to their rescue. Under Don Garcia de Toledo, 8000 men put ashore near St Paul's Bay, facing a pitched battle as they landed. But the tired and demoralised Turks were in no position to oppose trained and well-fed soldiers fresh for battle, and they were routed. Piali and Mustapha Pasha sailed home to disgrace. The Turks had lost almost 30,000 men. Of the nearly 9000 that made up the numbers of the defenders, just 600 remained.

Across Europe the crowned heads rejoiced as news of the victory spread. Grand Master Jean Parisot de la Valette was proclaimed a hero.

## A city named Valletta

With news of the Ottoman defeat, the crowned heads of Europe began bestowing largesse upon the Order. Even the Protestant queen of England, Elizabeth I, showed her gratitude at the conquest of the Infidel by sending as a gift a large sum of money. Within six years, as prosperity returned, so the new city of Valletta emerged and took the name of the brave Knight who lead them to victory.

Valletta quickly replaced Mdina as the Islands' first city. In 1622 its position of importance was ratified when the Bishop of Malta transferred the Curia there from Mdina.

The Order continued to fortify the Islands. A serious Turkish attempt to land was driven off in 1614 and, with this in mind, well into the 17C much of the building strategy was based on the premise that a Turkish threat remained imminent. In reality, after the defeat of the Turks by the Holy Alliance in the Battle of Lepanto in 1571, the Ottoman fighting spirit was destroyed. In fact by the end of the 17C the Turks had forged trading agreements with a number of Christian powers and were soon protesting about the way the Order's galleys behaved: like privateers, descending to plunder their ships.

Throughout the 17C the Order erected forts as well as lookout towers on strategic points on the coast. Around 1720 they added redoubts and batteries to these (most of which survive because the British quickly incorporated them into their own defensive system).

Malta became a busy trade centre and was known for its flourishing slave market. But the Islands were still reliant on foreign gifts and the incomes of the Knights themselves.

## The decline

While the Order was still building fortifications and bestowing great wealth to bring fine architecture and aesthetic design to the Islands, its role as Christian warrior was slipping into final decline. In 1720 Grand Master **Ramon Perellos y Roccaful** died. An elegant Spaniard, it was he who had ensured Mdina's cathedral was restored after an earthquake and acquired the great tapestries that hang in St John's Co-Cathedral and the Palace of the Grand Masters. It was he who insisted the fleet should be modernised.

But although Perellos brought grandeur and elegance to the Order, the Knights themselves had taken up a hedonistic life of gambling, drinking, womanising and duelling. The simplicity and celibacy that once had been an implicit part in their ordered lives was replaced by ostentatious living. Their last serious naval engagement came in the 1715–18 conflict when they joined the Venetian fleet off the Peloponnese in their war against the Turks. Their days of influence on diplomacy or even military matters were over.

Perelos's successor was **Marc Antonio Zondadari**, a nephew of Pope Alexander VII. In his brief reign he endeavoured to turn Malta into the most important trading centre in the Mediterranean. Then came the Portuguese Grand Master **Antonio Manoel de Vilhena** who used his immense wealth to build yet more magnificent edifices, places like the Manoel Theatre and Fort Manoel which, naturally, took his name.

By 1773, when **Grand Master Francisco Ximenes de Texada** headed the Order, its coffers were empty. His predecessor, **Manoel Pinto de Fonseca**, had lived in a lavish style, and the Knights, less and less monastic in outlook, made their lives as comfortable and luxurious as they could, a tendency which brought about constant conflict with the austere Inquisitor and the Bishop.

The Maltese were no longer in sympathy with the arrogant Knights, and in 1775 a number of Maltese clergy rebelled in what was termed 'The Priests' Revolt'. Grand Master Ximenes had the ringleaders executed. The situation was volatile.

As soon as **Emanuel de Rohan** was elected later that year he tried to placate the troubled population. He established a new municipal code and new laws and statutes, but it was too late. The Order's tenure of Malta had just four years remaining.

## Napoleon ends the Order's reign

In France the Revolution had already brought about the confiscation of the Order's wealth and property. The protection of the Pope in Rome now meant nothing, as his power too had already diminished. From Malta, Grand Master de Rohan had financed Louis XVI's abortive flight from France in 1791 by selling much of the Order's silver. When, six years later, **Ferdinand von Hompesch**, the German Grand Master, agreed to Tsar Paul I's offer to establish a Russian Orthodox Langue within this Christian Order, **Napoleon Bonaparte** was furious. So, in 1798, on his way to his Egyptian campaign, he called in at Malta. His intentions were clear.

On 9 June, as his armada of 472 ships gathered outside the Grand Harbour, Napoleon requested permission to enter for water and provisions. On board were 54,000 soldiers. French Knights in Malta already informed of Napoleon's plans prevailed upon the Grand Master to grant permission and, with much trepidation, he did so. Bonaparte and his armada sailed in. Two days later without a single shot fired, the Grand Master was forced to surrender the Islands. The Order had three days in which to leave, taking with them only their holy relics and personal possessions.

Napoleon was now possessor of the finest fortress island in the Mediterranean. The glorious days of the Order of St John were ended.

## Grand Masters of the Order of St John in Malta

| | |
|---|---|
| 1530–34 | Philippe Villiers de L'Isle Adam (French) |
| 1534–35 | Pierino del Ponte (Italian) |
| 1535–36 | Didier de Saint Jaille (French) |
| 1536–53 | Juan de Homedes (Spanish) |
| 1553–57 | Claude de la Sengle (French) |
| 1557–68 | Jean Parisot de la Valette (French) |
| 1568–72 | Pietro de Monte (Italian) |
| 1572–81 | Jean l'Evêque de la Cassière (French) |
| 1581–95 | Hugues Loubenx de Verdalle (French) |
| 1595–1601 | Martin Garzes (Spanish) |
| 1601–22 | Alof de Wignacourt (French) |
| 1622–23 | Luis Mendez de Vasconcellos (Portuguese) |
| 1623–36 | Antoine de Paule (French) |
| 1636–57 | Jean Paul de Lascaris Castellar (French) |
| 1657–60 | Martin de Redin (Spanish) |
| 1660 | Annet de Clermont de Chattes Gessan (French) |
| 1660–63 | Rafael Cotoner (Spanish) |
| 1663–80 | Nicolas Cotoner (Spanish) |
| 1680–90 | Gregorio Carafa (Italian) |
| 1690–97 | Adrien de Wignacourt (French) |
| 1697–1720 | Ramon Perellos y Roccaful (Spanish) |
| 1720–22 | Marc Antonio Zondadari (Italian) |
| 1722–36 | Antonio Manoel de Vilhena (Portuguese) |

| 1736–41 | Ramon Despuig (Spanish) |
| 1741–73 | Manoel Pinto de Fonseca (Portuguese) |
| 1773–75 | Francisco Ximenes de Texada (Spanish) |
| 1775–97 | Emanuel de Rohan Polduc (French) |
| 1797–98 | Ferdinand von Hompesch (German) |

---

### The Knights of Malta today

When the Order of St John was so ignominiously thrown out of Malta it entered a wilderness as it struggled to find a new home. Many Knights went to Rome, others back to their home countries to plead their Order's cause. As a result, a number of Orders sprang into being, all claiming to be the true heirs of the Order once based in Malta.

Many still exist, thriving as they strive to carry out charitable work. One, however, claims to be the truest of heirs: The Sovereign Military Hospitaller Order of St John of Jerusalem, Rhodes and Malta. Its headquarters, a *palazzo* on Rome's elegant shopping street, Via Condotti, is recognised by Italy as a sovereign state. The Order is headed by the Prince and Grand Master (for many years, Fra Andrew Bertie, from Britain).

This Order has more than 11,000 Roman Catholic members, men and women, and it cooperates with the other Christian and non-Catholic Orders of St John around the world. The work is humanitarian and includes running children's homes, refugee camps and leprosy hospitals in deprived countries.

In Malta known as SMOM the Order's bases are St John's Cavalier, Valletta, and a small section of Fort St Angelo which is on a 99-year lease with the added privilege of 'extraterritoriality' (similar to sovereign state).

---

## Enter the French

**Napoleon Bonaparte** did not plan to stay in Malta, but he did consider the island with its great harbours to be an excellent addition to the French empire. So while his fleet took on board the provisions it would need for his campaign in Egypt, he stationed himself for just a few days' respite in Palazzo Parisio in Valletta. Among his first actions were to appoint **General Claude Vaubois** Governor of Malta and give orders for the Islands to be stripped of their wealth. Paintings, tapestries and ornaments of gold and silver belonging to the Knights were the first to be seized. In France the Revolution had confiscated all the Order's possessions, and the same would happen in Malta. The wealth of the Order of St John would help to finance Napoleon's campaigns.

In June 1798 soldiers looted parish churches. They rampaged through the nation's archives trying to destroy documents that pertained to the royal houses of Europe or to the Order of St John. They caused havoc, and the Maltese were helpless.

When Napoleon left, he did so with great satisfaction. Not only did the strategically important fortress island now belong to France, much of its wealth did too. On board the *L'Orient* was all the Order's silver, including the famous silver service used by the Knights to feed the sick in their hospital, the *Sacra Infermeria*. On Bonaparte's orders the service had been melted down into bullion.

Two months later, however, it was all lost. **Admiral Horatio Nelson** with the Royal Navy had been pursuing the French fleet and finally encountered them outside Alexandria. In the Battle of the Nile that followed, as the French fleet was annihilated, so the *L'Orient* was sunk.

Angered by General Vaubois's imperious behaviour, the Maltese were further alienated when he created unpopular new laws and statutes. He even imposed the French language as the Islands' official language. Finally, they could take no more.

The Governor had decided to raise yet more money by auctioning the contents of the Carmelite Church in Mdina. To the Maltese this was sacrilegious and, led by the clergy, they rose in rebellion, taking to the streets of the city. In the ensuing turmoil, Captain Masson, the French officer in charge of the militia, was thrown from a window at no. 11 Villegaignon Street and killed. Immediately villagers outside the city walls joined in the uprising and when news reached General Vaubois, he quickly ordered the withdrawal of his force of 1000 men into Valletta and locked the city gates. His garrison was now, in effect, besieged.

The Maltese, having heard the heartening news of Nelson's victory at Alexandria, quickly sent a delegation to Naples to appeal to the French fleet's greatest enemy, the British Navy, for help. A British ship, *Orion*, was despatched and soon arrived to land 1000 muskets. Other ships supplied by Admiral Nelson and the King of Naples, under the command of Captain Alexander Ball, blockaded the Islands. Should French reinforcements arrive they would be prevented from putting ashore.

General Vaubois refused to be intimidated. In a show of bravado he executed a number of Maltese considered to be spies.

As two months passed the British began to lose patience with the resilient general. They sent in 1500 British troops under Major-General Pigot and also raised a local militia with volunteers known as the Maltese Light Infantry. But still Vaubois clung on.

Then grave news reached the general. Because of the sea blockade, no more than three days' rations remained in Valletta. In the great traditions of siege warfare, his force had been starved into submission.

He surrendered to the British on terms favourable to the French. His force was allowed to leave with all possessions and, much to the fury of the Maltese who were not consulted, they took with them with a considerable amount of the valuable items they had looted during their stay.

On 5 September 1800 the British flag flew over Valletta.

In October **Captain Alexander Ball** took responsibility for the Islands on behalf of England. Now the British were, if only temporarily, rulers of Malta.

## *French Commanders in Malta*

| | |
|---|---|
| 1798 | Napoleon Bonaparte |
| 1798–1800 | General Claude Vaubois |

## Under the British Flag

In October 1800 Captain Alexander Ball was appointed Britain's administrator of the Islands, a role he was honoured to accept. He could see Malta's strategic importance to Britain and, after his conflict with the French, was reluctant to allow it to fall into other hands.

But two years later, in the Treaty of Amiens that brought a fragile peace between England and France, it was agreed that Malta and its dependent islands should be returned to the Order of St John—this time under the formal protection of Naples or Russia. In that way, it was argued, neither France nor England would lose in the compromise Treaty.

The Maltese were furious. The Order of St John was penniless and decadent and the Maltese had come to dislike and distrust them. In the hands of the Knights they had no future to call their own. They would rather become a British Colony and have the stability and opportunities that such a protective arrangement would afford.

So while the Order of St John waited in Sicily for the Treaty to be ratified, Sir Alexander Ball (he had been knighted for his role in chasing Napoleon's troops out of Malta) begged his superiors for the fortress island to remain in Britain's hands. It took nearly 12 years for the situation to be resolved, and it was only after Napoleon had abdicated and the Treaty of Paris been signed in 1814 that the Islands were formally recognised as under British dominion. A new era had begun. **Sir Thomas Maitland**, an imperious man with an arrogant manner, known behind his back as King Tom, was appointed Britain's first governor. Immediately he began changing laws to match those of England.

The naval base and dockyard were soon established and when in 1869 the Suez Canal finally opened, the Grand Harbour grew yet more important as ships sailing between Britain and India began calling in for provisions. Like Aden on the other side of Suez, Malta was now a coaling station on this rich trading route.

But while Malta's fortunes were tied to those of Britain, and ultimate authority for governing the Islands would remain in London, it was always envisaged that the Maltese would have a say in the affairs of the colony. Establishing just how it could be done, however, was not an easy matter.

The first attempt at a form of autonomy was introduced by proclamation in 1835 and bitter divisions about the share of power took root. New constitutions were introduced, then revoked again, in 1849 and in 1887 as the war of words moved between the imperious Governor, Britain and the Maltese.

With the outbreak of **World War One** in 1914 the situation calmed down. The Islands became a sanctuary for the wounded and as such were known as the 'Nurse of the Mediterranean'. It was estimated that Malta cared for more than 25,000 sick and wounded brought in by hospital ships from the Dardanelles.

But by 1919 after war had ended, the economic situation had deteriorated, poverty had returned and there were riots. On 7 June British soldiers shot and killed four Maltese. **Sette Giugno** (7 June) is still commemorated as a public holiday.

In 1921 the situation was resolved. Malta was granted self-government in all matters of local concern; Britain would control everything else.

The system did not work any better than earlier attempts and the constitution was again suspended in 1930, restored in 1932, and suspended yet again in 1933. Apart from the natural difficulties of a population which could not be self-supporting without help from Britain, another problem concerned the official language. Britain wanted to replace Italian with English. Until then Italian had been the language of society and commerce and *Malti*, the Maltese language, the language of the working man. To compound matters further, many prominent Maltese believed their allegiance should be with Catholic Italy not Protestant Britain anyway.

World War once again united dissident voices.

## The Second Great Siege

On 10 June 1940, **Benito Mussolini**, Italy's Fascist Dictator, formally declared his intentions of allying his Italy to Adolf Hitler's Germany in the creation of an all-powerful Fascist Europe. The next morning the first bombs were dropped on Malta. Seven more air raids would follow that day.

In Mussolini's speeches he always referred to Malta as rightfully belonging to Italy. The little islands were less than 90km south of Sicily, spoke Italian and—perhaps more to the point—represented the most obvious stepping stone for the conquest of North Africa. Mussolini meant to have Malta.

The Islands were unprepared. As the bombs fell, only the guns of the anti-quated World War One survivor HMS *Terror*, berthed in Pietà Creek, joined the rapid anti-aircraft fire from Malta's artillery batteries. The three antiquated Gloucester Gladiator biplanes left behind when the carrier HMS *Glorious* sailed to Britain as Germany invaded Norway, joined in the mêlée. Nicknamed *Faith*, *Hope* and *Charity*, they did what they could, but *Charity* was lost. (One biplane, assumed to be *Faith*, is on display in Valletta's War Museum).

From that day, heavy bombardment continued. If the Great Siege of 1565 was based on the premise that blockading the islanders and bombing them unmerci-fully would force them to surrender when faced with starvation, so was the Second. Within 12 months more than 210 air raids were logged. The next year would be worse.

It was now that friction between the three British arms serving in Malta man-ifested itself. There were about 30,000 service personnel facing the enemy along-side the 250,000 civilians (minus a prominent handful known to be Italian sym-pathisers who were exiled to Kenya). The Army and Royal Air Force, fearing the Islands would be bombed into submission very quickly, favoured mass evacua-tion to safer territory. In fact many families had already been flown out at night to Kenya and further south. The Navy, however, respecting Malta's strategic posi-tion, favoured clinging on. Britain made the final decision. Governor Dobbie's Order for the Day stated:

> *The decision of His Majesty's Government to fight until our enemies are defeated will be heard with the greatest satisfaction by all ranks of the Garrison of Malta. I call on all Officers and other ranks to humbly seek the help of God, and in reliance on Him to do their duty unflinchingly.*

Immediately squadrons of new aeroplanes flew in to the strategically placed fortress from Britain.

The Germans saw Malta's strategic worth too. It was Malta-based recon-naissance planes that had located the Italian fleet sheltering at Taranto and caused the loss of two cruisers and three battleships. Malta should be taken at any cost.

In January 1941, ace pilots of the Luftwaffe now stationed in Sicily attacked the aircraft carrier HMS *Illustrious* as she sailed from Malta with a convoy to join the British campaign in Egypt. Badly damaged and with her flight decks out of action, she turned back to seek shelter in Dockyard Creek ready for the Luftwaffe the crew knew would return for the kill. When they did two weeks later, Malta was prepared. Every gun in every battery around the Grand Harbour fired an umbrella of exploding shells in the air above the carrier. No German pilot would risk flying through it.

Many, however, flew at rooftop level across Valletta below the artillery's 'box barrage'. It was the heaviest raid recorded to that day. Casualties were high and Vittoriosa, Senglea and Cospicua suffered such serious damage, it was decided to evacuate them. The *Illustrious* remained largely unscathed and, although the Luftwaffe came back to attack her again a few days later, she was able to slip out of harbour for Alexandria and then on to the United States for major repairs.

Meanwhile, in North Africa, Germany's Afrika Korps under the command of Field Marshall Rommel was attempting to sweep towards Tobruk and Alexandria. Although their convoys headed for Tobruk were skirting Malta at a distance and by night, they were falling prey to Malta-based submarines as well as aircraft. Supplies were having severe problems getting through.

Convoys carrying essential rations and ammunition were not reaching the Islands either. In 1941 it was calculated that the Luftwaffe attacked Malta three times a day. More than 960 attacks were counted with more allied shipping destroyed than ever before.

### Suffering and victory

In 1942, when Rommel's success in the desert seemed only a matter of time, yet more aircraft were despatched from Germany to Sicily. Malta could now be bombed into submission.

That January there were 499 raids, and by February there had been more than 80 days of continuous alert. In March and April more than 6700 tons of bombs were dropped, particularly around the Grand Harbour. The church bells which now rang only as air raid warnings seemed never to be silent. The Islands recorded 157 days of continuous bombardment. (London during the peak of its blitz recorded 57.)

Food rationing was acute. The government set up Victory Kitchens in an attempt to feed the locals a meagre hot meal. Milk, flour, eggs and fruit could only be found on the black market. Scabies and scurvy were rife. The situation was bleak.

In London, in a symbolic morale-boosting gesture on 15 April 1942, King George VI presented Malta and its population with the **George Cross**, Britain's highest civilian award. The citation read:

> *To honour her brave people, I award the George Cross to the Island Fortress of Malta to bear witness to a heroism and a devotion that will long be famous in history.*

In May, Field Marshall Viscount Gort VC replaced the ailing Dobbie as Governor and was presented with Dobbie's final situation report. In unequivocal terms is showed that the Islands had enough food to last until August. In three months they would have no food, no fuel and no ammunition. They would have to surrender. There was no other choice.

But, the prayers of the Maltese were answered—in an indirect way. Rommel and his panzers were fast advancing across North Africa. Tobruk had fallen to him in June and, with their desert campaign going well, the German High Command saw no hurry to press on with **Operation Herkules**, designed to bring Malta to its knees. Herkules was postponed.

By coincidence, in that lull, while Germany enjoyed its advances, the Allies despatched a convoy that just had to get through. Code-named **Operation Pedestal**, it had 14 supply ships with an escort of three aircraft carriers, two battleships, seven cruisers and 24 destroyers. Pedestal was the Islands' lifeline.

Day and night after passing Gibraltar the convoy was attacked. It suffered heavy losses; the carrier *Eagle* was sunk. Then, nearing Sicily, the larger ships turned back to join a major task force off Gibraltar. The remainder sailed on.

It was 13 August when the first ships were sighted off Malta. In came three supply ships, *Port Chalmers*, *Melbourne Star* and *Rochester Castle*. Two days later the *Brisbane Star* arrived and, far behind, came the charred hulk of the tanker *Ohio*, her rudder shot off and heavily listing, being towed into harbour by two minesweepers. In the charged hours it took, crowds lining the battlements wept, waved and cheered. Churchill recorded:

> *Thus in the end five gallant merchants ships of 14 got through with their precious cargoes. The loss of 350 officers and men and so many of the finest ships in the Merchant Navy and in the escorting fleet of the Royal Navy was grievous. The reward justified the price exacted. Revictualed and replenished with ammunition and essential stores, the strength of Malta revived.*

The day the last ship limped in was 15 August, the feast day of the Assumption, Santa Marija, one of the Islands' most celebrated religious holidays.

It is an epic story recounted each year in the local newspapers on the feast of Santa Marija, with the blackened hulk of tanker *Ohio* as the symbolic heroine of a time when supreme courage was expected of every man and woman.

Fortunately the Afrika Korps's campaign now faltered. As the surge of battle turned against them they found themselves retreating first to Tripoli and then to Tunisia. Montgomery's advance from El Alamein gathered momentum.

The changing tide of war was noticeable in Malta too. Four merchantmen sailing from Alexandria arrived unscathed carrying ammunition and food.

On 12 May 1943 the Afrika Korps finally surrendered—they could fight no more. Had Fortress Malta not stood in the way, the beleaguered 291,000 German and Italian troops might have been evacuated to Europe to fight again.

By the end of that year, while Field Marshall Montgomery and General Eisenhower planned the Allied advance through Sicily, King George VI flew in to visit his brave subjects and, a little later, what appeared to the Maltese to be thousands more troops arrived to swell the garrison. Then, on 9 July, the new faces were gone. The invasion of Italy had begun, and Malta was the springboard for the capture of Sicily.

On 8 September the Italian fleet surrendered. By coincidence this was the feast day of the Virgin Mary, the anniversary of Malta's great victory over the Turks in the Siege of 1565.

Days later the armistice between Italy and the Allies was signed aboard HMS *Nelson* in the Grand Harbour. For Malta the war was over.

## After the War

Britain gave the Islands £10 million towards rebuilding and restoration after the devastating wartime destruction they had suffered. There was a promise of a further £20 million to be delivered as it was required for improved housing and the infrastructure. In 1947 **self-government** was restored and the first election returned a Labour government under **Dr Paul Boffa**.

The main problems concerning the economy still had to be addressed. There were worries that the hardships that followed World War One might be repeated, although mass emigration to Australia and Canada would ease some of the problems of unemployment. (There are now as many Maltese and Gozitans living abroad as on the Maltese Islands.) But the future looked uncertain.

Self-government worked modestly well, and when in 1955 the Labour party was again returned to power, the volatile and charismatic **Dom Mintoff** became Prime Minister and made his first indelible mark on the local and international scene. He proposed a popular idea: that Malta should be integrated into the United Kingdom to become another county on the lines of Britain's Channel Islands. Economically this made sense to the Maltese, who now spoke English as a national language and considered themselves Britain's friends and allies, but the idea floundered. Although a national Referendum showed 67,607 votes out of 90,343 were in favour of the motion, the British government maintained they were not convinced the result truly reflected the feelings of the non-voters.

Relations between Britain and Malta then became strained, and were further aggravated when Britain announced it would be cutting back its armed forces and their base in Malta. With the immediate prospect of diminishing revenue and loss of jobs (the garrison was the Islands' greatest single employer), Mintoff lost his interest in union with Britain and called for full independence.

In 1959, political deadlock with Mintoff forced Britain to suspend the constitution, but a five-year plan was published giving a transition time towards **independence**.

On 21 September 1964, with a Nationalist government headed by **George Borg Olivier** now in power, Malta became independent while remaining a member of the Commonwealth. A defence agreement entitled British forces to remain in Malta for ten years and during that time Britain would provide capital aid up to a total of £50 million for the diversification of the economy; tourism was suggested.

The Malta Labour Party, still under the leadership of Dom Mintoff, returned to power in June 1971 and soon afterwards tenaciously renegotiated the 1964 agreements in order to provide Malta with higher remuneration for the use of its military facilities. Malta would receive £14 million annually in rent, plus £7 million as part grant and part soft loan. Italy, with whom Malta enjoyed good relations, promised a further £2.5 million in economic aid.

The British forces left Malta on 31 March 1979 after a presence of 180 years. Malta became a neutral and non-aligned **Republic**.

## Representatives of the Crown Civil Commissioners

| | |
|---|---|
| 1799–1801 | Captain Alexander Ball, RN, President of the Provisional Government |
| 1801–02 | Sir Charles Cameron |
| 1810–13 | Lieutenant-General Sir Hildebrand Oakes |

### Governors

| | |
|---|---|
| 1813–24 | Lieutenant-General The Hon. Sir Thomas Maitland |
| 1824–26 | General the Marquess of Hastings |
| 1827–36 | Major-General The Hon. Sir Frederic Ponsonby |
| 1836–43 | Lieutenant-General Sir Henry Bouverie |
| 1843–47 | Lieutenant-General Sir Patrick Stuart |
| 1847–51 | The Right Hon. Richard More O'Farrell |
| 1851–58 | Major-General Sir William Reid |
| 1858–64 | Lieutenant-General Sir John Gaspard le Marchant |
| 1864–67 | Lieutenant-General Sir Henry Storks |
| 1867–72 | General Sir Patrick Grant |
| 1872–78 | General Sir Charles Van Straubenzee |
| 1878–84 | General Sir Arthur Borton |
| 1884–88 | General Sir Lintorn Simmons |
| 1888–90 | Lieutenant-General Sir Henry Torrens |
| 1890–93 | Lieutenant-General Sir Henry Smyth |
| 1893–99 | General Sir Arthur Freemantle |
| 1899–1903 | Lieutenant-General Lord Grenfell |
| 1903–07 | General Sir Mansfield Clarke |
| 1907–09 | Lieutenant-General Sir Henry Grant |
| 1909–15 | General Sir Leslie Rundle |
| 1915–19 | Field-Marshal Lord Methuen |
| 1919–24 | Field-Marshal Viscount Plumer |
| 1924–27 | General Sir Walter Congreve |
| 1927–31 | General Sir John du Cane |
| 1931–36 | General Sir David Campbell |
| 1936–40 | General Sir Charles Bonham-Carter |
| 1940–42 | Lieutenant-General Sir William Dobbie |
| 1942–44 | Field-Marshal Viscount Gort |
| 1944–46 | Lieutenant-General Sir Edmond Schrieber |
| 1946–49 | Sir Francis (later Lord) Douglas |
| 1949–54 | Sir Gerald Creasy |
| 1954–59 | Major-General Sir Robert Laycock |
| 1959–62 | Admiral Sir Guy Grantham |
| 1962–64 | Sir Maurice Dorman |

### Governors-General

| | |
|---|---|
| 1964–71 | Sir Maurice Dorman (British) |
| 1971–74 | Sir Anthony Mamo (Maltese) |

# The Republic today

On 13 December 1974, Malta's parliament, the House of Representatives, changed the constitution. From that day the Islands of Malta would be a neutral and non-aligned democratic Republic within the Commonwealth. For the first time in their long history the Maltese were in charge of their own lives and destinies.

To replace the Governor-General, the (largely ceremonial) office of President was established and **Sir Anthony Mamo**, who was the first Maltese-born Governor-General (appointed in July 1971), became the first President.

To replace the loss in revenue with the departure of the British it was a time for aggressive promotion of the Islands, both as a tourist destination and as a base for manufacturing investment, especially the kind of light industry that would lessen unemployment figures by taking in the ever-constant numbers of a young female workforce that worked until marriage. Mistakes were made, but generally the Islands prospered. Tourism in particular, aimed at the middle market, took over, and package tour companies were courted.

At home the Maltese began to live in better comfort and style than ever they had before. Politically the Islands swung left to right and back again, but rarely with a majority of more than two seats. Voters here are born to their family's party and seldom change allegiance, so the arrival of first-time voters coming to the polling stations with their parents can change governments. Although there are three political parties, only the **Malta Labour Party** and **Partit Nazzjonalista** (Nationalists) win seats. The third party, **Alternattiva Demokratika**, has yet to win a seat.

On 16 July 1990, Malta applied for membership of the European Community, a natural step as the Islands have been a member of the United Nations since 1964 and the Council of Europe since 1965.

The two main parties are divided on how to achieve membership, if at all. The reluctant Labour Party believes all conditions of membership should be stated before entry; the Nationalist Party is prepared to talk once entry is achieved. However, the introduction of VAT, the removal of government subsidies on many products and other new measures are aimed at preparing the ground for eventual entry. A tentative date for membership is 2004.

When all the formalities and protocols are agreed and a date set for Malta's entry, the ruling Nationalist Party (as of the year 2000) has promised a national referendum asking the people if they want EU membership or not. The party is convinced the answer will be an overwhelming 'yes' vote. Leader of the Opposition, Dr Alfred Sant, said in 1999 that, whatever the outcome, when in power the Labour Party will pull Malta out of the EU. This might not be just the rhetoric of Opposition.

One of the problems of EU membership might have been the fact that Malta has declared itself neutral and non-aligned. This came about in a package deal imposed on the Nationalists in opposition by the Labour government just before the 1987 elections. Although he had already stood down as prime minister, the volatile Dom Mintoff brokered the discussions. In spite of proportional representation (but with the help of cleverly drawn electoral boundaries) Labour had held on to the majority of seats in parliament with only a minority of votes for five years. Seeking to rectify this anomaly, in behind-the-scenes discussion it was agreed that the party polling an absolute majority of votes should govern, if necessary through adding seats in the House of Representatives. In exchange for granting the Nationalists this opportunity for regaining power, it was agreed that Malta would declare itself a neutral state and would not participate in military alliances or permit the setting up of foreign military bases on its territory. As a result, the Nationalist Party, polling the largest number of votes, was returned to office.

Within days the then Prime Minister called a meeting for all diplomats accredited to the Islands to explain that Malta's neutrality was *sui generis*, that is, a unique type. Italy, a NATO member and financial benefactor, could come to its defence if so requested. Malta would also rewrite the Agreement of Friendship and Co-operation with the Libyan Jamahariya signed in Mintoff's reign. The Agreement would drop the clause combining the security interests of the two countries and so delete, as Italy saw it, the 'odd part of the equation'.

The intention then was for Malta to continue developing its bilateral and multilateral relationships with Europe and, in time, become a full member of the European Union. A statement in officialese added: 'Malta's European credentials are not in doubt. Its Western democratic values have deep roots that have withstood the test of provocation; and its neutral status and unpretentious but sober efforts for peaceful dialogue are a positive contribution to a new, larger and closer, but outward-looking Europe.'

Meanwhile, the Islands continued, and continue still, to flourish. Schooling remains compulsory up to the age of 16 and entries from government, church-run and private schools to the University of Malta are high. There are trade schools in every district and most towns and villages have a state primary school and kindergarten. The Islands remain Roman Catholic although church attendance is falling.

As in most countries, car ownership is increasing, with many families owning more than one vehicle. This is in part due to inefficient public transport, notably the antiquated buses much loved by tourists. Restaurants and cinemas flourish too, especially at weekends, a sign that economically the Maltese family feels comfortable. Having accepted English as one of two national languages, the Maltese are now in a position to teach it to students from all over Europe in English-as-a-foreign-language schools.

With sea and sun as the Islands' only resources, the tourism industry continues to be the centre of the economy. With more than 1 million visitors arriving each year, and with more money being invested on improving the facilities and the roads, there is a move to up-grade tourism from its mass-market base. This may be too late—the Islands have sacrificed beauty spots and aesthetic judgment in the name of business development—yet five-star hotels continue to open on prime sites and, even out of the July to October peak season, maintain high occupancy rates. New yacht marinas will soon be able to berth some of the world's largest yachts at competitive rates.

Malta International Airport is spacious and functional and a new sea terminal will soon be welcoming with similar efficiency the thousands of tourists each day as they arrive on giant cruise ships. Light industry continues to be a prime target for the government and, to generate overseas investment, there continue to be numerous inducements like 10-year corporate tax holidays, soft loans, investment and depreciation allowances and generous training grants. The dockyards, in a shrinking but competitive market, are facing today's challenges with some success as they bid to repair and service some of the world's largest tankers and cruise liners in the Grand Harbour. And the Malta Freeport in Marsaxlokk Bay is expanding as its success as a duty-free distribution and handling shipment zone becomes better known.

Malta has come a long way as a Republic and has the drive to go further still. These tiny Mediterranean islands have already achieved as much as many a larger country with greater resources. The next great challenge is to be a member of the European Union.

## Prime Ministers

| | |
|---|---|
| 1921–23 | Hon. Joseph Howard |
| 1923–24 | Hon. Francesco Buhagiar |
| 1924–27 | Hon. Sir Ugo Mifsud |
| 1927–32 | Hon. Sir Gerald Strickland (later Lord Strickland) |
| 1932–33 | Sir Ugo Mifsud |
| 1947–50 | Hon. Dr (later Sir) Paul Boffa |
| 1950 (Sept–Dec) | Hon. Dr Enrico Mizzi |
| 1950–55 | Hon. Dr Giorgio Borg Olivier |
| 1955–58 | Hon. Dom Mintoff |
| 1962–71 | Hon. Dr Giorgio Borg Olivier |
| 1971–84 | Hon. Dom Mintoff |
| 1984–87 | Hon. Dr Carmelo Mifsud Bonnici |
| 1987–97 | Hon. Dr Eddie Fenech Adami |
| 1997–98 | Hon. Alfred Sant |
| 1998 – | Hon. Dr Eddie Fenech Adami |

## Presidents

| | |
|---|---|
| 1974–76 | Sir Anthony Mamo |
| 1976–81 | Dr Anton Buttigieg |
| 1981–82 | Dr Albert V. Hyzler (Acting President, Dec–Feb) |
| 1982–87 | Miss Agatha Barbara |
| 1987–89 | Mr Paul Xuereb (Acting President) |
| 1989–94 | Dr Vincent Tabone |
| 1994–99 | Dr Ugo Mifsud Bonnici |
| 1999– | Prof Guido de Marco |

# Malta on business

## The Economy

Valletta is Malta's business centre, with the House of Representatives (parliament), ministerial offices, law courts and most company head offices within its fortified walls. The manufacturing industry is spread out across Malta and Gozo.

More than one-quarter of the gross national product is generated by the **tourism industry** which is also the Islands' largest employer. Other main sources of revenue are the Malta Freeport (see below), **agriculture** (including the export of most of the Islands' annual potato and onion crops to Holland, where they are highly praised), small industries and the national airline, Air Malta.

**Malta Drydocks**, the dockyards that for generations seemed to epitomise the Islands' fame and brought considerable revenue, have suffered as the drop in the shipping market seriously affected the industry in the Mediterranean.

However, aggressive management working for the yards to become more competitive has won additional contracts from countries as far apart as the United States and Ukraine, and the dockyards have been cited by *Lloyd's Report*, the international shipping industry newspaper, as performing well and with a positive future ahead. To protect and ensure this future, it is the government's intention to ask for a special transition period for this sector when Malta eventually joins the European Union.

## Doing business

A considerable amount of international business is done through the flourishing customs-free transshipment zone, the Malta Freeport, which handles freight from as far away as Japan. Many international companies have offshore arrangements here too and, with an eye to the future, HSBC, the Hong Kong banking group that took over the UK's Midland Bank, acquired majority share holding in Mid-Med Bank, the large Maltese bank. (Before nationalisation in the 1970s, it was Barclays Bank).

Local business is conducted efficiently with a fair amount carried out socially. It is worth remembering that the Islands are small, so many of the people you deal with in business are related to each other and that anyone they recommend could be a brother, cousin or relative. This may, or may not, be an advantage.

When doing business in Malta it is advisable first to take advice and carry out research that covers both legal and political aspects. The swings of political power can affect the success of a business venture.

However, many long-established foreign companies trade in Malta or have Maltese partners and are proof that profitable, successful business is possible.

## Setting up business

The Government actively seeks foreign investment and the setting up of small manufacturing units on the Maltese Islands. There is a large, young, adaptable workforce available.

Many attractive incentives have been introduced including tax-free concessions, soft loans and training grants. For further information contact: *Malta Development Corporation*, Villa Portelli, Kalkara. ☎ 667100. 🗎 667111. E-mail: mdc@maltanet.net

As part of government plans to further develop the Islands as an international financial and trading centre, laws have been enacted that, while they do not make Malta into an offshore centre, offer highly advantageous low-tax incentives.

For further information contact *Malta Financial Services*, Attard. ☎ 441155. 📄 441188.

### As a conference centre

Many of the five-star hotels offer excellent conference facilities and have teams set up specially to help organise conferences and free-time entertainment. Around St George's Bay, the two *Corinthia* hotels, the *Westin Dragonara* and the *Hilton Malta* have devoted considerable space and investment to updating the technical necessities required for international conferences and, of course, have ample quality rooms for delegates. Most have business centres too. Smaller hotels also have facilities and can tailor a conference to demand.

The government runs the *Mediterranean Conference Centre* in Valletta with well equipped halls that can seat from 70 to 1500 delegates, theatre style. This spectacular building was once was the old hospital of the Knights of the Order of St John. (No accommodation.)

Contact: *Mediterranean Conference Centre*, Triq l-Isptar, Valletta. ☎ 243840-6. 📄 245900.

### Malta Freeport

This successful government venture near Birżebbuġa in Marsaxlokk Harbour was set up as a customs-free zone that could handle bulk cargo in preparation for its redistribution in smaller loads or containers to Europe and North Africa. It has two terminals and oil tanking facilities.

The Freeport is free of all customs and excise dues, exchange control and other duties. The Freeport benefits, enacted by law, are guaranteed for 15 years.

Full information is available from *The Malta Freeport Corporation*, Freeport Centre, Kalafrana BBG 05. ☎ 650200. 📄 684814.

# Did you know?

The Maltese take their islands for granted. Visitors, however, may like to know more. For example:

**Band Clubs** Every town and village has one or two brass bands that play at important events, like a *festa* (see below). The bands are truly popular and their clubs often act as social centres. Rivalry is great and during a *festa* fights can occasionally break out in the streets as rival fans and clubs clash. The music is rousing but the bands move at a leisurely shuffle, taking time to stop and chat as well as enjoy a free drink. The noise they make is exhilarating and more than makes up for any lack of skill. As they march, so crowds follow.

**Churches** *'Wherever you are, you can see a church or a chapel.'* Although it may seem so, this is not quite true. Creating this impression are 313 churches in Malta (63 parishes) and 45 churches in Gozo (15 parishes). There are also five National parishes: English, French, German, Greek Catholic and Italian.

**The Eye of Osiris** On either side of the prow of every traditional Maltese fishing boat there is an eye. It may be painted, it may be embossed, but it will be there. This eye, the 'Eye of Osiris', wards off evil. (There is an example on our cover picture.)

How this simple superstition found its way to Malta is unclear. The eyes appear on fishing boats in many parts of the Mediterranean. Osiris is an ancient Egyptian god, known both as the god of fertility and the god of the dead. In this second role he wards off evil spirits.

Many of the Maltese boats are named after Roman Catholic saints and carry little shrines too. It is a perfect example of traditional superstition and religion working harmoniously together.

**The *festa*** This is the day—now by custom a weekend between May and September—when the parish celebrates its patron saint's feast day with bangs, bands, fireworks and processions. Once it was exclusively a religious event, but now a *festa* is simply a time for celebration. The weekend starts with petards exploding deafeningly in the sky as if war has been declared. In the evening when the church is lit up and all its silver is out on display, the crowds come out, the bands play and the saint's statue is paraded through the streets. Vendors sell everything from *pastizzi* (savoury hot pastry stuffed with ricotta cheese or mashed peas) to nougat that breaks the teeth. Around 23.00, each day ends with superb displays of fireworks. (See also p 36.)

**The *Gallarija*** The main characteristic of the domestic architecture until the advent of high-rise apartment blocks and cementstone and aluminium modern buildings, was the addition of the *gallarija*, the painted, wooden closed balcony that gives each façade such a charming appearance. Valletta's apartment blocks, with seven or eight storeys marked out by balconies, could not look more distinctive, or Maltese. At one time all houses, whatever the financial background, had to have a balcony. Many were left open, but by the 18C closed ones began to appear and as gentrification took hold early in the British years, they took on importance. Here a wife and daughters could sit in comparative privacy and watch the world go by. Initial costs, restoration and upkeep has made them less popular now but the government has made funds available for the restoration of old ones.

***Kaċċa*** Literally translated, 'hunting'. Although the Maltese would profess to love birds, only a few desultory sparrows, housemartins and homing pigeons dare fly the skies. The birds the Maltese love are songbirds like finches, canaries and budgerigars—in cages. Or large stuffed specimen in glass cabinets.

Twice a year as birds migrate to and from Europe and the warmer climes of Africa, Malta's *kaċċatur* (that is, the bird trappers and bird shooters characterised locally as 'hunters') take to—and often take over—the countryside. Nothing is safe and anything that flies is considered fair game. This is the *kaċċa*, Malta's answer, enthusiasts say, to fox hunting or bullfighting. The *kaċċatur* is the man, the *tal-kaċċa* his fine Maltese gundog.

The environmental group BirdLife is active, but bird shooters and trappers continue their slaughter for two reasons.

The first: although the government has declared official seasons (i.e. times of the year when shooting is prohibited) it is not a law enforced with any enthusiasm. In a country where every vote counts in a general election, neither of the two major parties would risk having this small but volatile fraternity vote against them. The *kaccatur* are vociferous in matters like joining the EU too. They are convinced EU regulations will outlaw 'hunting' even though, regretfully, this is not likely to happen.

The second reason: the *kaččatur* are often men given to violence. If you are in the countryside or on an unspoiled stretch of coast and you see 'hunters' with their rifles, or trappers sitting inside ramshackle stone hides with tiny songbirds as decoys in tiny cages on stone plinths in front of them, give them a wide berth. Everyone has a story to tell, but it is a fact, that sometimes fists are used or a shot fired in the general direction of the trespassers. It is not unusual either to come across the tattered remains of an owl, kestrel or homing pigeon.

**The Maltese Cross** The internationally distinctive Maltese Cross originated as the emblem of the Order of St John of Jerusalem. It was only as the Knights themselves became known as the Knights of Malta that the device took on the title Maltese Cross.

As the Order became established in the mid-13C, based in Acre, so their simple white cross on a scarlet background was replaced by the more dramatic eight-pointed cross. The four arms of the cross represent Prudence, Justice, Temperance and Fortitude, while the eight points represent the Beatitudes as taught by Christ in the Sermon on the Mount. This new cross, the Knights believed, symbolised Christianity rather than the plain cross of crucifixion.

Although the Maltese Cross features on tourist trophies and souvenirs of the Maltese Islands, it is still considered to be the insignia of the many and various Orders that now make up the Order of St John.

**Milestones** Although many are now being stolen to decorate private gardens, as you travel through the countryside you may notice tall granite milestones, particularly at crossroads. You will also not fail to notice that each one has been defaced and all its detail has been chipped away. No town or village name or distance is legible. This is because in World War Two the British were taking no chances. The theory was that if airborne German or Italian troops succeeded in landing on Malta or Gozo, they would get hopelessly lost without the information on the milestones. It is probably for the best that no record contains the name of the originator of this bizarre idea.

**Pink and blue ribbons** This is a charming custom. Often you will see a large pretty bow of pink or blue silk ribbon tied decoratively to a door knocker. It means a new daughter or son has been born to the family. If you see a big white one, a wedding is soon to take place. This is the bride's house.

**Rabbit stew and *lampuki* pie** These are two favourite Maltese dishes that sometimes make an appearance on menus.

Rabbit stew is simply that—pieces of rabbit casseroled with wine and vegetables. *Lampuki* pie is a pastry-covered fish pie made with lots of vegetables (from cauliflower to olives) and filleted *lampuki*. *Lampuka* (singular) and *lampuki* (plural) are dolphin fish (not to be confused with the mammal). In France the fish are *coriphène*, in Italy *lampuga*. The *lampuki* season is September.

Let a Maltese or a Gozitan guide you to other local dishes: they can be excellent. (See also *Food and drink* and *Where to eat*.)

**Super Five** The Maltese enjoy gambling. On all main streets a Lotto office opens for business three days a week selling tickets for the Saturday numbers draw. 'Super Five' is a Wednesday draw where, for 50 cents a ticket, you can win a tidy sum. Select the correct five numbers out of 36; it is that simple. Many weeks no one has the correct five, so the prize money is carried forward. It can add up considerably. You do not have to be Maltese or Gozitan to buy a ticket.

**Superstitions and customs** There are any number you will come across. Some seek the protection of the Lord, others ward off evil.

Making the sign of the cross as soon as the bus starts up, for example, and crossing yourself again as you pass a church, puts you firmly in the hands of the Lord. In the countryside bulls' horns tied to the roof of a farmhouse ward off evil. (Some have an effigy of the Virgin Mary on one of the walls too, for double insurance.)

Then look at the churches. They have two clocks, one real, the other false— this way the devil does not know what the time is. Nor must you wear green if someone in the family is doing school or university examinations; *unlucky*.

# Additional reading

Countless books, both fiction and non-fiction, have been written about or mention the Islands of Malta and Gozo.

Much has been written about the archaeology too and the outstanding importance of the temples. Many of those learned archaeological tomes are now out of date as carbon dating has proved Maltese temples to be much older than was once considered. (See the study: *Before Civilization* by Colin Renfrew.)

The following books are available in Malta at **Sapienza's Bookshop**, 26 Republic Street, Valletta ☎ 233621, ▤ 246182

Other titles not mentioned may now be out of print.

## Archaeology

*Malta: An Archaeological Guide* by David Trump (Revised 1990. Progress Press, Malta). Definitive look at the Islands' prehistoric remains. An important study.
*Before Civilization* by Colin Renfrew. (Penguin, 1990). Proof that Malta and Gozo's temples are the oldest free-standing monuments known to man.

## Architecture

*Malta: a guide to the Fortifications* by Quentin Hughes (Said International, 1993). Excellent guide to the Islands' forts with photographs and drawings that bring to life the part each played in history.
*British Military Architecture in Malta* by Stephen C Spiteri (Malta, 1996). Learned study concentrating on the British years when the Islands were a fortified garrison.
*5,000 years of Architecture in Malta* by Leonard Mahoney (Valletta Publishing, 1996). Eminent Maltese architect studies the great civil, religious and military buildings.

## History

*The Story of Malta* by Brian Blouet (Revised 1981. Progress Press, Malta). Well-written comprehensive history.
*The Great Siege: Malta 1565* by Ernle Bradford (Penguin, 1964). The most readable account written of the fight between the Christian and Ottoman Turk forces based largely on the eyewitness account of Father Balbi di Correggio.
*The Cross and the Ensign: a Naval history of Malta, 1798–1979* by Peter Elliott. (Harper Collins, 1980). Well-researched details of Malta's connection with the British Royal Navy.
*Siege: Malta 1940–1943* by Ernle Bradford (Penguin, 1987). Bradford's skill brings to life Malta's second great siege.
*Malta Convoy* by Peter Shankland & Anthony Hunter (Collins, 1961). Evocative account of Operation Pedestal, the convoy that saved the besieged islanders from starvation in 1942 as it braved enemy action and decimation crossing the Mediterranean.
*Malta Convoys 1940–1943* by Richard Wooodman (John Murray, London. 1999). A graphic account based on personal experience and recently declassified documents.
*Malta: a Thorn in Rommel's Side* by Laddie Lucas (Penguin, 1992). Enthralling account by wartime pilot and commander of Malta's most successful squadron

of the dark days when Malta was the most bombed place on earth.

*The Temple of the Knights of Malta* with text by Nicholas de Piro and photographs by Daniel Cilia (Miranda Publications, 1999). Seriously expensive photographic study of St John's Co-Cathedral in coffee-table presentation.

## Other

*Art in Malta* by Giovanni Bonello (Fondazzjoni Patrimonju Malti, Malta, 1999). Stimulating reappraisal (and occasional reattribution) of Malta's art treasures.

*The Dghajsa and other traditional Maltese Boats* by Joseph Muscat (Fondazzjoni Patrimonju Malti, Malta, 1999). Well-illustrated, learned look at Maltese boats and their origins.

*The Kappilan of Malta* by Nicholas Monsarrat (Pan, 1994). A moving love story set against the backdrop of World War Two.

*Malta 360°* with superb gatefold photographs by Attilio Boccazzi-Varotto and text by Geoffrey Aquilina Ross (Priuli & Verlucca, 1985). Giant (and expensive) coffee-table book with sweeping pictures that shows the island as never seen before.

*The Maltese Islands from the Air* with photographs by Jonathan Beacom (Proud Publishing, Malta. 1994). Aerial tour of the Islands; superb vistas, surprising detail. Text by Geofffrey Aquilina Ross.

*Saints and Fireworks* by Jeremy Boissevain (Progress Press, Malta. Reprint 1996). Full of information and entertaining too. A look at the roles played by religion and politics in Malta's rural life.

# MALTA

# Valletta

### City of the Knights

Sir Walter Scott wrote to a friend that Valletta was 'a city built by gentlemen for gentlemen', and even now, behind the disfiguring plethora of shopfronts, neon signs and all manner of electrical and telephone wiring, Valletta is a city of stupendous architecture. It has much to offer anyone who explores.

The capital sits on what was known as **Mount Sceberras**, a 43m-high rocky mound that is the promontory separating the superb Grand Harbour that gave the Islands their fame from the more tranquil harbour of Marsamxett where, today, varieties of boats set out on day cruises from Sliema's waterfront.

Established on what was barren ground by Grand Master Jean Parisot de la Valette on 28 March 1566, the city was designed by Italian architect Francesco Laparelli but completed with much vigour and style around 1571 by his Maltese assistant, Gerolamo Cassar. (See *The Order of St John*, p 59.)

At that time Valletta's street plan was considered revolutionary in its simplicity. It consists of a rectangular grid of straight streets stretching the length of the city, from City Gate to Fort St Elmo, crossed at right angles by streets that run side to side, from harbour to harbour. In this formation there are squares of open ground designed to face the prominent buildings. Centuries later New York would be designed in the same manner.

The straight streets follow the natural terrain within the walls. As a result many are steep and often have picturesquely shallow steps that were created to allow men encumbered by weighty armour to ascend or descend with less difficulty than they would on steps of standard height. Byron called them 'cursed streets of stairs'.

At the seaward point of the promontory is Fort St Elmo, and—another legacy of the Knights—the whole city is surrounded by high stone bastion walls to make it impregnable.

---

### Arrive by ferry

Going to the city by car during office hours means facing severe parking restrictions (tow zones operate) unless you use the underground car park by the bus terminus and War Memorial (you cannot miss this eyesore).

An alternative is to start your visit by ferry from Sliema. Take the shuttle (it leaves every 30 minutes, weather permitting) from Sliema's Ferries. The 10-minute trip is enjoyable. However be warned: there is a steep hill to negotiate from the quay into the city.

## How to see Valletta

Two routes will lead you to the major sites. See the other places mentioned later or on another day.

1 • The Republic Street walk
2 • The Merchants Street walk

If time is limited use the Check List below to see Valletta's most important sites. Enjoy the cafés and restaurants at the same time.

### Check list

What to see if your time is limited:

St John's Co-Cathedral
Palace of the Grand Masters
The Grand Harbour from the Upper Barrakka Gardens
The church of St Paul Shipwrecked
Auberge de Castille
The Manoel Theatre
The Mediterranean Conference Centre (the Knights' Sacra Infermeria)

### History

When the Knights of the Order of St John of Jerusalem arrived in October 1530, only a simple watchtower stood on the tip of the rocky peninsula. At that time most of the Islands' population of 12,000 lived and worked around **Vittoriosa** (known then as Borgo (in Italian) or Birgu (the Maltese derivation), a small conurbation on the south side of the harbour where there were sheltered creeks for ships and boats and a dilapidated Castel St Angelo offered modest protection should warmongering forces attack. With the arrival of the Knights, grand buildings were erected and **Senglea** (L'Isla) and **Cospicua** (Bormla) began to take shape to accommodate the growing number of residents.

But the Knights, who knew that the Ottoman Turks were preparing to pursue them and wage war in their attempt to conquer the Christian empire, decided that a fort would be needed to guard the entrance to the great harbour. Fort St Elmo was commissioned. By 1551 it was built.

The Order was aware that the rocky ridge of Mount Sceberras was important in strategic terms and that from its imposing height mortar fire could dominate the harbour and destroy any ship within it. A number of plans were drawn up for an additional fort on the ridge too, including one in 1562 by Baldassare Lanci of Urbino which had the blessing of Pope Pius IV obtained by the Knights at the Council of Trent. But in 1565, when the Turkish force did set foot on Maltese soil, work had still not begun and the enemy occupied the peninsula. The strategic position was secured as their base.

When, after feats of incredible bravery, the Knights and their Maltese allies obtained victory and watched the remains of the Turkish force set sail, the Order of St John speedily took over the terrain. Mount Sceberras would never again fall into enemy hands.

To answer their call for help, the Pope sent Francesco Laparelli, a pupil of Michelangelo, to Malta and, within a few days, he presented a plan for a fortified city.

On 28 March 1566 the foundation stone was laid and, when eventually the city took shape, it was named Valletta in honour of the glorious French knight, Grand Master Jean Parisot de la Valette, who had lead them to victory in the Great Siege.

## The city walls

The fortifications of Valletta were carried out to the designs of the illustrious Francesco Laparelli between 1566 and 1570 and, for the most part, are structurally still as they were conceived. Gates were added or widened later to give easier access to the city as the threat of attack receded.

For the best vantage point of Valletta's defences you should try to see them first from a distance, as from Sliema. This gives an idea of the magnitude of the work carried out.

(Similar fortifications can be seen on the far side of the Grand Harbour from Upper Barrakka Gardens, with Fort Ricasoli at the entrance to the harbour and Fort St Angelo and the Senglea peninsula at its centre. If, on a cool day, you want varied panoramas of the two harbours and the magnitude of the construction, an enjoyable walk is along the walls circling Valletta. Allow nearly two hours to complete the circuit.)

Malta's forts and fortifications are excellent examples of military architecture dating from the late 16C. They have changed little and most bastions and curtains in Valletta are marked with their names. In this context, although *bastion* is commonly used to indicate any sheer, high wall erected by the Knights, a number of words are more definitive:

- **Bastion**  A fortified stone wall thrusting out from the line of fortifications
- **Cavalier**  A defence work behind and higher than a bastion. It might be a gun emplacement or simply a stronghold for troops and arms
- **Counterguard**  An acutely angled, many-sided, stonework set lower and in front of a bastion as first line of defence
- **Curtain**  The sheer stone wall linking the bastions
- **Parapet**  The low, indented wall on top of a rampart used by defenders to fire down on the enemy
- **Rampart**  A flat-topped defensive mound
- **Ravelin**  The v-shaped protrusion in front of the curtain with open access for defenders at its rear

## The city

The city of Valletta is wrapped in the defensive stone walls built by the Order of St John. There are a number of entrances from land and sea although City Gate, where the central bus terminal and underground car park are located, is considered the entrance for pedestrians. Vehicles entering the city use the more attractive entrance into Valletta that sweeps up Gerolamo Cassar Avenue from the War Memorial outside Floriana to the square in front of Auberge de Castille. As there is limited parking space in the city, entering with a car during office hours cannot be recommended.

Cut into the section of the walls (St James's Curtain), City Gate leads on to **Republic Street**, (in Maltese Triq ir-Republikka) the main thoroughfare that runs along the spine of the of the city to Fort St Elmo.

Depending on who ruled the Islands, so the name of this important street was changed. To the Knights it was *Strada San Giorgio* in Italian, to the French during their brief occupation it was *Rue de la République*, and then for a long while the Maltese called it *Strada Reale* until, under the British mantle, it became *Kingsway*. When the Islands became a republic in 1974 it changed again. Now, mostly pedestrianised, it is the city's main shopping street and is dotted with places of historical interest as well as cafés and a **McDonald's** that sits harmoniously within its surroundings.

**City Gate** was once a grandiose Baroque stone edifice with three narrow entrances, two for pedestrians, one for vehicles, and was reached by a narrow stone bridge that replaced the original drawbridge over the 17m deep and 9m wide dry moat. This ditch, that stretches from harbour to harbour, was carved out of the solid rock by Turkish slaves. When the drawbridge was raised, this side of Valletta was impregnable.

Regrettably, in the pre-preservation days of the mid-1960s the superb stonework was demolished and replaced by an ugly utilitarian entrance that would permit heavy commercial vehicles to enter the city. Successive governments have promised to rectify this blot and undoubtedly one day a new gate will be commissioned, but it would not appear to be a priority.

Meanwhile, the **bus terminus** outside the Gate fills the air with diesel fumes and the imposing **Triton Fountain,** designed by Maltese sculptor Vincent Apap (c1950), acts as the bus roundabout. On the days when this fountain with its three classic Tritons holding a giant dish is operational, it is a welcoming sight and in keeping with the spirit of the city. A few metres away, by the other blot on the landscape that is the underground car park, a glistening, gilded eagle hovers on a tall stone column. This is the **Royal Air Force Memorial** commemorating the fallen in World War Two.

# The Republic Street walk

As a pedestrian, having negotiated the bus terminus, you enter through City Gate into a shambolic open space that is used as a car park unless a public event is scheduled to take place there. This is **Freedom Square**. Like City Gate, it is unattractive and was built in the mid-1960s. Don't be dismayed by this greeting: the treasures of Valletta lie ahead.

Alongside the square are the remains of the **Royal Opera House**, a gracious building that was destroyed by enemy aircraft in 1942. It is destined to be restored and will form an integral part of the National Arts Centre taking shape in St James Cavalier (see p 109); so help is at hand.

Designed by Britain's E.M. Barry, the opera house was built between 1861 and 1864 on the site that was once the Auberge d'Angleterre, the lodgings of the British Knights. It was the Islands' great social centre where balls, concerts and operas took place. When redeveloped, a theatre will be at its core with shops and other commercial interests around to sustain it financially.

This is where **Republic Street** really starts. It is hard to imagine now, but this was a street where society once lived, the home of prominent families. The Neo-classical **Palazzo Ferreria** opposite the opera house ruins is an example of such a home. Acquired by the government in lieu of death duties and now the Ministry for Social Welfare, the *palazzo* is on a site where the knights had their gun foundry. Further along, where a plethora of clothing shops and cafés flourish, there were small hotels and clubs where gentlemen would go to smoke tobacco. In those days Valletta was an elegant city.

In South Street, on the left, as you continue along Republic Street, is the **Museum of Fine Arts** in a historic *palazzo* (see p 115). In Republic Street itself, you'll see on the right the church of **Santa Barbara**, once the church of the Langue of Provence. (A *Langue* was a national branch of the Order of St John's Hospitallers. See *The Order of St John*, p 59.) Designed by Giuseppe Bonici around 1739, the simple church offers Masses in English, French and German.

Opposite, is the church of **St Francis** with a constant, large congregation. Rebuilt with affection in 1681, its ceiling is celebrated, but a more recent painting was completed early this century by Giuseppe Cali (1846–1930), a Neapolitan born in Malta. It shows Christ triumphant in heaven holding a cross in one hand while blessing the faithful with the other. St Francis is among the devoted crowd.

On the same side is the **National Museum of Archaeology**, once the Auberge de Provence, designed by Maltese architect Gerolamo Cassar in 1571. It took five years to complete but was later considerably modified. It has an austere façade with imposing portals flanked by shopfronts. (See p 114.)

On your right you now come to the first of the city's great treasures in St John's Square.

## St John's Co-Cathedral

The exterior of the cathedral looks austere simply because, unlike the decorative work associated with other churches of this stature, its long, plain frontage is unadorned. The flat plainness of the external walls masks the wealth, splendour and opulence of the interior, and even the two brass cannons framing the entrance portico at the top of the sweep of steps in no way prepare you for what is inside.

The architect, Gerolamo Cassar, was by trade a military architect, a man whose work centred on defence and the creation of fortresses that would withstand any enemy. This may explain why the exterior is so austere. The portico and twin bell towers are a much later addition. William Makepeace Thackeray reported in 1846:

> *The Church of St John, though not handsome without, is magnificent within. A noble hall covered with a rich embroidery of carving. It seemed to me fitting place for this wealthy body of aristocratic soldiers who made their devotions as it were on parade, and on their knees, and never forgot their epaulets on their quarters of nobility.*

### History of the Cathedral

Work began in November 1573 to Cassar's designs with monies donated by the reigning Grand Master, Jean l'Evêque de la Cassière from France. It was originally conceived simply as the church belonging to the religious Order of St John of Jerusalem and it was consecrated as such on 20 February 1578. Each Langue of the Order was allocated a chapel. With time, and with the considerable wealth endowed by the Knights, it grew in importance. As Valletta itself began to replace Mdina as the Islands' recognised capital, Valletta's church, though it would remain a conventual church, began to take over the importance of Mdina's gracious older cathedral.

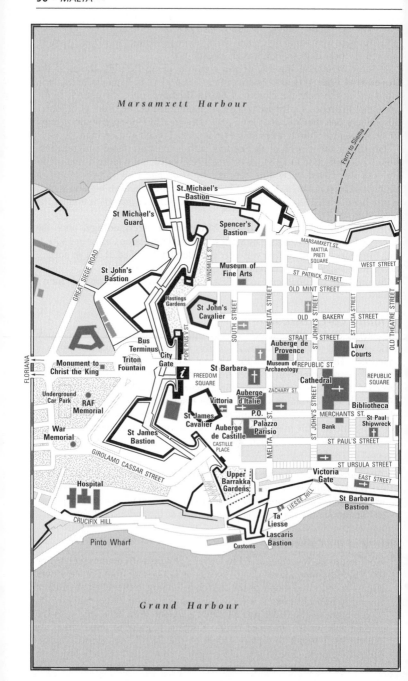

*Marsamxett Harbour*

Ferry to Sliema

St Michael's
Bastion

St Michael's
Guard

Spencer's
Bastion

MARSAMXETT ST.
MATTIA
PRETI
SQUARE

WEST STREET

St John's
Bastion

WINDMILLS ST.

Museum of
Fine Arts

ST PATRICK STREET

OLD MINT STREET

MELITA STREET

SOUTH STREET

Hastings
Gardens

St John's
Cavalier

OLD

BAKERY

ST JOHN'S STREET

ST LUCIA STREET

OLD THEATRE STREET

STREET

GREAT SIEGE ROAD

Bus
Terminus

City
Gate

POPE PIUS V ST.

STRAIT

STREET

Auberge de
Provence

Museum of
Archaeology

Law
Courts

Triton
Fountain

FLORIANA

Monument to
Christ the King

St Barbara

FREEDOM
SQUARE

REPUBLIC ST.

ZACHARY ST.

Cathedral

REPUBLIC
SQUARE

Underground
Car Park

RAF
Memorial

Vittoria

Auberge
d'Italie

P.O.

Bibliotheca

MERCHANTS ST.

St Paul
Shipwreck

War
Memorial

St James
Cavalier

Auberge
de Castille

Palazzo
Parisio

CASTILLE
PLACE

Bank

MELITA ST.

ST PAUL'S STREET

St James
Bastion

GIROLAMO CASSAR STREET

ST URSULA STREET

Victoria
Gate

EAST STREET

Hospital

Upper
Barrakka
Gardens

LIESSE HILL

St Barbara
Bastion

CRUCIFIX HILL

Ta'
Liesse

Customs

Lascaris
Bastion

Pinto Wharf

*Grand Harbour*

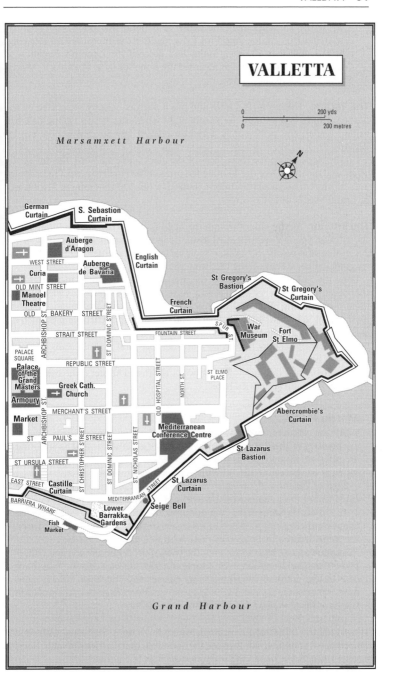

# VALLETTA

0        200 yds

0        200 metres

N

*Marsamxett Harbour*

German Curtain

S. Sebastion Curtain

Auberge d'Aragon

WEST STREET

Curia

OLD MINT STREET

English Curtain

Manoel Theatre

Auberge de Bavaria

St Gregory's Bastion

St Gregory's Curtain

OLD

BAKERY STREET

ARCHBISHOP ST.

ST DOMINIC STREET

French Curtain

FOUNTAIN STREET

SPUR ST.

War Museum

Fort St Elmo

STRAIT STREET

PALACE SQUARE

REPUBLIC STREET

OLD HOSPITAL STREET

NORTH ST.

ST ELMO PLACE

Palace of the Grand Masters

Greek Cath. Church

Armoury

ARCHBISHOP ST.

MERCHANT'S STREET

Abercrombie's Curtain

Market

ST

PAUL'S STREET

ST CHRISTOPHER STREET

ST DOMINIC STREET

ST NICHOLAS STREET

Mediterranean Conference Centre

St Lazarus Bastion

ST URSULA STREET

EAST STREET

Castille Curtain

MEDITERRANEAN STREET

St Lazarus Curtain

BARRIERA WHARF

Lower Barrakka Gardens

Seige Bell

Fish Market

*Grand Harbour*

In 1816, 18 years after the Order of St John had been ignominiously despatched from Malta, Pope Pius VII recognised the importance of this great religious edifice in Catholic Malta and decreed the church's elevation to Conventual-cathedral. It was awarded the same status as St Paul's in Mdina, giving Malta two cathedrals.

**The façade** This projects a little and has a narrow balcony supported by the portico. Above is a window to provide light for Mattia Preti's ceiling (see box below) and in the pediment is a bronze bust of the Saviour by Alessandro Algardi.

On the clock tower, the three faces of the clock mark the hour, the day of the week, and the date. Over the door are the arms of the Papal Nuncio, Fra Ludovico Torres, who consecrated the church, flanked by those of the Order of St John and of Grand Master de la Cassière.

**The interior** As you enter through the main door into the soft light that bathes the interior, you are overwhelmed instantly by the magnificent harmony of the decoration and colour. Sir Walter Scott exclaimed in a letter: 'This is the most magnificent place I saw in my life.' Now you see why.

From the richly painted vault to the mosaic of multicoloured memorial slabs that cover the floor, every detail proclaims that, to the Knights, this was the most important building of all. Each successive Grand Master added to its embellishment on his appointment, as did each and every Knight when he presented his *gioja*, or joyous gift, as he was honour bound to do when promoted within the Order. The Knights may have been a brotherhood that took up arms of war to preserve Christianity, but the Order was, above all, a religious brotherhood and this was to be their testimony. All but two of the Grand Masters who commanded the Order in Malta are buried here.

### Mattia Preti

While the cathedral owes its splendour to Mattia Preti, one of the outstanding painters of the Italian Seicento, it is said the cathedral had as profound an effect on the artist as his works have had on Malta. The best examples of his work are here and the cathedral is his artistic triumph.

Born in Calabria in 1613, Preti studied in Rome and Naples where he came under the influence of the works of Caravaggio and painters of the 16C. An outstanding artist, his masterworks are in Naples and dispersed about southern Italy. As much of his legacy in Malta is painted directly onto the stone, it can only be seen by those who seek it out.

As you enter St John's following the traffic flow to the left, the first chapel you enter (No. 2) contains the simple tomb of Mattia Preti. He may have embellished many of the island's fine palaces and churches, but his commemorative stone is plain. Perhaps it was considered that the cathedral itself stands as his memorial. He died in Malta in 1699.

The plan of the cathedral is a rectangle with a single nave, 58m long, with six side chapels in bays on either side between the thick walls that buttress the vault. Narrow passages were cut into the walls to connect each set of chapels.

As you enter, pause to take in the great sweeping picture. Do not be swept on by other visitors. What greets you is awesome.

**The vault**  St John's stood plain and unadorned for nearly 80 years until Grand Master Rafael Cotoner commissioned Mattia Preti (see box) to decorate the vast expanse of ceiling. In five years, between 1662 and 1667, with consummate artistry and draughtsmanship, he made it into a superbly colourful spectacle. He turned the uncompromisingly shaped vaulted ceiling into separate canvases by the simple device of painting in architectural details like cornices, decorated archways and balustraded balconies, and then filled the ceiling with paintings depicting 18 episodes in the *Life of St John the Baptist*. The narrative moves from John's birth through to the Dance of Salome and John's Beheading. Around them are figures of saints and heroes. Preti painted in oil directly on to the stonework which he had primed first. The Spanish brothers, Rafael and Nicolas Cotoner, who were Grand Masters in succession, paid for the work.

**The pavement**  The floor of the cathedral—the pavement—is made up of a colourful tapestry of 400 marble memorial slabs that commemorate the dignitaries of the Order. Some are macabre, some dramatic, but all have a story of chivalry to tell. They were made by craftsmen from marble of every hue, and are adorned with coats of arms, heraldic devices, military and naval trophies, instruments of war, figures of angels, crowns, skeletons, symbols of death, and much more. The effect is remarkable.

Because of wear and tear caused by the shoes of both daily worshippers and visitors to the cathedral, measures are now being taken to stop the floor deteriorating. Visitors should walk only in designated carpeted areas.

**The high altar**  At the centre of this magnificent building is a wonderful feast of opulence in the name of the Lord, the holy sanctuary with the high altar (No. 1).

The focal point of the cathedral, it is raised on four steps, enclosed by a marble balustrade. Its two bronze lecterns were originally presented by Francis of Lorraine in 1557 to the conventual church of Birgu (Vittoriosa), but were moved here when the Knights established Valletta.

The altar itself, dated 1686, is made of lapis lazuli and other marbles adorned with a gilt bronze relief of the *Last Supper*. Behind is the magnificent marble group of the *Baptism of Christ* by Giuseppe Mazzuoli (1644–1725) backed by a splendid bronze *Gloria* by Giovanni Giardini da Forti (1646–1721). On the beautifully carved wooden lectern there are scenes from the *Life of John the Baptist*. A monstrance made by Gian Lorenzo Bernini for the reliquary containing the right hand of John the Baptist once adorned the altar too but is now in the **St John's Museum** (see p 97). The reliquary itself, however, was looted by Napoleon's troops and then lost when the warship *Orient* was sunk by Nelson's fleet in Aboukir Bay (Egypt).

- At various times of the year, usually from the feast of Corpus Christi in early June to the Feast of St Peter and St Paul on 28 June, the walls of the nave are hung with impressive Flemish tapestries by Judocus de Vos (1697). On show normally in the St John's Museum, the tapestries are based on paintings by Rubens and Poussin.

# ST JOHN'S CO-CATHEDRAL

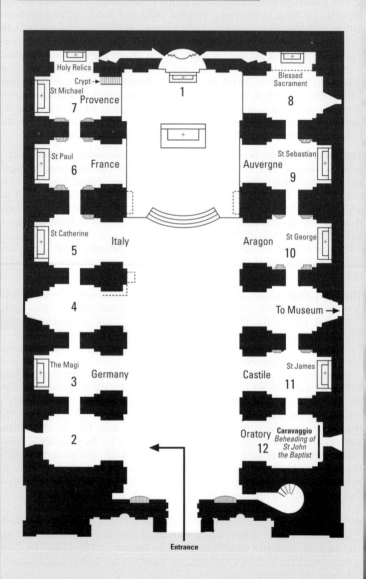

Holy Relics

Crypt →

St Michael
Provence
7

St Paul
France
6

St Catherine
Italy
5

4

The Magi
Germany
3

2

1

Blessed
Sacrament
8

St Sebastian
Auvergne
9

St George
Aragon
10

To Museum →

St James
Castile
11

Oratory **Caravaggio**
*Beheading of
St John
the Baptist*
12

Entrance

## A tour of the cathedral

The **second chapel** (No. 3) is that of the Langue of Germany. Dedicated to The Magi, it has an early 18C white marble altar with late 17C altarpiece depicting the *Adoration of the Magi*. The imposing bronze and black marble mausoleum honours Marc Antonio Zondadari, Grand Master, 1720–22.

The **third bay** (No. 4) contains the north door of the cathedral leading from Great Siege Square. Passing through, you next come to the chapel of the Langue of Italy dedicated to St Catherine (No. 5). Here the altarpiece, the *Mystic Marriage of St Catherine*, is another Preti masterpiece. The monument by Algardi honours Gregorio Carafa, Grand Master, 1680–90. Its marble relief shows the galleys of the Order of St John at the Battle of the Dardanelles in 1656. Carafa was the Captain General of the fleet.

You then enter the **fifth bay**, the **Chapel of France**, dedicated to St Paul (No. 6). It was stripped of its Baroque decoration around 1840 but contains the tomb of Grand Master Emanuel de Rohan Polduc who laid the foundation of the Maltese civil code, as well as the tomb of Louis Charles d'Orléans, Vicomte de Beaujolais, the brother of King Louis-Philippe of France, who died in Malta in 1808. His full-length figure, by Jean-Jacques Pradier, was added to the tomb in 1844.

The **sixth chapel** on this side is the **Chapel of Provence** dedicated to St Michael (No. 7) with, to one side, the **Chapel of the Holy Relics** dedicated to St Charles Borromeo. The chapel belonged briefly to the Anglo-Bavarian Langue, 1784–98. The wooden figure of St John the Baptist on the wall came from the poop of the carrack in which the Knights sailed from Rhodes.

From the Chapel of Provence you descend into the **crypt** which contains the tombs of 11 of the Grand Masters who served in Malta. The medieval style of their sarcophagi with full-length effigies are enveloped by Nasini's exuberant decoration. Among the Grand Masters are Villiers de l'Isle Adam (hero of the defence of Rhodes), Jean Parisot de La Valette (commander during the Great Siege of Malta) and Jean l'Evêque de la Cassière (founder of the cathedral). There is only one person here below the rank of Grand Master, Sir Oliver Starkey who was secretary to La Valette.

Across the High Altar is the **seventh bay**, the **Chapel of the Blessed Sacrament**, enclosed by a screen and gates of silver (1752) (No. 8). Story has it that these gates were painted black in 1798 to look like wrought iron to escape the notice of the French, who were stripping the Islands of all its treasures. The chapel was originally dedicated to Our Lady of Phileremos in honour of an icon brought from Rhodes, but that was removed by Grand Master Hompesch when the Order was despatched from Malta. (The icon was later presented to Tsar Paul I of Russia when he became protector of the Order.) The 15C crucifix painted in tempera also came from Rhodes, while the keys on the walls were acquired by Admiral Gattinara in 1601 after being taken from Turkish fortresses at Mahometta (Hammamet in Tunisia), Lepanto (Navpaktos in Greece) and Passava (near Gytheion in the Peloponnese). The *Madonna di Carafa* was bequeathed by Gerolamo Carafa, prior of Barletta, in 1617, and was moved here in 1954 from the Chapel of Italy.

Next is the **Chapel of Auvergne** (No. 9). Dedicated to St Sebastian, it has two lunettes of scenes from his life by Giuseppe d'Arena. The altarpiece is also attributed to him. The monument is to Grand Master Clermont de Chattes Gessan who reigned for four months in 1660. An epitaph in the floor marks the grave of Melchior de Robles y Pereira who was killed during the Great Siege.

The next bay is the **Chapel of Aragon, Catalonia and Navarre** dedicated to St George (No. 10). Its altarpiece of St George is by Mattia Preti who painted it in Naples before 1657 and sent it originally to Malta as an example of his work. The other paintings, also by Preti, are later.

The chapel contains two of the most impressive marble and bronze monuments to Grand Masters. Both are superb examples of Italian Baroque sculpture and have all manner of decoration, effigies, banners, cherubs and cannon. One commemorates Nicolas Cotoner (ascribed to Domenico Guidi) and the other Ramon Perellos (by Giuseppe Mazzuoli of Volterra).

The next bay is an entrance to the St John's Museum (see p 97) and bookshop with, alongside, the **Chapel of Castile, Leon and Portugal** (No. 11), dedicated to St James and decorated by Preti. It holds two dramatic monuments to Grand Masters, one to Manoel Pinto de Fonseca (Grand Master, 1741–73), and the other to Manoel de Vilhena (1722–36). The Byzantine icon on the altar was brought to Malta in 1760 by Christian slaves escaping from a Turkish man-of-war.

Now you come to the **Oratory** (No. 12), which in December 1999 was declared an integral part of the museum. It contains one of Malta's greatest treasures, the magnificent *Beheading of St John the Baptist* by Caravaggio.

In 1603 this inner chapel was designated as a suitable place for knightly devotions and instructions to novices and, until it was decorated in the grand manner by Mattia Preti, it remained starkly plain. His eight paintings adorning its walls and ceiling changed it from a plain oratory into a fitting showcase for what is often referred to as the most important painting of the 17C.

---

### The Beheading of St John

Michelangelo Merisi da Caravaggio (1573–1610) came to Malta in July 1607 as a guest of Grand Master Alof de Wignacourt (whose portrait by Caravaggio hangs in the Louvre in Paris). He was already a celebrated painter in Rome but known as much for his riotous life as for his artistic talent. In effect, he was given to a life of pleasure.

On his arrival he began work on the *Beheading of St John* and a year later was received into the Order of St John of Jerusalem by special permission of the Pope who was prepared to overlook his past indiscretions. But in spite of his attention to his devotions, in 1610 Caravaggio's unruly behaviour caused him to be imprisoned in Fort St Angelo. He escaped and fled to Porto Ercole in Italy where, only 38, he died of malaria just days before a papal pardon was delivered.

The *Beheading of St John* is a masterpiece of exceptional drama and realism. Although it depicts a grim subject, complete with Salome and executioner, Caravaggio imbues in the painting's other characters a sense of tortured emotion as they participate in the desolate act in prison.

The great painting hung in the cathedral for nearly 300 years before being taken to Italy in 1956 for (ineffectual) restoration. On its return it was placed in the National Museum by the government of the day, but the ecclesiastical outcry at what was seen as an act of sacrilege reached the Pope in Rome and, in due course, the masterpiece was returned to the church. In 1999 it was again taken to Italy for restoration and, after being exhibited in Florence and Naples, is back in position.

The Oratory is a superb chapel with subtle lighting that does justice to both Mattia Preti and Caravaggio, whose haunting masterpiece *St Jerome* also occasionally hangs here.

*St Jerome* used to hang in the chapel of the Langue of Italy as it was a gift of an Italian Knight, Ippolito Malaspina, who donated it to the chapel. His escutcheon is on the painting. The ecclesiastical authorities moved it to the Oratory believing this location to be more secure. (*St Jerome* was stolen in the 1980s and recovered by a stroke of luck.) It will be moved again.

## St John's Museum

The highlight of the museum is the collection of 29 **Flemish tapestries** commissioned by Grand Master Perellos upon his election in 1697. Made in Belgium by Jodicos de Vos, 14 are square panels based on drawings by Rubens and depict the *Life of Christ* as well as illustrate allegories like the *Triumph of Chastity* and the *Destruction of Idolatry.* Another, based on a work by Poussin, commemorates the *Last Supper.* The remainder, which punctuate the sequence of Christ's life, show the Virgin Mary, the Disciples and the benefactor Grand Master Perellos himself.

Other exhibits include vestments, illuminated choral books (antiphonals) and the only church silver remaining after Bonaparte ransacked the church in 1787 in order to finance his Egyptian campaign.

After visiting St John's, turn right on Republic Street into **Great Siege Square** where an allegorical bronze group by eminent Maltese sculptor Antonio Sciortino commemorates the dead of the Great Siege of 1565. Facing it, across the road is a tall, pillared modern building. This is the **Law Courts**, built in 1967 on the site of the Auberge of Auvergne (1574) which was ruined, like much of the city, in 1942.

It is probably now time for a cooling drink or coffee, and as you reach **Misraħ ir-Repubblika** (Republic Square) you have a choice of cafés. The square is covered with tables sheltering under colourful umbrellas. Those in the centre belong to *Caffè Cordina*, the city's premier café (see p 28). Sit at one of the tables outside or enter the bustling café itself. Enter anyway, just to see what they are offering as snacks. You can stand at the bar like the locals (it costs less than being seated at a table, inside or out), but if you do you must pay for your drink and snack first in the Italian manner. The staff will guide you.

A marble statue of **Queen Victoria** by Giuseppe Valenti stands in the middle of the square, a resting place for Valletta's pigeons. This was Queen's Square in British times.

## The Bibliotheca

As its backdrop, the arcaded square has the solid façade of the Bibliotheca, also known as the National Library or the Biblioteka Nazzjonali (open to visitors during office hours, approximately 08.30–17.00 in winter, 08.30–13.00 in summer; closed holidays).

Designed for the Order in 1786 by Stefano Ittar, an architect from Calabria in southern Italy, it took 10 years to complete and was the last civil building the Order was to commission. Inside, the collections include 300,000 books and documents.

## History of the Library

In 1555, before Valletta was built, the Knights created a library as a repository for the books bequeathed by their deceased brethren, and in 1612, to safeguard this wealth, the Order passed a statute forbidding the sale of any of a Knight's books at his death.

By 1760 with the bequest of Cardinal Giocchino Portocarrero's 5670 volumes and, three years later, 9700 volumes from Guerin de Tencin's estate, a new building was essential. Two decades later it was commissioned.

Despite serious losses during the French occupation when Malta's treasures were looted, and despite instructions being issued by Napoleon for all records pertaining to the Knights to be destroyed, documents in the Bibliotheca include all written records of the Order from 1107 to 1798. It is presumed the Knights who were given these orders ignored them.

The most important items are the bull of Paschal II instituting the Order of St John (1113) and the Act of Donation (1530) when Malta was given to the Order by the Emperor Charles V. Of considerable interest is the signed bull and accompanying letter in which Henry VIII proclaimed himself head of the Church of England. There is always a changing display of documents and books and one beautiful exhibit is the illuminated Life of St Anthony the Abbot, by Master Robin Fournier of Avignon (1426).

Unfortunately, recent lax security has meant that many more treasured items and maps have disappeared.

Under the arches that shelter the entrance to the Bibliotheca is an old café, now transformed into the *Café Premier Complex* with a café and a multimedia experience devoted to the life and times of the Knights. Billed as a walk-through attraction, *The Great Siege of Malta and The Knights of St John* attempts to relive the days of the Knights and bring the Siege to life with sound, video and light effects.

Now you come to Valletta's other great treasure house on Misrah il-Palaż (Palace Square), the Palace of the Grand Masters (see below).

Sadly, the square is largely used as a car park for members of parliament and their staff. In the past it was the focal point of all national occasions and has seen historical events such as the day in 1798 when Dun (Father) Mikiel Xerri and 33 compatriots were shot there by the beleaguered French after they tried and failed to open the city gates to rebel islanders attempting to overthrow their oppressors. And it has been the scene of military parades, including the momentous occasion when the islanders were awarded the George Cross for bravery in World War Two.

At the centre of the square is a building that is known as the **Main Guard** after its British years when a ceremonial guard was stationed there. The Latin inscription on its portico, put there in 1814 by the British, records the cession of Malta to Great Britain. The building is currently used as offices of Valletta's administration. Next to it, screened by trees is the **Italian Cultural Institute**, an attractive one-storey building from the 17C, formerly the Chancellery of the Order of St John. It has a fine painted ceiling in the main hall by Tuscan painter Nicolo Nasini da Siena, completed in 1725. Visitors are welcome.

On the corner to the right, on **Archbishop Street**, is the flamboyant but sadly decaying **Hostel de Verdelin**, designed by Francesco Buonamici who introduced the Baroque style of architecture to Malta. The building contains a club and a small theatre which screens a dramatically moving 45-minute film, *The Wartime Experience*, an archive film account of the bravery of the Maltese nation and British services during World War Two. There are hourly performances.

But it is the Palace of the Grand Masters overlooking the square that you must visit.

## The Palace of the Grand Masters

● **State Rooms open** 1 Oct–15 June, Mon–Wed 08.30–15.45, Thur–Fri 08.30–16.00; 16 June–30 Sept, Mon–Fri 08.30–13.00. Entrance fee.

In 1571, six years after the victorious outcome of the Great Siege, the Order of St John considered the new city safe enough to become their new headquarters instead of Birgu. To create a suitably magisterial palace, Grand Master Pietro del Monte purchased a recently erected house at the centre of the city and commissioned Gerolamo Cassar, who was already responsible for establishing Valletta's splendid architectural roots, to make this house a fitting place for future Grand Masters.

Like the plainness that masks St John's Co-Cathedral, its frontage in no way signals what lies behind. The façade is 89m long and had it not been for the dressed corner stones and the two arched gateways that were introduced later to replace a single archway, and the addition of two long wooden balconies in the time of Grand Master Pinto de Fonseca (1741–73), the façade would be austere indeed.

The interior however makes up for this apparent oversight and renders the palace fitting offices for heads of state.

Until 1798 when the Order of St John was despatched, each Grand Master was based here, and it was the office of the British Governor until the departure of the British garrison in 1964. Today it houses the office of the President of the Republic as well as Malta's parliament, the House of Representatives. All state occasions take place here.

The gateway on the right as you face the palace leads to the sombre, unprepossessing **Prince Alfred's Courtyard**, renamed by the British after Queen Victoria's son, who visited Malta in 1858. Once (but no longer,)it was graced with orange trees to perfume the air. In the bell tower above, placed there by Grand Master Pinto de Fonseca in 1745, a charming clock has four bronze Moors to strike the quarter hours on gongs alongside four dials that register the time, day and month as well as phases of the moon.

Between two stone lions in the courtyard, an entrance leads to a modern staircase and the **Great Hall of the Knights**, which runs the full length of the palace. This is now the **House of Representatives**. If you enter, the public gallery is on the right and looks, theatre style, directly on to the floor of the House. At the centre is the Speaker's chair with the Government members' pews to the left and the Opposition to the right.

Also in Prince Alfred's Courtyard is the entrance to The Armoury in what was formerly the stables.

## The Armoury

- **Open** 1 Oct–15 June, Mon–Sat 08.15–17.00, Sun 08.15–16.15; 16 June–30 Sept, daily 07.45–14.00.

A statute of 1551 decreed that all arms and armour belonging to the Knights should be pooled and kept in serviceable condition at the public expense for future use. The collection, now reduced by years of neglect from around 25,000 suits to under 6000 pieces, ranks in interest, if not richness, with those of the Armeria Real in Madrid and the Royal Armories in Leeds.

On show are remarkable suits of armour including ceremonial suits made for Grand Masters La Valette and Wignacourt. (Alof Wignacourt's, made by the best Milanese craftsmen of the day, is inlaid with gold.) There is also sapping armour of immense weight belonging to Wignacourt and fragments supposedly worn by Dragut Rais when he commanded the Ottoman force during the Great Siege. Making up the remarkable collection are all manner of swords, halberds and arquebuses as well as trophies and captured arms taken from Ottoman forces.

The Armoury narrowly escaped total removal in 1827 when plans were made to ship it to the Tower of London and again in 1846 when similar plans were proposed for Britain's Woolwich Arsenal. The impressive collection was rehoused here in 1974 having been moved from the Great Hall where the armour was being adversely affected by damp and mildew.

The ceremonial (and main) entrance to the palace is on the left leading into **Neptune's Courtyard** where, amid ailing hibiscus and palm trees, there is a bronze statue of *Neptune* attributed to Giambologna. Amateur historians suggest the attribution is wrong, however; they say the subject is in fact Admiral Andrea Doria, a friend of La Valette's, who was much given to taking off his clothes and posing as Neptune with a trident in his hand. Were that so, the work could be that of Leone Leoni, the admiral's personal sculptor.

The statue was originally the centrepiece of a fountain in the old fish market, placed there by Grand Master Wignacourt in 1615, but moved to the palace in 1861. Behind Neptune in the arcade is a marble fountain originally used to water horses and embellished with an elaborately carved escutcheon of Grand Master Ramon Perellos.

In a corner of this courtyard a superb circular staircase rises to the *piano nobile*, the first floor, of the palace with marble steps shallow enough for a man in full armour to ascend. It was also, it is said, wide enough to accommodate litters carrying knights with gout.

It is in this courtyard that guides for tours of the palace can be found, but the stairs are likely to prove difficult for anyone with a physical disability. There is no other suitable entrance.

On the *piano nobile*, **corridors** overlooking Neptune's Courtyard are lined with portraits of Grand Masters and aristocrats as well as with suits of armour. The ceilings were painted by Nicolo Nasini da Siena around 1720, and most of the lunettes above the windows depict victorious naval battles of the Order.

To the left, a set of doors leads into the Supreme Council Chamber of the Order of St John, known today as the **Throne Room** (or sometimes the **Hall of St Michael and St George**). Its magnificent frieze shows 12 important incidents of the Great Siege and was painted between 1576 and 1581, not long after the siege was lifted, by Matteo Perez d'Aleccio, a pupil of Michelangelo. The scenes illustrate the dramatic episodes following the arrival of the Turkish armada in May and lead up to the Order's final victory with the retreat of the enemy force on 8 September.

The Chamber acquired the name of Hall of St Michael and St George in 1818, when the first investiture of a newly created British chivalric order was held here. The throne used by the President is on a dais at one end, while at the other is a charming sculptured wooden gallery with six painted panels depicting scenes from Genesis. This gallery, it is believed, was formerly in the palace chapel and came originally from the galley *Grand Carrack* in which the Order retreated from Rhodes.

To one side of this great room are the Hall of the Ambassadors (or Red Room) and the Pages' Room (or Yellow Room).

The **Red Room** was the Grand Master's audience chamber. Below the coffered ceiling runs a frieze by Perez d'Aleccio with scenes from the Order's history between 1309 and 1524. Portraits on the walls include *Louis XV* of France (by Jean Baptiste van Loo), *Catherine II* of Russia (by Levitzky) and *Alof de Wignacourt* (by Leonello Spada), who wears the suit of armour now in the Armoury.

The **Yellow Room** was the *Paggeria* or Pages' Room where 16 boys enrolled by their noble fathers as pages would wait until summoned. The boys were taken at the age of 12 on the understanding that on reaching 18 they could apply to become Knights.

The **State Dining Room** leading off the Throne Room was seriously damaged during World War Two. On its walls are paintings of Malta's presidents.

Off the secondary corridor is the **Council Chamber of the Order**, known as the **Tapestry Chamber** because of a set of the impressive Gobelins tapestries that hang here. These were presented by Grand Master Perellos in 1697 and are signed by Le Blondel. Known as *Les Tentures des Indes*, the magnificent works show jungle and hunting scenes from South America, India and the Caribbean. They are rich with life, exotic flora and action. Above them the frieze shows galleys in victorious action against the Turkish Ottoman force.

This is a palace of surprising wealth and grandeur. It must be seen.

On leaving the palace continue down Republic Street to Fort St Elmo. If you want to avoid the steep downward slope of the hill, you could at this point instead visit other places of interest within this remarkable city by checking the map. (See *Alternative Route*, p 106.)

As the street descends it becomes less interesting, but to your right, is the **Borsa** (Exchange), with its grand façade, facing a charming building from the turn of the last century that is the headquarters of HSBC, one of the Islands' banks.

As you progress, you come to **Casa Rocca Piccola**, the family home of Marquis de Piro. The building has seen many uses in its long history but the de Piro family have lovingly restored it to a gracious patrician home with family possessions and treasures. (Open Mon–Sat, 10.00–13.00. Tours on the hour. Entrance fee.)

Finally you come to the road on the bastion walls that encircles the city. Across the harbour to your left is Sliema. To the right is Fort St Elmo.

## Fort St Elmo

- **Open** Every weekend, Sat 10.00–17.00, Sun 09.00–17.00

### History of the fort

Early records show that in 1481 a watchtower stood on this advantageous tip of the promontory that separates two of the island's impressive harbours. It took its name from the small chapel also there, dedicated to St Elmo, the patron saint of sailors.

The fort began to take shape in 1488. In 1551, in keeping with its strategic importance facing the sea and commanding the entrance to both harbours, it was strengthened for the Order of St John by the Spanish military engineer, Pedro Pardo, who created a traditional fort linked with a wooden bridge to the land side across a man-made ditch. Unfortunately, the fort was exposed to enemy fire from the heights of Mount Sceberras that rose behind it, but this was the fort that would so bravely withstand the might of the Ottoman Turkish forces when they attacked.

In May 1565, when the Turkish force arrived to conquer the Islands and the Christian Order, the commanders took stock of the defenders' positions. Part of their force they established in fields to the south of the Order's land base at Birgu (see *The Three Cities*, p 159). Another large section was positioned on Mount Sceberras but sited above Fort St Elmo on the Marsamxett flank of the hill so the natural high ground in between could act as a screen for its mortar batteries which might otherwise have come under sight and fire of the mortar on Fort St Angelo. Unwittingly this particular precautionary measure initially favoured the Knights. It left communication open between Birgu and Fort St Elmo and the defenders used it to full advantage.

On 3 June, after assembling their finest men, the Turks attacked and captured the first line of defence around Fort St Elmo. Had it not been for a Spanish officer who held the drawbridge single-handedly, the enemy would have captured the fort itself. In the ensuing bombardment great stretches of the fort's ramparts were reduced to rubble.

It was now that Dragut Rais, aged 80 but still Suleiman the Magnificent's greatest commander, arrived with his additional troops and took stock of the Ottoman position. In his opinion many tactical miscalculations had been made and to rectify the situation he set about further strengthening the Turkish hold on the island.

He constructed two batteries to face Fort St Elmo, the first on the northern point of Marsamxett harbour (Tignè) and the second on Ricasoli Point. The Ottoman force now commanded entrance to both harbours. He also extended the lines in front of St Elmo in order to cut the garrison's link by boat with Birgu across the harbour.

While he was directing these works, however, fate took a hand. Dragut was struck by rocks thrown up by mortar bombardment and fell mortally wounded. One of the greatest warriors of the century, and La Valette's supreme enemy, was dead.

As news reached them morale rose high within the ranks of the defenders. But it was a short respite. On 23 June 1565 Fort St Elmo was stormed and fell. It was the eve of the feast day of the Order's patron saint, St John. In the course of the battle, the Turks lost 8000 men, a quarter of their force. As for the defenders, only four Maltese escaped, swimming to Fort St Angelo. In the 31 days the fort was bombarded, 1500 Christian lives were lost, including 89 Knights. The Ottoman commander Mustapha Pasha recorded, as he faced the task of conquering the next fortress, Fort St Angelo: 'If so small a son cost us so dear, what must we pay for so large a father?'

After the final victory and the lifting of the siege in September, the Order put into effect many changes in the island's defensive lines. The battery in Marsamxett harbour soon became Fort Tignè, with Dragut Point marking where Dragut was mortally wounded, and Fort Ricasoli was established across the main harbour to strengthen its defence.

Under Grand Master Alof de Wignacourt the bastions were reinforced, and by 1687 St Elmo was totally enclosed, taking on the completed star shape it has today. Later Grand Master Perellos would add further works. The fort was no longer the vulnerable fortress that faced the Ottoman might with such bravery.

Between 1871 and 1875 the British made further changes and later it became the headquarters of the Maltese army.

St Elmo is a fortress of magnificent military architecture but it is in a pitifully neglected state. It has been singled out by the International Council on Monuments and Sites as one of ten sites on Malta and Gozo in danger of disintegration through neglect and misuse.

The road to the main entrance to **Upper Fort St Elmo** passes across the underground granaries where the Order stored the vital grain needed to sustain the garrison. Each storage hole is cut deep into the rock and covered by a circular stone slab. A section of this upper part of the fort is now home to the Police Academy and not open to visitors.

**Lower St Elmo** is reached by the road where Republic Street joins the fortifications. It houses the War Museum (see p 117). Alongside it is the entrance used by squatters who have taken over the fort's neglected buildings for various dubious purposes.

---

## In Guardia

On certain days each month a full-scale military re-enactment in period costume takes place at Fort St Elmo. Known as *In Guardia*, the full ceremonial event includes musketry and gunnery drills, presentation of the colours and a rousing *Feux de Joie* (ceremonial gun salute). At 11.00 and 20.00. Entrance Lm1.

---

Fort St Elmo overlooks the **St Elmo Breakwater** jutting out to sea at the entrance of the Grand Harbour, built between 1903 and 1906 to protect the harbour's great reaches and creeks from violent northeasterly gales. An iron bridge once linked the stone breakwater to the mainland with supporting stanchions placed so as to allow small boats to sail through, close to the shoreline. The breakwater remains, but the bridge was brought down in World War Two during a brave but foolhardy raid by explosive Italian E-boats attacking the entrance on the night of 25 July 1941. That night the guns of Fort St Elmo were victorious once more.

## *The Sacra Infermeria (Mediterranean Conference Centre)*

Facing into the Grand Harbour alongside Fort St Elmo you now come to the Mediterranean Conference Centre, once the Great Hospital of the Order of St John, the Sacra Infermeria. This is yet another magnificent building behind a plain façade.

### History of the hospital

When the Order set about building their new city, one of the first priorities was a hospital. The Knights may have become famed as soldiers and defenders of the Faith, but they were Hospitallers first and foremost. It was their duty to care for the sick. In order to carry out their charitable works, a great hospital was essential.

As the city took shape, in 1574 they laid the foundations for the Sacra Infermeria (the Holy Infirmary). Its architect is unknown but its design seems to have been inspired by the Santo Spirito hospital in Rome. Soon, not only was it providing nursing of the highest standards of its day but, as extensions were added, it came to have the longest hospital ward (with an unsupported roof) in Europe (155m). In winter the ward was hung with 131 pieces of woollen tapestry and in summer with paintings by Mattia Preti. It was so special that in 1666 it was said to have 'one of the grandest interiors in the world'; patients ate from silver plate. Within two centuries it would grow in size to be able to care for 914 patients in an emergency.

The Infermeria housed only male patients but there was no class discrimination, nor was there one based on nationality. Lords and paupers were treated equally. However, although the hospital would take patients of any religion, non-Catholics were only permitted to stay in the Great Ward for a total of three days unless they were prepared to accept religious instruction from one of the Order's chaplains. No records exist of any conversions taking place.

In 1676, under Grand Master Nicolas Cotoner, a School of Anatomy and Surgery was established. Decades later this would be transformed into the University of Malta.

When Napoleon Bonaparte arrived in 1798 en route to Egypt and chased the Order from Malta, he declared that in future the Sacra Infermeria would serve only French troops. No sooner had his troops ejected its patients than they melted down the silver plate to fund the Egyptian campaign. The days of being of service to the civilian population were over. When Britain chased the French out two years later, they turned the Infermeria into the British Military Hospital, which it remained until 1920.

During World War Two large sections of the building were flattened during the relentless bombing raids on the Grand Harbour and what was left of it became an entertainments hall for allied troops. This was where they came for film shows, concert parties and dances.

Today the restored Sacra Infermeria is an excellent example of the grand scale of architecture created by the Knights. Its corridors are redolent with history. With its capability now to be a centre for international conferences as well as remaining a historical site, it has won the prestigious international Europa Nostra Award for excellent restoration and adaptation. As the Mediterranean Conference Centre, its great rooms make it ideal for large conferences, and musicals and opera are often staged in the large auditorium.

In the Magazine Ward there is also a permanent exhibition entitled '*The Knights Hospitallers*', with the episodes and personalities that make up the history of the Knights. (Open Mon–Fri, 09.30–16.00. Entrance fee.)

On another level, with its own entrance on the bastion walls, another theatre shows '*The Malta Experience*', an audio-visual show giving a fascinating record of Malta's history from the earliest times. Hourly performances in 13 languages (with headphones) last 50 minutes and are an excellent way of learning all about the Islands.

Follow St Lazarus Bastion alongside the Mediterranean Conference Centre and you come to the **Siege Bell Memorial**, overlooking the Grand Harbour just below **Lower Barrakka Gardens**.

Dedicated to the men who lost their lives in the wartime convoys of 1940–43, the Memorial was unveiled by Queen Elizabeth II on a visit in May 1992 marking the 50th anniversary of the award of the George Cross to the Islands. It consists of a Neo-classical cupola enclosing a 12-ton bell and, between the cupola and the harbour, a monumental bronze catafalque with a recumbent figure. The monument was funded by the George Cross Island Association and the Maltese and British governments. The Siege Bell is rung every Sunday at noon.

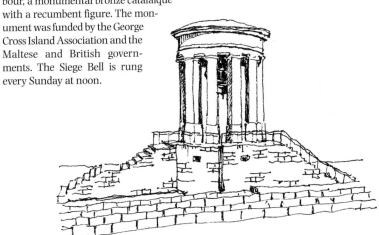

*The Siege Bell Memorial, Valletta*

Above on St Christopher's Bastion, the Lower Barrakka Gardens have an excellent view of the harbour and its entrance. At their centre, an incongruous memorial in the form of a Doric temple commemorates Sir Alexander Ball who was Britain's first Governor of the Islands. It was he who led the siege that defeated the French in 1800, and in recognition he was appointed the first civil commissioner.

If you progress down the hill below the Bell you come to **Barriera Wharf** where the fish market occupies an area that, before 1643, was used as a place of quarantine. Grand Master Lascaris made this wharf into a commercial centre, building warehouses along the road he had cut through the bastion named after him. On Lascaris Wharf the **Custom House**, the impressive work of Giuseppe

Bonici (1774), is still in use. A lift precariously attached to the outside of the bastion wall once carried passengers from this level to the Upper Barrakka Gardens. To no one's surprise it was declared unsafe and never replaced.

Follow the high road, and you come to **Santa Barbara Bastion**, with houses that are much sought after as they are considered to have the best location in Valletta. Continuing on the road below the limestone walls of a Franciscan convent and the church of **Ta' Giezu** (sometimes written as Ta'Ġesu), you come to the **Victoria Gate**, another access to the city. (In fact, due to the one-way system, this is the exit from the city. Entrance is along Barriera Wharf by the fish market.) In the times of the Knights, as the original Del Monte Gate, it gave the only access from the harbour. The new gate and road were constructed between 1884 and 1887 for vehicles.

The charming little church of **Notre-Dame de Liesse** outside the gate was rebuilt in 1740 at the expense of the Langue of France. Its low dome moulded with bands of curved stone is best seen from the Upper Barrakka Gardens above.

From here, return to the city. As a reward enjoy lunch or refreshments at one of the listed Valletta restaurants or cafés (see *Where to eat*, pp 23–28).

# An alternative route

Having visited the Palace of the Grand Masters, instead of following Republic Street further, you can visit the other places of interest located on the map.

For example, outside the palace, to the left alongside the cafés, there is Triq tat-Teatru l-Antik (Old Theatre Street) that leads to Malta's national theatre, Teatru Manoel (the Manoel Theatre) and to St Paul's Anglican Cathedral.

The first narrow street that crosses your front has some passing interest, even if only for curiosity value. This is **Triq id-Dejqa**, once known as Strada Stretta, then as **Strait Street** when it became more (in)famous as '**The Gut**'. Even in the days of the Knights this street had a dubious reputation. As duelling was forbidden, Knights went there to disguise their duels as quarrels brought on by colliding with each other in the narrow lane. Between and during both World Wars, it was known to servicemen everywhere as The Gut (assumed to be an abbreviation of 'The Gutter'), a place where bars, dance halls, cheap lodging houses and ever-friendly hostesses offered their wares day or night. With the departure of the British services business dwindled and disappeared. All that remains are peeling shopfronts and the occasional hostess who has seen far better days.

On the next corner, Triq l-Ilfran (Old Bakery Street), is the Manoel Theatre complex with its charming shop, theatre museum and courtyard café that serves excellent light refreshments.

## Manoel Theatre

Built in only ten months in 1731, Teatru Manoel is, as everyone says, 'a gem of a theatre' and one of the oldest theatres still presenting productions in Europe. It opened its doors with the opera *Merope*, given by the Knights of the Italian Langue. In those early days the Grand Master and his Knights would attend performances given in the flickering light of hundreds of candles and then retire to dine in one of the nearby Auberges. Today theatregoers book tables at nearby restaurants (see *Where to eat*, pp 23–28).

The theatre has seen a richly varied life. In the early days of British rule it served as a ballroom as well as a theatre, but as the decades passed it fell into great neglect becoming for a while a doss house and then a cinema.

Magnificent restoration work in 1960 returned the theatre to its former splendour, making it once more a fine Baroque gem. In its foyer stands a bust of Grand Master Manoel de Vilhena, the original patron, whose exhortation above the door in Latin says: 'For the honest recreation of the people'.

An elegant place, its oval auditorium seats 600 and has 45 boxes rising in tiers above the stalls. Each box is decorated in muted tones of cream and green with a pastoral panel on its front. From the gilded ceiling hangs a grand crystal chandelier.

During the theatre season, October to May, there are performances of drama, ballet and opera, as well as orchestral concerts. In the **Sala Isouard**, on the second floor above the courtyard café, there are regular classical recitals, many at midday.

Among the luminaries who have graced the boards here are singers and musicians Mirella Freni, Cecilia Gasdia, Yehudi Menuhin, André Segovia, Yvonne Kenny, Mstislav Rostropovich, John Ogdon and Vladimir Ashkenazy as well as Britain's National Theatre, the Bolshoi Ballet and the Berlin State Opera Ballet. The Manoel Theatre also takes an orchestra on tour overseas.

It is always worth checking the Manoel's programme. Tuesday nights are usually given to concerts while larger productions, including touring productions, perform Friday to Sunday. The programme is varied and advance booking is essential for operas or star name performances, but there may always be seats available on the night. Tickets are considerably cheaper than those in most European cities; students pay half price.

- The Booking Office (with telephone and credit card facilities) opens daily, office hours. ☎ 222618. Guided tours of Theatre Mon–Sat 10.30–11.30. Museum open: Mon–Sat 10.00–12.30 and 16.00–18.00. Entrance fee.

A few steps further brings you to the church of **Our Lady of Mount Carmel** with a dome that dominates Valletta's skyline and dwarfs the slim spire of its neighbour, St Paul's Anglican Cathedral. The church, built according to designs by Gerolamo Cassar, was damaged by bombs in World War Two. The dome is a recent addition and said by wagging tongues to have been designed on its grandiose scale simply to put Anglican neighbours in their place.

On the corner, with its entrance on what is now Pjazza Independenza (Independence Square), is **St Paul's Anglican Cathedral** occupying the site that was once the Auberge d'Allemagne. The auberge was demolished in 1838 to make way for the church. Designed along classic lines but with the addition of a Gothic spire by Richard Lankersheer, it was built between 1839 and 1841 by William Scamp with funds provided by the dowager Queen Adelaide, widow of William IV. An aunt of Queen Victoria, the ageing queen visited Malta to convalesce after illness.

In the square is a monument to Dun Mikiel Xerri one of 33 Maltese executed by the French during their brief tenure (see pp 66–67). At the rear of the cathedral, beyond the apse, is St Paul's Building, an apartment block with a plaque that commemorates a visit by Sir Walter Scott in 1831 when the Beverley Hotel occupied this position.

Facing the cathedral on the Square is the **Auberge d'Aragon**, now ministerial offices. An elegant building, the small *palazzo* was designed by Gerolamo Cassar and is regarded as one of his more discreet works. On a good day the doorman might let you see the courtyard.

A deep sweep of steps alongside the *palazzo* descends to the city walls and, after a five-minute stroll, to Fort St Elmo. But, follow Triq l-Arcisqof (Archbishop's Street) and you head back to Republic Street passing the gloomy **Archbishop's Palace** designed by Tommaso Dingli in 1622. Its post-World War Two restorations and additions were carried out in 1953.

## The Merchants Street walk

While the Republic Street route brings you to the major sites and sights, this second tour shows you yet more facets of this extraordinary city. When its restoration work is completed, Valletta will be a city to match some of the finest in Europe.

Start at the **Upper Barrakka Gardens**. These are simple gardens with a magnificent panoramic view from a colonnaded open terrace that perches above the Grand Harbour. In British times ceremonial gun salutes would be fired from its lower terrace. To your left is the harbour entrance with **Fort Ricasoli** on the far side. In front of you are **Fort St Angelo** and **The Three Cities** and across the water to your right, Malta's famous **dockyards**. Decimated in World War Two, they now refit and repair tankers and liners. And beneath you, deep in the fortifications itself, are the **Lascaris War Rooms** where strategic planning took place in World War Two (see *Valletta Museums*, p 117).

The gardens were originally the playground of the Knights of the Italian Langue, and in 1661 the space was given roofed arcades to afford them some shade. Not longer after, however, there were divisions among the Knights and after a plot to overthrow Grand Master Ximenes was uncovered, the roof was removed as a form of punishment. The event, known as the Priest's Revolt (see p 64), was hatched on this playground.

Visitors come for the view, but among the statues in the gardens are *Les Gavroches*, a work considered the masterpiece of Maltese sculptor Antonio Sciortino, and a bust of Sir Winston Churchill.

The entrance to the gardens is on Castille Place, dominated by the **Auberge de Castile et Leon**, the finest and most imposing example of symmetrical Maltese

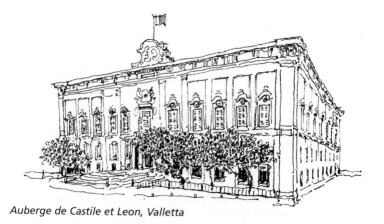

*Auberge de Castile et Leon, Valletta*

Baroque architecture in the city. It is now the Office of the Prime Minister.

The original building on this site was designated as the palace for the Grand Master but in 1741, according to notarial deeds, under instructions from the flamboyant Grand Master Manoel Pinto de Fonseca it was given considerable embellishment and decoration by the master mason Domenico Cachia. The Portuguese Grand Master had decided the building was to become the auberge of the Knights of Spain and Portugal.

The imposing portal set at its centre is flanked by bronze cannons dating from 1756 with, conspicuously displayed above, the arms, bust and escutcheon of the benefactor, Grand Master Manoel Pinto de Fonseca.

At the gate to the gardens are the temple-like premises of the **Malta Stock Exchange**, once the Garrison Church. Across the square opposite Castille are the imposing plain walls of **St James Cavalier** which, together with **St John's Cavalier** on the far side of Republic Street, formed an integral part of the Knights' defensive system within the city. St James Cavalier is taking on a new role as the **National Arts Centre** with exhibition halls, theatre and café; it was recently the government printing press and, before that, the British forces NAAFI shop. St John's Cavalier is a base for the Sovereign Military Order of Malta. On the bastion walls behind St John's Cavalier are **Hastings Gardens**, the haunt of romantic couples in the evenings. The gardens contain a monument to the Marquis of Hastings, Governor of the Islands, 1824–26.

Where **Merchants Street** begins, a pair of charming, small but important buildings illustrate the city's historical heritage. These are the churches of St Catherine and Our Lady of Victories.

As you face the ruins of the Royal Opera House, **Our Lady of Victories**, or **La Vittoria**, is on the left. This was the first building erected in Valletta and dedicated in thanksgiving for the Turkish defeat in the Great Siege. Before his remains were transferred to the cathedral, the siege's heroic Grand Master, Jean Parisot de la Valette, was interred here. The church's façade was altered around 1690 on the instructions of Grand Master Ramon Perellos when he had the bust of Pope Innocent XI placed above the central window. After decades of neglect, the church is being restored to its former simple glory.

Across the narrow road is the church of **St Catherine** attached to the Auberge d'Italie, home of the Langue of Italy. Designed by Gerolamo Cassar in 1576, its porch to the design of Romano Carapecchia was added in 1713. The interior, octagonal in plan, has an altarpiece of the *Martyrdom of St Catherine* by Mattia Preti and *Our Lady of Sorrows* by Benedetto Luti. In keeping with the church's roots, Mass here is said in Italian.

On Merchants Street, **Auberge d'Italie**, like so many Valletta buildings, has seen better days. It is now the **General Post Office** and houses some government offices. Designed by Gerolamo Cassar in 1574 as a single-storey *palazzo*, the auberge was enlarged with the addition of a second storey by the Italian Grand Master Gregorio Carafa in 1683. While embellishing the façade with Baroque decoration, he used the opportunity to have his effigy placed above the portal.

Facing the Post Office is the **Palazzo Parisio**, which is in the process of total restoration; the sober building is the Ministry of Foreign Affairs and many foreign dignitaries call there. In June 1798 this was where Napoleon Bonaparte set up his headquarters on his way to his Egyptian campaign.

On the next corner, truly neglected except by the city's pigeons, is the Baroque church of **St James**. Built originally for the Knights of Castile and Leon in 1612, it was redesigned by Giovanni Barbara in 1710.

On weekday mornings you now come to the street market known as the ***monti*** selling all manner of T-shirts, CDs, clothing and household goods. (On Sundays, in a larger form, it moves to outside the city's walls, alongside the bus terminus.) Some of the designer names on goods may even be genuine, and pirated copies of CDs, cassette tapes and videos are almost a thing of the past.

Then, on the corner of St John's Street where the steps descend to the city walls, there is the **Castellania**. Like many of the grand buildings, it is currently government offices but in the times of the Knights the *palazzo* housed the Law Courts (and prisons) presided over by a Castellano.

Begun in 1748 by Francesco Zerafa and completed by Giuseppe Bonici in 1760, the Castellania was the court of civil and criminal law. To emphasise the sincerity of the building's business, the figures of Justice and Truth stand on either side of the balcony. Once an escutcheon and bust celebrating Grand Master Pinto de Fonseca adorned the façade too, but they were removed by the French in 1798. After the Priest's Revolt many of the accused were put to death by the garrotte in the Castellania dungeons and their heads placed on spears outside in order to demonstrate the power of the Order and the Church. On the corner of the building is a pillory stone and, one storey high further along the street, a hook. It is believed that this hook was used to suspend a cage in which convicted felons were imprisoned for all to see.

Further along, masked by the street market stalls, is (on the left) the former **Banca Giuratale**, an elegant *palazzo* built by Grand Master Zondadari around 1720. It houses the Public Registry and Record Office and its condition matches its stolid current role. Facing it, in an equally tired condition, is another *palazzo*, this one containing the *Monte di Pietà*, the government-run pawnbroker with roots that go back to the late 16C. Their jewellery sales are well attended.

In St Paul's Street and running parallel to the Monte di Pietà, is a charmingly ornate church, the Collegiate church of **St Paul Shipwrecked**. Originally a simple church built to the designs of Gerolamo Cassar for the religious Order of Carmelites, St Paul Shipwrecked became the church of the rich Order of Jesuits in 1639. Work was immediately begun to rebuild it on a grander scale to plans by Garagona and, later, Lorenzo Gafà. It took 40 years to complete.

The church contains the magnificent **altarpiece of the Shipwreck** by Matteo Perez d'Aleccio, but it is the relic of the saint's wrist held in a **jewelled reliquary** that is of special reverence in Malta, where St Paul introduced Christianity when he was shipwrecked en route to trial in Rome. On 10 February each year, a date proclaimed by decree of the Pope in 1692, there is special veneration of this reliquary. On that day all the wealth of gold and silver ornaments owned by this church is displayed. It is a remarkable sight.

Also in the church is a part of the original column on which the saint is said to have been martyred outside Rome. The eccentric, over-dressed façade to the designs of Nicola Zammit was added to the church in 1885.

On Merchants Street at the rear of the Palace of the Grand Masters you next come to the **covered market**, built in iron between 1859 and 1862. Until the 1970s this was a thriving food market with stalls selling excellent selections of meat, fish, dairy produce and vegetables. After a considerable cleanout in the name of hygiene and a few years as a Made-in-Malta centre, it is a shadow of its former self.

Then in St Paul Street there is the **Old University**. With the blessing of Pope Clement VIII, the Jesuits established Malta's first College in 1592 as the *Collegium Melitensia Societatis Jesu* with faculties for letters, philosophy and theology. In 1769, after the expulsion of the Jesuits from the island, Grand Master Manoel Pinto raised the college to university status and incorporated the School of Anatomy that had been founded by Grand Master Nicolas Cotoner as the faculty of Medicine. (The Jesuits did not return until the Islands came under British rule.) In the late 1960s the much expanded university moved to a modern, pur-pose-built complex at Tal-Qroqq, Msida, and the original building is now the Centre for International Studies.

The Jesuit buildings, now a monastery, and the superb Church of **Ta'Giezu** attached to it, remain substantially unaltered. Reputed to have been built in 1592–1600, to designs by Gian Francesco Buonamico, its structure and interior resemble the Jesuit church in Rome. In the left transept an inscription records the consecration here of Fabio Chigi as Inquisitor of the Order. (He was later elevated to Pope Alexander VII.) Above the high altar, the *Circumcision* is attributed to Baldassare Peruzzi, while in the chapel of St Ignatius (right) the altarpiece is by Romanelli and in the neighbouring chapel the altarpiece and two lunettes are by Mattia Preti.

If you turn back into Archbishop Street, alongside the palace, there is **Our Lady of Damascus**, the Greek Catholic Church. This houses the ancient icon of *Our Lady* treasured by the Order of St John.

Turn into Republic Street again, where cafés and restaurants beckon.

---

### See Valletta from the sea

One of the best views of Valletta is from the sea. For centuries this was mariners' and travellers' first sighting of the city and it remains impressive even now. Boat excursions set out daily from Sliema's Ferries with tours of Marsamxett Harbour and the Grand Harbour. Guides are well informed and it is a very enjoyable way of seeing history. (See *Boat cruises*, p 9.)

---

# Floriana

Outside the walls of the city, Floriana is Valletta's suburb. Unless you have busi-ness here (the British High Commission and the embassies of Italy and the United States are here, for example) or you are paying a parking fine at the Police Headquarters, it is not a place you would normally visit. But it does have some points of interest.

## History

In 1634 when rumours swept the Mediterranean region that a second Turkish invasion was imminent, the incumbent Grand Master, Antoine de Paule, sought help in the customary manner from Rome. To defend this Christian outpost Pope Urban VIII sent his renowned military engineer Paolo Floriani with speedy despatch, to prepare plans for additional defences that would make Valletta impregnable. These plans included walls that would stretch across the whole peninsula, from harbour to harbour, on high ground—and at high cost. It was estimated that the expense of doing this would be as great as the cost of the complete walls circling the city of Valletta.

Within two years, however, work was halted as it was decided that the Margherita Lines around Vittoriosa on the south of the harbour were the priority. Work was begun again only after a visit by Giovanni de Medici in 1640, and the Floriana Lines were eventually completed to Floriani's design by Don Carlos Gruenenberg and a French military engineer De Tignè. Within the fortified stone walls, the streets were laid out to a plan drawn up in 1724 and, although much was destroyed in World War Two, many of the central blocks of buildings date from before 1760.

To get to Valletta you would normally travel through Porte des Bombes and Floriana. **Portes des Bombes**, a magnificent gate, was erected in 1697–1720 as part of the city's outer ring of defence. Today, separated from the walls on either side by wide roads, **Bombi**, as the locals call it, is a traffic island allowing cars to pass in and out of the city. For the purposes of seeing Floriana, it is probably easier to use Valletta as the starting point.

Leave Valletta on Gerolamo Cassar Avenue, the sweeping road facing Auberge de Castile; below, to your left, are the narrow terraces that make the small but pleasant **Kalkara Gardens** alongside the Sir Paul Boffa Hospital. You have a fine view of the Grand Harbour here, similar to the one from Upper Barrakka Gardens. Below is **Pinto Wharf** where cruise ships dwarf the quay as they land their passengers.

## A walk around Floriana

For a pleasant walk in the spring or autumn when it is not too hot, you could start at Valletta's City Gate and stroll through the gardens that are bounded on one side by **The Mall** (outside the Meridien Phoenicia Hotel) and **Sarria Street** (alongside the underground car park) on the other.

In the garden, with its back to Valletta, is the statue of *Cristo Re* (Christ the King), a monument by one of Malta's eminent sculptors, Antonio Sciortino. It was commissioned to commemorate the International Eucharistic Congress of 1913, and when it was unveiled in 1917 a crowd of 40,000 gathered to applaud.

A more abstract monument commemorates Malta's Independence at the entrance to the second section of the gardens. Inside their walls, more memorials honour various Maltese worthies, including Sir Adrian Dingli, whose effigy was unveiled by Edward VII during his visit to Malta as king in 1907.

These gardens were once the **Maglio Gardens**, part of an enclosed area created by Grand Master Jean Lascaris. He subscribed to the belief that sport helped keep the mind off pleasures corporal, so created a sports area where knights could play *palla a maglio* (pall-mall). To exhort the knights further he had inscribed in Latin on its walls:

*Here perish sloth, here perish Cupid's darts,*
*Knights, on you this place I now bestow,*
*Here play your games and harden your warrior hearts,*
*Let not wine, women or dice bring you low.*

To the right is what was, in British times, a huge parade ground. Now, as **Independence Arena**, it is a football ground. To the left is St Publius Square known to all as the **Granaries**. Under what is mostly car park space, there are subterranean granaries constructed by the Knights for storage in the same manner as those outside Fort St Elmo. The backdrop here is **St Publius** itself, the huge parish church of Floriana, erected in 1733–68. Its design is attributed to Giuseppe Bonici but the façade is recent having sustained damage in the World War Two. The side chapels and their external screen walls were added in 1856.

Beyond St Publius is the little church of **Sarria**, built on a circular plan by Mattia Preti in 1678. He adorned it with seven vigorous paintings.

At the end of the Mall is a circular water tower that once formed part of the **Wignacourt aqueduct** which brought water to Valletta from the hilly ground near Mdina. The incongruous but not unpleasing Gothic edifice facing it was once a Methodist church but is now a cultural centre. On the bastion walls here are the **Argotti Botanical Gardens** with a collection of cacti, exotic trees and the flora of the Islands.

Follow the road that circles the Arena and you come to Police Headquarters (where documents are stamped and car fines are paid) to descend steeply through what was Salvatore Bastion to Sa Maison Road, passing the charming **Sa Maison Garden** (which supplies other public gardens) and on to **Pietà Creek**. The goods-only Gozo ferry uses this quay.

The road then leads on to Msida and the yacht marina.

## From the Great Siege Road to Fort St Elmo

For an alternative walk, from the corner of the Meridien Hotel, take the **Great Siege Road** that descends to pass the British Army's former barracks (now government offices) and follow the walls that ring Valletta. To the right rises St John's Bastion and St Michael's Counterguard, while to the left, on St Roque's cove facing the Msida creek, is the Excelsior Hotel. Ahead is Manoel Island.

On this road is the entrance to the slave-made **Great Ditch** that passes between St Michael's Counterguard and St Michael's Bastion and under City Gate bridge and Gerolamo Cassar Avenue to reach Lascaris Wharf. It has restricted access.

Further along (you are now in Valletta again) is an area that was once known as the **Mandraċċ**. Here, where Mattia Preti Square is today, a natural cleft in the rocky surface was partly worked in the hope of forming a *Manderaggio*, or sheltered harbour. Builders were expected to take stone from this site for houses. The project was never completed and the area was abandoned. In later years a slum dwelling developed in the sunken ground; it was redeveloped with municipal apartment blocks in the 1970s. It is here that a steep slope leads down to the ferry shuttle service to Sliema.

From Mattia Preti Square, the road winds its way below St Paul's Anglican Cathedral along the German Curtain. On the corner is Palazzo Carnerio (1696), a private house that became the **Auberge de Bavaria**, home of the Anglo-Bavarian Langue during the Langue's brief existence in 1783–98. A dull building, it is government offices.

Follow the road further and you come to Fort St Elmo.

# Valletta Museums

## National Museum of Archaeology

- **Open** 1 Oct–15 June, Mon–Sat 08.15–17.00, Sun 08.15–16.15; 16 June–
  30 Sept, daily 07.45–14.00. Entrance fee: Lm1.50. Free under-19s or over-
  65s. Tickets include entrance to Palace of the Grand Masters. Auberge de
  Provence, Republic Street. ☎ 221623.

The building itself is one of the exhibits. It was designed in 1571 by Gerolamo
Cassar and built by the Knights of Provence four years later. Cassar, Malta's most
prestigious early architect, had been trained in both architecture and military
engineering by the Italian Francesco Laparelli, who had worked for the Medicis
and Pope Pius IV. Cassar collaborated with Michelangelo on the building of
St Peter's in Rome, before being sent by the Pope to design the defences of Malta.

Like most buildings in the city it has seen a considerable number of uses, the
most recent being as the Union Club where Maltese gentry and British officers
and their wives would meet to dine, dance and play cards.

The building has been meticulously restored and the archaeological treasures
found in Malta and Gozo from the Stone and Bronze Ages and the Phoenician,
Roman, early Christian, medieval and Baroque periods are being returned to it in
protracted stages.

The first exhibits to be put back on show are the earliest and these are the most
important since they are unique to Malta.

Almost the whole of the ground floor is given over to the Islands' remarkable
prehistoric **Temple Period (4100–2500 BC)**, when a profusion of massive
structures were built which are now recognised as the oldest stone buildings in
the world. In the entrance hall two great bowls and a pair of finely carved stone
screens from the last of the temples, **Tarxien**, set the scene.

**Room 1** On entering Room One turn sharp left for the earliest exhibits, which
date from the time of the first settlers on the Islands (5000–4100 BC), then return
to the display of carved stones, which once adorned the temples. The carvings, all
created with stone tools, range from the earliest simple decoration of pitted dots to
friezes of the animals that were sacrificed in the temples. At the far end of the
room, look out for the heavily spiralled block with a loose, semi-circular segment
at its base. A sacrificial flint knife was discovered in the niche behind this cover.

**Room 2** shows how the temples were built and the great stones levered into
place. The first showcase on the right is of particular interest, with models of the
temples (found inside the temples) and what looks remarkably like an architect's
ground plan carved in stone. There are also models of the temples, more prized
carvings and a choice selection of pottery, all showing animals or birds.

**Room 3** has a display of cult statues, splendidly obese figures which once
presided over the temples. The largest, in a pleated skirt, would have stood nearly
three metres high before it lost its torso. They used to be called 'fat ladies' but
since many of them have insignificant breasts, they are now more cautiously
called 'fat figures' (see also p 114). Don't miss the undoubtedly female figures in
the small showcase on the far left. The smaller one, a mere twist of clay, is the
very embodiment of woman. The larger one is called the *Malta Venus*. Some
prime phalluses, two of them in their own shrine, and two 'Sleeping Ladies' statuettes, in a small darkened room on the right, should also not be missed.

**Room 4** has jewellery, pottery, temple builders' tools of bone, obsidian and chert, and two extremely intriguing items: a piece of pottery decorated with a solar wheel and a stone carved with stars, moon and sight lines.

As the museum completes its changes, all the remarkable finds will find their place in this restored *palazzo*. Phoenician, Roman, early Christian, medieval and Baroque treasures will be revealed. It is a major project.

## Museum of Fine Arts

This *palazzo* was among the first to be erected in Valletta after the Order of St John gave up Vittoriosa in 1571. The site was acquired by Fra Jean de Soubiran who commissioned one of the first, but simple, private palaces in the new city. Later it became the property of the Order who leased it to various knights.

Between 1761 and 1763 most of the *palazzo* was demolished in order to be rebuilt into its present patrician form (possibly to designs by Andrea Belli) and since then has always played an important part in the city's life.

It was once the home of the Comte de Beaujolais, brother of the future King Louis Philippe of France who, in fact, died there in 1808. It was then taken over by the British and, on 1 January 1821, was leased to the Naval Authorities, becoming the official residence of the Admiral Commander-in-Chief and renamed **Admiralty House**. When the Islands became a Republic in 1964 it was returned to the Maltese Government, and by 1972 it had taken on its new role as Museum of Fine Arts.

Today the compact *palazzo* contains some of Malta's national collections of works of art and historical curiosities. (The rest has still to be housed.)

● **Open** 1 Oct–15 June, Mon–Sat 08.15–17.00, Sun 08.15–16.15; 16 June–30 Sept, daily 07.45–14.00. South Street. ☎ 233034.

Start the tour on the first floor. The galleries here display paintings from the 14C–17C as well as important works by **Mattia Preti**.

**Room 2** The first gallery has a charming collection of 14C works including the *Scourging of Christ* attributed to Maestro de Capodonico from the School of Le Marche, and leads into Room 2 which contains 15C works. Here the *Madonna and Child with Saints* by Domenico de Michelino is particularly fine, and on the wall facing the entrance is an exciting long panoramic scene, *The Nativity* by Maestro Alberto.

**Room 3** has 16C paintings of the Florentine, North Italian and Roman Schools. On display is a portrait of a child attributed to Santi di Tito and a portrait of the Grand Master Verdalla. The showcase contains two important drawings by Perugino and Vittore Carpaccio's study of a figure in his *Legend of St Ursula* (on show in the Accademia, Venice).

**Rooms 4 and 6** are devoted to works of the Venetian School. Significant works are by Domenico Tintoretto, Palma il Giovane and Pietro Liberi. *The Raising of Lazarus* by Mannerist painter Andrea Vicentino, one of Tintoretto's chief pupils, is especially dramatic.

**Room 5** Is devoted to the Dutch School. *Portrait of a Lady* is painted in the style of Holbein and once labelled as his work. It is now accredited to Jan van Scorel. Other interesting works are by William Key, Paul Brill, Johann Rottenhammer and David Teniers.

**Room 6** Returns to works of the Venetian School, including paintings by

Francesco Maffei and Bernardino Licinio. The ivory crucifixes are from the 18C. The 17C relief of the *Nativity* is by Antonio Giorgetti.

**Room 7** Contains four paintings, including a well-known *Madonna and Child* by Carlo Maratta from Ancona and another superb *Madonna and Child* of the Italian School. The **Sciortino Room** (**Room 7A**), on the terrace overlooking the harbour, has casts by the Maltese sculptor Antonio Sciortino who made a name for himself in Rome when he was President of the British Academy there.

Rooms 8, 9 and 10 are among the most spacious galleries in the museum. They display the largest canvases, mainly biblical scenes and religious allegories.

**Room 8** Has the *Martyrdom of St Agatha* by Giovanni Baglione. The artist has included himself in the scene, on the left dressed in armour. On the right of the gallery is a violent composition, *Judith*, by Louis Valentin, a French artist and follower of Caravaggio. Of special interest is the monumental *Christ holding the Cross* by the 17C Bolognese artist, Guido Reni. There is another version of this in the Academia de San Fernando in Madrid, recorded in the Spanish Royal Inventory in 1666 as being by Reni. Close examination of the two paintings has shown the Maltese painting to be the original.

Also here, the *Allegory of the City of Antwerp* by Theodar van Thulden is noted for its superb composition, as is the portrait of *Grand Master Wignacourt* attributed to Leonello Spada, who came with Caravaggio to Malta. Wignacourt wears his famous armour which is on display in the Palace Armoury (see p 100). Caravaggio also painted two portraits of Wignacourt but they are not in Malta.

**Rooms 9 and 10** have four large canvases on religious themes by the Flemish artist Matthias Stomer, including the *Beheading of St John*. There is also an elegant small landscape with figures by Neapolitan painter and engraver Salvator Rosa, and a delightful *St John* by Pachecco de Rosa. The collections in the showcase include *bozzetti* for sculptures in the style of Bernini by the Maltese 17C sculptor Melchiore Gafa and his contemporary, Giuseppe Mazzuoli. Many of Gafa's major works are in Rome.

**Room 11** is dominated by a large painting of *Cain and Abel* attributed to the school of Caravaggio. Other paintings include *St Francis de Paul* by Ribera and a portrait by Bernardo Strozzi. Note the sculpture of *St Luke* by Pietro Papaleo.

**Rooms 12 and 13** contain treasured works by the Italian artist **Mattia Preti** 1613–99, who transformed the interior of the Co-Cathedral of St John into a marvel of Baroque decoration and painted some of the finest works in Malta. Few museums can match the quality of this work. For emotional impact, look for *The Incredulity of St Thomas*, and for sheer force, *The Martyrdom of S Catherine*.

Down to the ground floor.

**Room 14** displays works by the French artist Antoine de Favray, 1716–98, most of which are portraits in the Grand Manner tradition. He was also known for the delightful way he captured interior settings in his portraits.

**Room 15** is devoted to 18C French works: *Fire on the Tiber* is by Joseph Vernet, the two landscapes by Hubert Robert, and the pastoral scene by François Boucher. In the display case are antique fob watches, snuff boxes, fans and combs.

**Rooms 16 and 17** are devoted to 18C Italian painters including Trevisan, Andrea Belvedere and Carlo Antonio Tavella. Dominating Room 17 is an impressive large canvas by Francesco de Mura of the *Allegory of Malta*. Here too is *St Margaret of Cortona* by Giovanni Domenico Tiepolo.

**Room 18** continues the Italian theme and contains two Impressionist paintings by De Nittis.

**Room 19** has views of Valletta by Louis du Cros painted in the 19C.

Rooms 20 to 24 are devoted to works by Maltese artists from the 17C to the 20C.

**Room 20** has important works by Stefano Erardi and Giorgio Pullicino. Other works of interest are by Giuseppe Hyzler and Giuseppe Grech.

**Room 21** contains the Caruana Dingli Bequest, charming paintings donated by a family involved in the arts.

**Room 23** contains work by 20C Maltese artists include sculptures by Antonio Sciortino (d. 1945), and paintings by Edward Caruana Dingli (d. 1950) and Willie Apap (d. 1970).

**Room 24** is used as an exhibition hall.

At basement level, Rooms 25 to 30, are devoted to unique memorabilia of the Order of St John in Malta, 1530–1798. These are divided into Religion, Hospital, Army and Minor Arts. Among them are impressive collections of majolica medicinal jars, silver implements and instruments.

The **Loggia** is often used as an exhibition gallery for up-and-coming painters.

## War Museum

- **Open** 1 Oct–15 June, Mon–Sat 08.15–17.00, Sun 08.15–16.15; 16 June–30 Sept, daily 07.45–14.00. Lower Fort St Elmo. ☎ 222430.

In 1975 a voluntary association, the National Museum Association, established this small museum to commemorate the World War Two siege when the Axis Powers attempted to take Malta. With donations, it has since grown with a small collection of exhibits dating from 1798 to 1945. It attracts numerous visitors, war veterans and historians from all over the world.

During the Second Siege in 1942 there were 3343 air raids and 16,000 tons of bombs were dropped. In April that year more than 11,000 buildings were destroyed or damaged. The Royal Opera House, the Law Courts and some of the Auberges suffered direct hits. More than 2500 enemy aircraft were shot down by the Islands' defence provided by British and Maltese services.

Exhibits include many interesting items of the war-torn days including Britain's highest decoration for civilian gallantry, the **George Cross**, awarded to the entire population by King George VI on 15 April 1942 (see p 70).

One exhibit in particular evokes the early days of bravery, the restored Gloucester Gladiator bi-plane nicknamed *Faith* which with two other Gladiators *Hope* and *Charity* formed Malta's only aerial defence when Italy declared war on 10 June 1940. There is also the Jeep used in Operation Husky by General Dwight D. Eisenhower before the invasion of Sicily in July 1943. Among the numerous donations is a Captain's uniform donated by Earl Mountbatten of Burma.

## Lascaris War Rooms

- **Open** Mon–Fri, 09.30–16.00, Sat–Sun 09.30–12.30. Entrance fee: Adults Lm1.75, children 85 cents. Upper Barrakka. ☎ 234936.

The War Rooms are deep within the massive Lascaris Bastion built by the Knights below the Upper Barrakka Gardens. During World War Two this was the Allied

Command headquarters and operation rooms of the Air Force and Navy in the Mediterranean. It was from here that the defence of Malta and the invasion of Sicily were planned and co-ordinated. The Rooms have been sympathetically reassembled with figures crouched over the planning tables and sound effects recreating the atmosphere. It is a must-see for anyone serving in World War Two or researching history of that period.

**St John's Museum**, see p 97.

# Mdina and its environs

Mdina is the gracious and quiet medieval walled city at the centre of Malta, still a home to many. From here, you can walk into the bustling town of Rabat with its remarkable eerie catacombs. Time permitting (and with a car) take a look at Verdala Castle overlooking Buskett Gardens; once the Grand Master's superb country home, it is now the President's summer residence. Then go on to Dingli Cliffs with their ancient Cart Ruts and spectacular landscape.

Cars are not permitted into Mdina. Park in Rabat outside the city gate near the bus terminus.

- Bus 80 or 81 (from Valletta) serves Mdina and Rabat.

## Mdina

The Roman town at the centre of Malta was called *Melita*, the name the Romans also gave the island. When the Aghlabid Arabs took over they called it *Medina*, and during the reign of the Knights of the Order of St John, the dignified city became known as *Città Vecchia* (Old City) to distinguish it from the new city, Valletta. It was also once known as *Città Notabile* (see *History of Mdina*, below). Finally one name prevailed—the old Maltese one, Mdina. Since Arab times the Maltese had always corrupted the Arabic version, and that is the name that stuck.

### History of Mdina

Mdina is one of the world's finest examples of a still-inhabited medieval walled city. There are no offices, few shops, no market. Just formidable *palazzi* family homes, a superb cathedral, some museums, a graceful hotel and, to cater for the many daily visitors, a small selection of cafés, restaurants and multivision shows that re-create Mdina's sometimes violent history. It was— and still is—the home of many of the oldest Maltese families.

Because of its position on a ridge overlooking the countryside, there have been settlements here since the Bronze Age. Perched at 150m, it was always considered simple to defend, and its elevated position made it also a more bearable place to live in the heat of the summer than were the hamlets in the flat countryside. It was here, in AD 60, that the head man Publius welcomed

St Paul after his shipwreck and became the first person in Malta to be converted to Christianity by Paul.

In AD 870, after the Aghlabid Arabs took possession of the Islands, the new rulers concentrated on strengthening the city walls. The hamlet alongside Mdina where the growing population also lived they called Rabat, the name still used today.

With time the city grew and flourished; it was a place where the wealthy wanted to live. Imposing houses began to give it a patrician air.

According to legend, in 1429 when the Saracens attacked the city, attempting to subdue the island, the inhabitants of Mdina faced them with great stoicism. St Paul had appeared to them riding a white stallion, brandishing a flaming sword and exhorting them to be brave. Fired by this holy vision, the trusting citizens refused to surrender. In recognition of this impeccable behaviour, King Alfonso V of Aragon, who now owned the Islands, rewarded the city with an honorific title: *Città Notabile* (meaning 'Honoured City').

In 1565, during the Great Siege, the city acquitted itself equally well. Cavalry stationed within its walls made regular sorties to the countryside attacking the Turks, and their skirmishes helped turn the tide of war. As the capital, Mdina became the seat of power of the ecclesiastical, military and civil authorities.

The streets were built deliberately narrow and angled, so that while the limited ground space would be used to best advantage for the essential buildings, the narrowness and corners would prevent an arrow being shot any great distance. The narrowness had an additional advantage much appreciated by the residents: it encouraged cooling draughts of air to circulate while neighbouring buildings cast shadows on each other—a blessing when trying to keep cool in summer.

The city's fortifications were completed after the Great Siege. As the Order of St John built Valletta, they also strengthened Mdina's ring of impregnable bastion walls.

For many years Mdina was also known as 'the Silent City' because nothing much ever happened there. Its narrow streets were unsuitable for more than domestic traffic and busy commerce never became a part of daily life.

This is not quite true today. Although only residents may enter with cars, not-so-silent multivision shows, restaurants and cafés have opened up in the historic buildings and brought new life with them.

There are three entrances to Mdina: the Main Gate, the Greek's Gate and the 'hole in the wall'. The **Main Gate** leads from the patch of greenery known as **Howard Gardens** outside the walls (in Rabat), which is Mdina's car park and bus terminal. The **Greek's Gate** opens below into the wide ditch that cuts off the city from Rabat, while the **hole in the wall** is exactly that, a small entrance cut into the lower walls to allow residents to get to the nearby railway station with least effort. That was in the 1920s when Malta's steam railway operated between Valletta and Mdina.

## The Walled City

Enter Mdina through Main Gate. As you approach the narrow stone bridge you face three bastions: San Pietro on the left, de Redin in the centre and del Palazzo on the right. The bridge crosses the dry moat originally dug by the Arabs to separate their town from the high plateau. (The ditch is now partly planted and has

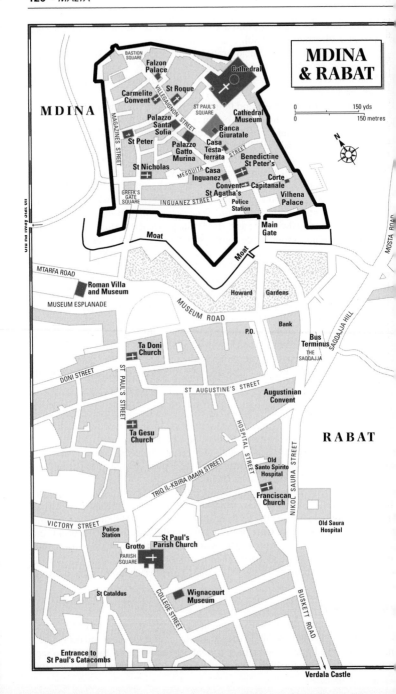

# MDINA & RABAT

## MDINA

BASTION SQUARE

Falzon Palace

Cathedral

St Roque

Carmelite Convent

VILLEGAIGNON STREET

ST PAUL'S SQUARE

Cathedral Museum

MAGAZINES STREET

Palazzo Santa Sofia

St Peter

Banca Giuratale

Palazzo Gatto Murina

Casa Testaferrata

MESQUITA STREET

Benedictine St Peter's

St Nicholas

Casa Inguanez

Convent

Corte Capitanale

GREEK'S GATE SQUARE

St Agatha's

Vilhena Palace

INGUANEZ STREET

Police Station

Main Gate

Moat

Moat

0    150 yds
0    150 metres

N

MTARFA ROAD

Roman Villa and Museum

MUSEUM ESPLANADE

Howard

Gardens

MUSEUM ROAD

MOSTA ROAD

P.O.

Bank

Bus Terminus

THE SAQQAJJA

SAQQAJJA HILL

Ta Doni Church

DONI STREET

ST PAUL'S STREET

ST AUGUSTINE'S STREET

Augustinian Convent

## RABAT

Ta Gesu Church

HOSPITAL STREET

NIKOL SAURA STREET

Old Santo Spirito Hospital

TRIQ IL-KBIRA (MAIN STREET)

Franciscan Church

Old Saura Hospital

VICTORY STREET

Police Station

Grotto

St Paul's Parish Church

PARISH SQUARE

COLLEGE STREET

BUSKETT ROAD

St Cataldus

Wignacourt Museum

Entrance to St Paul's Catacombs

Verdala Castle

tennis courts.) By the gate you can see the markings of an earlier entrance and drawbridge that once stood there.

Erected in 1724, the **Main Gate** bears the arms of Grand Master Manoel de Vilhena who, with no sense of humility, embellished many of the island's great buildings with his coat of arms. Inside the gate there are the arms of Antonio de Inguanez displayed according to the plaque (but no one is sure why) on the orders of King Alfonso V (of Aragon). The present escutcheon is comparatively recent. It was put there on the orders of the British governor, Sir Lintorn Simmons in 1886 as the original was defaced by the French when they endeavoured to remove all traces of the Order of St John in 1798. Above the plaque, three sculptured figures represent St Paul, St Publius and St Agatha, Mdina's most venerated saints.

Through the gate you enter the tiny **Misraħ St Publius** (St Publius Square) with, on the left, the **Torre dello Standardo** (Tower of the Standard), once the city's gatehouse but now the police station. It dates from the early 16C, and would have flown flags to warn farmers in the countryside of corsair or Turkish invasion. Grand Master Vilhena's arms were added later.

Characters in costume usually approach you here to encourage you to visit the *Mdina Dungeons* below the old **Courts of Justice** on the square or any of the other multivision shows in Mdina. The Dungeons are a scary and gruesome exhibition, not suitable for anyone with a vivid imagination or nervous disposition. (Open daily 09.30–21.00. Entrance fee.)

To the right is the Magisterial Palace, **Palazzo Vilhena**, built for the Grand Master by Giovanni Barbara. Behind its gateway the elegant building occupies three sides of an open courtyard. The façade's doorway is embellished, naturally, with a bronze portrait medallion of Vilhena. Malta's original governing body, the *Università* (Commune), convened here until it was devastated, like much of Mdina, in an earthquake in 1693. The Università had a council of *jurats* (that is, officers sworn in as magistrates) elected from the heads of Mdina's families. It was known as the *Consiglio populare* and had the right to appoint judges, impose taxes and submit recommendations to the king. It was here in September 1798, after the spontaneous uprising against the French, that the citizens declared a National Assembly and took the decision to approach Admiral Nelson for England's help in removing the French.

Until the 1960s the *palazzo* was the Connaught Hospital; it then became the dull **National Museum of Natural History** with a collection of stuffed birds, insects and other fauna common to the Islands, items of Maltese geology, a collection of minerals, and dioramas of mammals and fish. It is currently closed for restoration. A major problem is the threat of subsidence of one small corner of the building.

In front of you in the square are the massive walls of the sombre **St Peter's Monastery**, the Convent of the Sisters of St Benedict and home for about 20 nuns belonging to the enclosed order. Their seclusion is so strict that until recently the only men permitted to enter were doctors, plumbers or builders, and then only with the permission of the Archbishop. Even after death the sisters would be buried within the convent walls. The building dates from before 1418 when it was a women's hospital but it was altered in the 17C.

## Triq Villegaignon (Villegaignon Street)

Like Republic Street in Valletta, Triq Villegaignon cuts the city in two parts and is the street to follow as you explore. Along its length are many of Malta's finest houses preserved by the families who have inherited them through the generations. Many are reputed to contain paintings and silver that would be welcomed by museums in any country. Keeping up with today's demands, a number have opened, or are due to open, their doors to commerce as the charms of financial inducement become more widely understood by the residents and their families.

Villegaignon Street was named after a French Knight, Nicolas Durand de Villegaignon (1510–71). It was he who bravely led the defence of Mdina against a Turkish attack in 1551 and found further fame establishing the city of Nouvelle-Genève in Brazil (renamed Rio de Janeiro after its capture by the Portuguese).

Villegaignon Street starts by the convent of the Sisters of St Benedict and leads eventually to **Bastion Square** (officially Misraḥ tas-Sur) with spectacular views across the countryside. There are a number of cafés on the walls, which also have excellent views.

On the corner by the convent is the little **Chapel of St Agatha** with an altarpiece by Giuseppe d'Arena. The original church, built in 1417, was remodelled in 1694 to the design of Lorenzo Gafa. St Agatha is said to have fled to Malta from Sicily in AD 249 when Emperor Decius demanded she marry Quintanus, governor of Catania. She refused. When she did finally return to her country, she was imprisoned, had her left breast cut off and was then burned to death. Statues of St Agatha show her either covering her breast or holding the shears that severed it.

In the nunnery wall is the inconspicuous entrance of the **Church of St Benedict** that was once attached to the women's hospital. The altarpiece, *The Madonna with St Benedict, St Peter and Santa Scholastica*, is by Mattia Preti.

On the left at No. 6, a discreet façade disguises the **Casa Inguanez**, home of the oldest titled Mdina family. They were created barons of Dyar-il-Bniet in 1350, and the position of *Capitano della Verga*, the head of the *Università*, was held by a Baron Inguanez until the family were supplanted by the Order of St John in 1530. Alfonso V of Aragon stayed in this *palazzo* in 1432 and, in the same room in 1927, so did his distant relative, King Alfonso XIII of Spain.

On the corner of Casa Inguanez is Triq Mesquita leading to Triq Gatto Murina with the graceful **Palazzo Gatto-Murina**. The *palazzo* is a fine example of 14C workmanship and now houses a six-language multivision show, *Tales of the Silent City* (open daily: 09.30–16.30. Entrance fee).

In Mesquita Square, '*The Mdina Experience*' is an audio-visual presentation (in many languages) covering 3000 years of Mdina's history (open daily. Entrance fee).

No. 11 is known as the **house of Notary Bezzina**. It was once the office of the Captain of the Rod (the chief magistrate) and it was from a first-floor window here that Captain Masson, the unfortunate Commander of the French garrison, was hurled to his death by an infuriated mob on 2 September 1798, precipitating the riot that sparked the Maltese uprising against the French. The 'defenestration' came about when the French began auctioning tapestries looted from the nearby **Carmelite Church**, causing the city's residents to riot. Citizens outside the city walls joined in and the French retreated to the safety of Valletta.

Now you come to **St Paul's Square**, the spacious *misraḥ* with Mdina's superb Cathedral.

## *Mdina Cathedral*

### History of the Cathedral

Mdina Cathedral dedicated to St Paul is believed to stand on the site of the house belonging to Publius, head man of Mdina. When St Paul visited the house in AD 60, he found Publius' father in bed with fever and healed him. Publius was St Paul's first Christian convert in Malta and later became first Bishop of Malta.

It is considered a sacred site; a temple is believed to have stood here for many centuries before being replaced by a church in the 4C. In the religious hierarchy the church has always been the See of a bishop, though before 1530 it was rare for the titular bishop to live in Malta. The See became an archbishopric in 1797 and a metropolitan province in 1944.

In January 1693 a massive earthquake devastated much of Malta and Gozo (as well as the central Mediterranean region) and the city's Siculo-Norman cathedral was destroyed. From its ruins a few years later rose this yet greater cathedral designed by Maltese architect Lorenzo Gafa. Work started in 1697 and was completed in 1702. Only the apse at the back of the cathedral survived the earthquake. Gafa had strengthened this structure while restoring the church in 1681.

Lorenzo Gafa was 58 when he commenced this work and his maturity and wealth of experience in church building shows. It is an architectural masterpiece with a magnificent Baroque dome creating the city's unique silhouette that, for centuries, painters have sought to capture.

Seen from a distance rising high on Mdina's skyline, the cathedral majestically dominates the surrounding countryside. As you stand on the square facing the cathedral, however, it presents a dignified, if sombre, Baroque façade similar to St John's Co-Cathedral in Valletta.

The cathedral sits at the end of the large square with two **cannons** dating from the early 17C at the top of its short flight of steps. The cannons were taken to London for display at the Artillery Museum in Woolwich, London, and only returned in 1888 on the instructions of Malta's British governor. Over the main door are the escutcheons of Grand Master Ramon Perelos who was head of the Order at the time it was built (left), and of Bishop Cocco Palmieri who consecrated the church (right).

The slightly recessed side bays of the cathedral have twin towers with richly ornamented spires holding six bells, the oldest of which was cast in Venice

*The Cathedral of Mdina*

in 1370. A curious detail is the way the clock dials touch the cornice. No one is sure why, but it is suggested that this may have been Gafa's device for creating the illusion that the squat bell towers are taller than they really are. Both the clock and calendar clock were made by Sapiano, a Maltese clockmaker.

What gives the cathedral its particular distinction, however, is the way its octagonal dome has eight heavy stone scrolls acting like flying buttresses above the high drum, sweeping upwards to its lantern light. It is a fine sight.

**The interior**  Entrance is usually through the left door, except for important services, weddings and funerals when the centre door is opened to give an impressive flourish.

The cathedral is in the form of a cross with a central vaulted nave and two aisles of delightful small side chapels. Like St John's Co-Cathedral, it is paved with a patchwork of inlaid multicoloured marble slabs but here, instead of commemorating grand or brave knights, the slabs commemorate leading Maltese ecclesiastics—bishops, prelates, monsignors and canons—as well as prominent laymen. The ceiling is frescoed with scenes from the *Life of St Paul* by Sicilian brothers, Antonio and Vincenzo Manno (completed in 1794), but the painting of the interior of the dome, *The Divine Mission of the Church*, is recent. It was painted by Mario Caffaro Rore in 1955 after the original was ruined by rain seeping through the porous limestone.

Two interesting relics survived the 1693 earthquake intact. One is the white marble **baptismal font** (No. 1) which was made in the workshop of Antonello Gagini in Palermo and presented to the church by Bishop Giacomo Valguarnera in 1495. The second is the superbly carved solid Irish oak **sacristy door** (No. 2) made around 1520. This was the main door of the original cathedral.

Mattia Preti who was responsible for much of Malta's splendour seems at his finest here. His painting in the **Chapel of the Annunciation** (No. 3) depicts the miraculous appearance of St Paul to the citizens of Mdina during the Saracen raid of 1422, while the **altarpiece** (No. 5) depicts *The Conversion of St Paul* and the **apse** offers a superbly dramatic view of St Paul's shipwreck. (The **Royal Arms of Spain** at the apex of arch surrounding the apse record the generosity of Emperor Charles V in giving the Islands as a home to the Order of St John in 1530.)

On the chancel arch the two oval portraits of St Peter and St Paul are not paintings but mosaics (1873), while in the **Chapel of the Blessed Sacrament** (No. 4) the jewelled icon of the Madonna is wishfully attributed to St Luke.

On the **high altar** during feast days and holy days, the **ceremonial silver** includes towering candlesticks and a set of silver statues of the Virgin and the Apostles which once belonged to St John's and are attributed to Benvenuto Cellini. On special days a silver cross purportedly carried in the First Crusade of 1099 by Godfrey de Bouillon takes its place here. On these days the aisle chapels are hung with crimson damask, giving the cathedral a rich, if overdressed, effect.

The marquetry stalls date from 1481, but the panels were replaced in 1876 by a benefactor, Emanuele Decelis.

The **Chapel of the Crucifix** (No. 6), to the side of the main altar, contains an interesting painting of St Paul that was formerly the centre panel of the main altarpiece. The crucifix is the work of Fra Innocenzo da Petralia, a Franciscan monk, in the 17C.

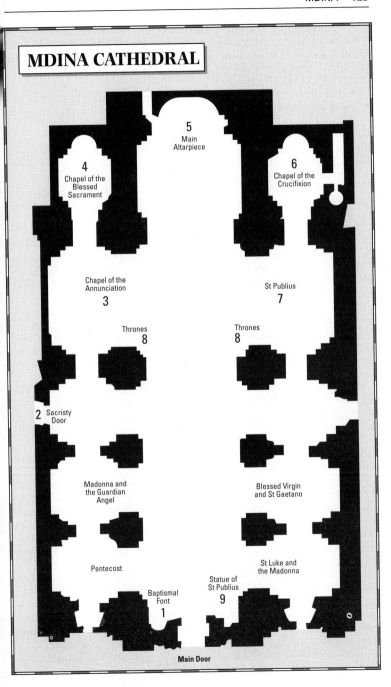

# MDINA CATHEDRAL

**5**
Main
Altarpiece

**4**
Chapel of the
Blessed
Sacrament

**6**
Chapel of the
Crucifixion

Chapel of the
Annunciation
**3**

St Publius
**7**

Thrones
**8**

Thrones
**8**

**2** Sacristy
Door

Madonna and
the Guardian
Angel

Blessed Virgin
and St Gaetano

Pentecost

St Luke and
the Madonna

Statue of
St Publius
**9**

Baptismal
Font
**1**

**Main Door**

The **altarpiece** in the next chapel (No. 7) showing the *Martyrdom of St Publius* may be by Preti but experts are uncertain. The statue of *St Publius* by the main door and the two lecterns of *St Luke* and *St John* (No. 9) by the main altar are by Giuseppe Valenti. (He also made the statue of Queen Victoria in Misrah ir-Republikka, Valletta.)

The two **thrones** (No. 8) presiding over the congregation are reserved for the Bishop of Malta and the Grand Master.

## Continuation of Villegaignon Street

Where Triq Villegaignon meets St Paul's Square is the **Banca Giuratale**. It was built in 1730 to the design of François de Mondion for Grand Master de Vilhena to house the *Università* when he took over the ruins of their *palazzo* by the Main Gate. Further along, on the corner of Holy Cross Street, is **Palazzo Santa Sofia** reputed to be the oldest house in Mdina. Its ground floor is 13C (the upper floor was added in 1938).

Even among the grand houses religion plays its part. On the right is the tiny **Church of St Roque** that once formed a part of the Chapel of Santa Maria della Porta at the Main Gate. When Grand Master de Vilhena replaced the old gate in 1728, the chapel dedicated to the patron saint of diseases was moved. Known locally as **Madonna tad-Dawl** (the Madonna of the Light), the altarpiece has a painting by the Portuguese artist Emanuel Pereira.

On a much larger scale is the **Carmelite Church** with its priory. The mendicant Carmelite order arrived from Sicily in 1370 and lived in Rabat outside the city walls until a home was found for them in Mdina in 1659. It was not until 1690, however, that this priory and the church dedicated to Our Lady of Mount Carmel, were completed. They are to the design of a brother monk, Francesco Sammut.

The richly ornamented church has four side chapels and seven altars. The main altarpiece is an 18C painting of *The Annunciation* by Stefano Erardi. The paintings of *St Simon* and *St Elijah* are by the 19C Maltese artist Michele Bellanti. The belfry was re-erected in 1857 after being brought down the previous year by another earthquake.

Across the road in the 17C **Palazzo Notabile** are a café and a walk-through museum called *Medieval Times Adventure* (open daily 09.30–16.30. Entrance fee).

Next you come to **Palazzo Falzon**, known as the **Norman House**. In the 14C the building had just one floor; the upper floor was added in the 15C so that the family could live above the kitchens. It is said to be the house occupied by Grand Master de L'Isle Adam on his first arrival in Malta in 1530. It is now a private museum containing Maltese scenes by 18C and 19C artists, furniture and other historic domestic items (open Mon–Fri: 10.30–17.00. Entrance free, donations appreciated).

At the end of the street is **Bastion Square**, once an artillery position, where everyone gathers for one of the finest panoramas of Malta. To your left, across the valley, is **Mtarfa**, an expanding residential area that was once British army barracks dominated by the David Bruce Military Hospital. In the middle distance is **Mosta Dome** (see p 156), while to the right below, the **Ta'Qali Crafts Village** stands on what was Ta'Qali airfield where fighter planes were stationed in World War Two. In the distance is Valletta, and on a clear day, some say, you can see the plumes of smoke rising above Mount Etna in Sicily.

Bastions Street to the right leads back to the cathedral, passing two patrician houses linked by a bridge across the street. The houses are now a girls' school. In the tiny square to the left is the entrance to a tunnel under De Redin Bastion by which the rebel Maltese forces penetrated the city in 1798.

Cross the front of the cathedral and you come to the imposing **Archbishop's Palace** (1722), his official residence. Across the road, where St Paul Street begins, is the cathedral museum.

## Mdina Cathedral Museum

• **Open** Mon–Fri 09.00–16.30, Sat 09.00–14.00. Entrance Lm1 ☎ 454697.

Built in 1733 to the instructions of Bishop de Bussan, the building was created as a seminary, but rather than in contemplative simplicity, it was conceived in impressive Baroque style with florid Sicilian decorations. A concave window and balcony on the first floor supported by two Atlantean figures give it grand style.

On its wall a plaque states that the building stands on the foundations of a house dated AD 679. It was the site of the home of Marcus Tullius Aristotle, where Cicero stayed around 73 BC while preparing his case against the notorious Gaius Verres, the Roman Governor of Sicily, who had plundered the Temple of Juno (thought to have been at Marsaxlokk). Verres fled before he could be brought to trial.

The collections in the museum are more important than they might at first appear. There are drawings, paintings and engravings, many of them the bequest of Count Saverio Marchesi (in 1833), notably woodcuts by Dürer and engravings from them by Marc Antonio Raimondi, engravings by Goya after Velazquez, and a drawing signed and dated 1581 by Luca Cambiaso. There are also the archives from the Inquisition.

Among works that graced the cathedral before the earthquake shook it to its foundations are *Virgin at Prayer* by Sassoferrato, donated in 1687, and late 14C Spanish painted panels depicting the life of St Paul from the main altarpiece. There are inlaid panels from the choir stalls by Parisio and Pierantonio Calatura of Catania, and vestments decorated with fine specimens of ancient lace. The manuscripts include 11C–12C antiphonals and homilies and a codex of the four Gospels. A portable altar decorated with Byzantine enamel may have been used in the galleys of the Order. Among the silver plate collection is a remarkable set of 15 statues made in Rome in 1748. There is a fine collection of coins and medals spanning the history of Malta.

**St Paul's Street** leads you into a charming small square with the *Xara Palace Hotel*, formerly the home of the Moscati-Parisio family. As Mdina's only hotel it had seen better days, but in late 1999 it reopened its doors, this time as an elegantly appointed hotel with a well-considered rooftop restaurant. The graceful **Herald's Loggia,** which is part of the hotel, was where the *banditore*, the town crier, proclaimed the *bandi* that were the laws governing public life decreed by the *Università*.

Opposite stands the **Corte Capitanale** where figures of Mercy and Justice and the inscription '*Legibus et Armis*' recall its former function as a criminal court. It is now local council offices. Beneath it are dungeons from an earlier building.

### The other side of Villegaignon Street

The western half of Mdina, to the left of Villegaignon Street as you enter, is pleasant to explore. These are the streets that still live up to Mdina's claim to be the Silent City. Life here is tranquil. There are fine 16C and 17C buildings, family homes that are delightful examples of Maltese architecture and show how local craftsmen used Malta's limestone to its best effect. Look for impressive window mouldings and armorial bearings carved in high relief. The little **Chapel of St Nicholas** off Mesquita Street served this quarter. Established in 1550 it was remodelled in 1692.

Magazines Street, leading to **Greek's Gate**, is where the city's munitions were kept (the doors to the original magazines still have Roman numerals). The gate was cut through the walls by Grand Master de Vilhena and is named after the Greek community that lived there. At No. 14, **Casa Magazini**, is the excellent *Knights of Malta* walk-through series of tableaux that show the life and times of the knights (open daily 10.30–16.00. Entrance fee).

Also off Magazines Street is the more recent entrance into the city, the west gate known as the **hole in the wall**. It was cut in the 1920s to allow easier access to the railway station for passengers taking the Valletta–Mdina train. The old station is on the road leading to Mtarfa.

# Rabat

Rabat (see map on p 128) is the district's commercial centre with banks, offices, souvenir shops, a vegetable market and inexpensive restaurants. (One such restaurant, *Veduta*, in the car park outside Mdina's main gate, offers superb views and pizzas on its terrace.) It also has a number of catacombs.

Under the Aragonese kings a number of religious orders came to Malta and settled in Rabat, its cool rural setting (and available space) being more conducive to learning and meditation than Mdina. Many imposing buildings are, or were, monasteries, priories and nunneries, or hospitals run by a religious order. The most interesting perhaps is the **priory of St Dominic** in Pjazza St Dominku (St Dominic Square), a particularly fine 16C Baroque church with monastic cloisters attached. During the brief French occupation the priory was—somewhat unwillingly—turned into a hospital. Napoleon had declared that religious orders were permitted only one religious house each, and as the Dominican order had one in Valletta too, the priory here temporarily changed its role.

In St Augustine's Street there is the great **Augustinian church**, designed by Gerolamo Cassar in 1571, with a gilded barrel vault.

In Nicolo Saura Street is the former **Santo Spirito Hospital**, the first hospital built in Malta. Records show it was functioning in 1370. It closed in 1968.

Start a visit to Rabat by leaving Mdina by either the Main Gate or the Greek's Gate and stroll towards the downward slope that leads on to Mtarfa. Follow the signs to the **Roman Villa** and **Museum of Roman Antiquities**

• **Open** 1 Oct–15 June, Mon–Sat 08.15–17.00, Sun 08.15–16.15; 16 June–30 Sept, daily 07.45–14.00).

Calling this a villa has given a grandiose title to what would have been a large house belonging to a wealthy family. Its size and delightful view along a valley suggest a Roman merchant might have lived there.

During excavations in 1881 a number of interesting mosaics were uncovered, and around 1922 as another excavation was taking place, it was decided to construct a museum to contain the site and the objects from the Roman period found here and elsewhere around the Islands. There are marble statues and busts, terracotta ornaments, Roman glassware, pottery, amphorae and agricultural fragments.

The town of Rabat starts at the top of **Saqqajja**, the hill on the main road from Valletta and the centre of the island. At the base of hill, to your left as you rise, is **Racecourse Street** leading to the village of Siggiewi. It is traditional for crowds to gather here on 29 June for a few hours of horse and donkey races held in the street. This is the feast day of St Peter and St Paul, known as *L-Imnarja* (see Buskett Gardens below). The **grandstand** where the Grand Master would have sat during the Order's reign is on the corner of Saqqajja Hill and Racecourse Street.

From Saqqajja, follow Triq il-Kbira (Main Street) and you come to the imposing parish **Church of St Paul** with its venerated grotto (open hours of worship. Entrance free, but donations accepted).

The church was built at the expense of a noblewoman, Cosmana Navarra, and has been altered a number of times. It is probably the first church in Malta to have been built in the shape of the Latin-cross. Lorenzo Gafa is credited with designing the vault and dome in 1692. Above the high altar, an enormous and famous painting of *The Shipwreck of St Paul* by Stefano Erardi (1683) shows St Paul throwing off the viper that bit him before declaring that henceforth all snakes in Malta would be non-poisonous (and they have been). In the background Paul's ship is seen floundering on Malta's rock.

The **grotto** beneath the church is where tradition says St Paul lived in austere simplicity during his three months in Malta. Tradition also says that St Paul's venerable presence caused the stone of the cave to have miraculous healing powers, and no matter how much the surface of the walls is scratched by pilgrims seeking flakes to take away, the grotto remains miraculously the same size.

The statue of St Paul is a gift from Grand Master Pinto in 1748. The model of a silver galley hanging from the ceiling was a gift of the Sovereign Military Order of St John in 1960 to mark the 1900-year anniversary of the shipwreck. Pope John Paul II came here to pray in May 1990.

Attached to the church is the **sanctuary of St Publius**, built in 1617 with money raised by a pious hermit.

In about 1600 Juan Beneguas came from Spain to become a Knight of the Order of St John. On visiting the grotto he was so moved by the experience that he gave up the trappings of wealth and his knightly ambition to devote his life to his religion. With financial help from the Pope and fellow Knights he was able to build the sanctuary to be dedicated to St Publius. Lorenzo Gafa completed its design in 1692. The **altarpiece** is by Mattia Preti.

The crypt contains traces of frescoes and a marble statue of St Paul by Gafa's brother Melchiore that was the gift of Grand Master Pinto.

Also by St Paul's Collegiate Church on the parish square is the little known but charming **Wignacourt College Museum** (open Mon–Sat 10.00–15.00. Entrance 50 cents). Built at the same time as the church, it was the college where Knights who were to become monks would stay. Inside is a varied collection of paintings and records of the building's own history.

### The Catacombs of St Cataldus, St Paul and St Agatha

Follow the signs (look for them at the top of Saqqija Hill and on parish square). These underground burial places are truly fascinating if macabre, with vaulted tunnels, tombs cut into the stone, niches and canopied burial tombs. Because their gruesome association made them places to shun, in times of religious intolerance Christians would often use them to hold their religious services. St Agatha's catacomb is the largest and probably to be avoided by anyone prone to claustrophobia.

The little church of **St Cataldus** was built in the 18C on the site of a church reputed to have been built in AD 400. Beneath it, in what is believed to be originally a Punic burial ground, are **catacombs** dug out in the late 2C and early 3C. It is in this catacomb that you first see one of the agape tables that are unique to Malta. Open daily. Donations accepted.

---

#### Agape tables

These are round tables with semi-circular benches found at the entrance to a catacomb. Although they would have been used for religious rites, when priest, family and friends would gather to mourn, the table would also be laden with food and wine when they later feasted. It is believed that later Christians might also have used these tables for feasting when celebrating the Last Supper.

---

Follow St Agatha's Street. On the left is the entrance to **St Paul's Catacombs**, an extensive system of passageways with window alcoves (arcosolium tombs) used as burial places around the 4C. In the main crypt there are more agape tables and, down a few steps into what is termed a chapel, there is what appears to be an altar. In this crypt are tombs for infants and children (loculi) and if you follow the long corridors they lead to canopied tombs. More than a thousand people were buried here. Open daily. Entrance Lm1.

Further on, to the right, are the most interesting **St Agatha's Catacombs** with their museum. These catacombs are reputed to be where young Agatha lived after fleeing from Sicily to avoid persecution by the Emperor Decius. She is said to have spent her time praying and preaching before returning to Sicily and a grim death (see p 122). Entrance is through the crypt. Inside, you find a chamber containing 32 painted frescoes, some dating from the 12C. There is also the marble statue of St Agatha attributed to Antonello Gagini which was placed where it could be seen on the walls of Mdina when the city was being besieged in 1551.

Further on in this amazing network of galleries and claustrophobic passageways are more frescoes. It is believed that the necropolis covers nearly 4000sq m but only a small part is open to visitors.

The **museum** has a charm of its own. There are vestments, Punic pottery, Roman glass oil lamps and coins. The metre-high solid alabaster statue of St Agatha (carved in 1666) was originally on the crypt's altarpiece. (Open Mon–Fri 09.00–12.00 and 13.00–17.00, Sat 09.00–13.00. Entrance 50 cents.)

After a quick look in the souvenir and craft shops, retrace your steps to the top of the hill and head for Verdala Castle and Buskett Gardens, Dingli Cliffs and Clapham Junction with its Cart Ruts.

# Beyond Rabat

## *Verdala Castle*

Leave Rabat on the Buskett Road that starts at St Dominic's Priory. If you take the No 81 bus, get off at St Dominic's; the walk to the castle and gardens is then about 1.25km.

Verdala Castle was built as a summer residence for Grand Master Hugues Loubenx de Verdalle, a French cardinal who much enjoyed the pleasures of life. Designed by Gerolamo Cassar in 1586, the year he died, it is a comfortable palace created in the traditional form of a fortified medieval keep surrounded by a dry moat. It was not really designed to withstand an assault, although its four corner towers would be excellent firing positions for muskets if required. The palace stands in the idyllic setting of Buskett Gardens, a *boschetto* of citrus and pine (see below).

The Grand Master commissioned the castle as somewhere he could spend the hot months of summer when life in Valletta became unbearable. Perched above the *boschetto*, it could not have been a better location. In those days wildlife was abundant and the Grand Master or his guests would hunt. A decade earlier Grand Master la Valette came here to hunt too, with bow and arrow, but he was content to live in something much smaller. Today the castle is the President of Malta's official summer residence (open only for charitable events when the President is not in residence).

The main room on the **ground floor** is huge and served as a dining room—which it still does on official occasions. The frescoes show illustrious scenes from Grand Master Verdala's life, taking him from artillery officer to Grand Master and Cardinal. The ceiling is currently under restoration because its earlier indecorous Greek mythological figures offended Lady Bonham-Carter, wife of the British Governor, and she ordered them to be painted over. However, restoration has discovered that some of the mythological figures were themselves painted over even earlier frescoes, possibly of a religious nature. These may yet be revealed.

The **first floor** is reached by a sweeping oval staircase which has broad shallow steps like those in the Palace in Valletta, shallow enough to be climbed by a Knight dressed in armour and unable to bend his knees. The ceiling of the drawing room is 7.5m high with 3.3m tall doors bearing the crest of the Portuguese Grand Master Vilhena, who added his own embellishments when he came to reign. A chessboard and other insets carved into the floor were done by high-ranking French officers imprisoned here by the British during their naval blockade in 1800. In the living quarters are pictures of other Grand Masters who lived in the summer palace as well as four small suits of armour, each weighing approximately 32kg. On either side there are small circular staircases. One is an escape route for the Grand Master, the other leads to a small torture chamber—a room no Grand Master, it would appear, could be without.

From the roof there are spectacular views of the whole island.

In the grounds is the **Chapel of St Anthony the Abbot,** built in the 16C. Inside, undergoing much needed restoration, is a *Madonna and Child* by Mattia Preti.

## *Buskett Gardens*

Buskett is Malta's largest wooded area and a delightful, verdant spot to picnic, summer or winter (open daily. Entrance free, ample parking). The amounts of litter will confirm its popularity. There are no flowers, just trees like citrus, fir and cypress, and the occasional Judas tree. In spring, water trickles through a stream that runs down the valley.

For more than 300 years *L'Imnarja*, the feast day of Saints Peter and Paul, has been celebrated here in a giant get-together. (The name *L'Imnarja* comes from the Latin *illuminaria*, when the clergy would light up the churches of Mdina and Rabat with lanterns and flaming torches to honour the saints.)

Traditionally the morning of 29 June starts with horse and donkey races on Racecourse Street by Rabat's Saqqijja Hill (see above). Then during the afternoon crowds gather in Buskett to fry rabbit, drink home-made wine, play *tombla* and sit out well into the night listening to *ghannej* (singers of a traditional form of Maltese folk singing).

### Dingli Cliffs

As you leave Buskett take the signposted high road until you reach Dingli Cliffs. This stretch of dramatic coastline has sheer cliffs which, at around 250m, make it the highest spot in Malta; there are some wonderful walks in the cooler months, with superb panoramic views. In the spring it is covered with a colourful profusion of wild flowers.

At some distance away to your left as you face the sea are the Neolithic temples of **Ħaġar Qim** and **Mnajdra** (see *The Neolithic Temples*). But follow the signs to the right and you come to **Clapham Junction** where no fewer than 30 parallel **cart ruts** resembling tramways run in parallel lines or intersect eachother (see *Ancient Malta*, p 50). The average gauge is about 140cm, while the width varies from about 10cm to 60cm. Some are shallow but others are up to 60cm deep.

Not far away is *Bobbyland*, an inexpensive, and therefore crowded, truly casual restaurant known for its simple fare. Specialities: rabbit and lamb.

The main road here turns to the small quiet village of **Dingli** and then Rabat.

# The northeast coast

## The resort towns

**Sliema** is the resort town with the widest selection of shops and cafés catering for the Maltese rather than the tourist. Sliema is also where most visitors gravitate if they want a little of the life that revolves around cafés and shopping, or are planning to take one of the boat trips that leave from the Ferries waterfront.

Established at the turn of the 20C, when families wanted summer residences by the sea away from the oppressive heat of Valletta, it quickly became fashionable. Today Sliema is Malta's prime middle-class residential area, where apartments facing the sea or looking across the harbour towards Valletta sell for seriously high sums of money. Sliema, and these apartments in particular, are considered *the* places to live. When the tourists have gone home and the cold weather envelopes the Islands, which it can do from January to March, Sliema is still alive.

As the hospitality business gathered momentum in the late 1970s, business interests began catering for tourists as well as the Maltese, and commercial development spread along the coast—to St Julians, Paceville and St George's Bay, the only areas available that were inexpensively ripe for change. Because of this success, even today, decades later, a considerable amount of demolition and rebuilding takes place on a daily basis in the name of supply, demand and profit. Many streets can seem permanently blocked with cranes, cement mixers and trucks delivering cream-coloured limestone. It is along here rather than in homely Sliema that you will find the widest selection in Malta of restaurants (at every price), cafés, discos, and three-, four- and five-star hotels.

If you want to shop for anything more than souvenirs, however, Sliema is where you head.

## Gwardamanġa, Pietà, Msida and Ta'Xbiex

If you were travelling from Valletta to Sliema you would pass through Floriana and Porte des Bombes on the main road that travels through the creeks of Pietà and Msida. Going downhill you pass Ta' Braxxia Anglican Cemetery and come to **Gwardamanġa**, a crowded district of narrow streets on raised ground with offices and homes above **Pietà Creek** where the cargo ferry service to Gozo leaves from Sa Maison quay.

At the centre of Gwardamanġa is **St Luke's Hospital** (built in 1938), the Islands' main hospital with its medical school. Medical treatment is rated very highly although the hospital suffers from overcrowding. A new hospital will open at Ta'Qroqq near Msida soon to share the load.

There is nothing to see in Gwardamanġa, although on Gwardamanġa Hill is the dilapidated **Villa Guardamangia** reputed to have once been the residence of a Grand Master's food taster, but more famously associated with Queen Elizabeth II. She lived here in the early days of her marriage when, as Princess Elizabeth-housewife, she accompanied Prince Philip on his posting as a naval officer. His ship was berthed in Sliema creek.

Further along is Msida Marina, the Islands' largest yacht marina to date (see *Practical Information*, p 16). The marina is well served and has a waiting list for permanent berths. In the narrow strip of gardens to one side are a monument to peace made of coralline limestone and a defused war-time torpedo, a reminder that this was once the British Navy's torpedo depot and submarines were based here. Overlooking the reach of the creek is Msida's parish Church of **St Joseph** (1893) with two altarpieces by one of Malta's favourite painters Giuseppe Cali (1846–1930), who was born in Malta to Italian parents.

Dividing the traffic by the church is the Msida Roundabout (at the centre of which is the Workers Monument unveiled in 1980). Birkirkara lies straight ahead, but traffic lights offer access to the Regional Road leading up to the University at Ta' Qroqq, St Julians and the coast road to St Paul's Bay, or the one-way main road system into Sliema.

Follow the main road to Sliema and you travel through Msida to Gzira. For Ta'Xbiex turn right at the top of the hill.

**Ta'Xbiex** is a residential district with a mixture of smart villas (some are embassies or ambassadors' residences), apartment buildings and blocks of government housing. The Marina continues along the Ta'Xbiex shoreline as far as **Christopher's**, one of Malta's most highly rated and costly restaurants, (see

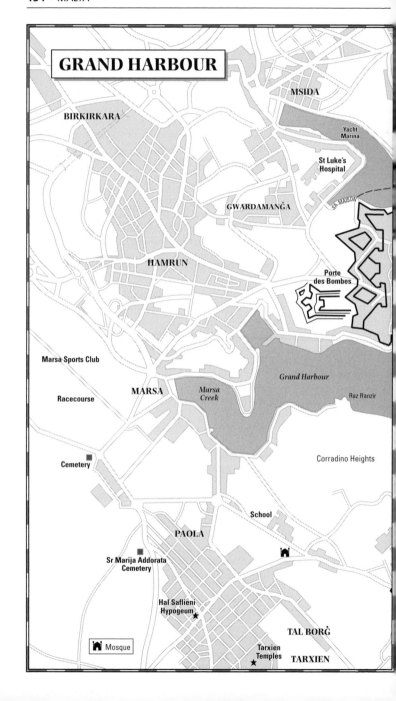

# GRAND HARBOUR

MSIDA

BIRKIRKARA

Yacht Marina

St Luke's Hospital

GWARDAMANĠA

SA MAISON

HAMRUN

Porte des Bombes

Marsa Sports Club

Grand Harbour

MARSA

Marsa Creek

Ras Ħanzir

Racecourse

Corradino Heights

Cemetery

School

PAOLA

Sa Marija Addorata Cemetery

Hal Saflieni Hypogeum

TAL BORĠ

Mosque

Tarxien Temples

TARXIEN

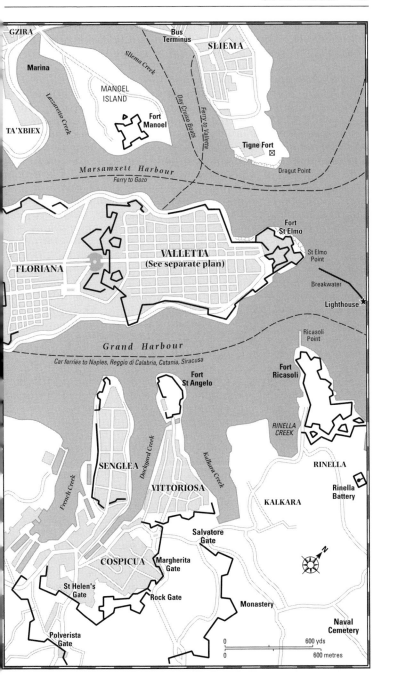

*Where to eat*, p 26). The *Black Pearl*, a three-masted schooner used in the Robin Williams film *Popeye*, shot in Malta, is also there like a landmark. *Black Pearl* had a habit of sinking so now, safely ashore, it too is a restaurant.

## Gżira and Manoel Island

Where Ta'Xbiex ends there is a small neglected patch of gardens with a sad children's playground, the Yacht Marina Gardens; **Gżira** begins here.

A crowded district with cramped streets and small traditional houses, this was once an area where British naval ratings would rent apartments for their families. It also had seedy bars with hostesses to cater for a sailor's needs. Now it is mostly residential with nothing more rousing than karaoke bars, inexpensive eating places and *Chez Philippe*, facing Manoel Island bridge, which is the lunchtime bistro for the smart set.

Cross the short stone bridge and you are on **Manoel Island**. Plans have been approved by the government and Planning Authority for this tiny historic piece of island to become a new development area with high-rise apartments and shopping centres, instead of the open-air community space local residents had hoped for. Its character will be lost permanently but the current neglected state of **Fort Manoel** and the **Lazzaretto** (see below) could already be said to be an act of vandalism. The developers guarantee that a certain amount of the fort and the ancient isolation hospital form a part of their plans, but the light industry (boat building and *Phoenician Glass*) will be moved away, probably to Marsaxlokk.

The **Manoel Island Yacht Yard** (☎ 334454), considered to have one of the best yacht slip facilities in the central Mediterranean, is scheduled to remain. The Yacht Yard has seven slipways for vessels up to 55m, 400 tons displacement. There is wintering space for 200 yachts, 16m LOA (length over all) and 2.7m draught. Lifting capacity on hard, 40 tons

The **Royal Malta Yacht Club** (☎ 333109) may stay on the island too, but will be relocated. Currently at the *Couvre Porte* facing Valletta, it has Manoel Island's prime site, perfect for starting regattas and international events for big yachts like the Middle Sea Race. Founded in 1835, the RMYC has a clubhouse to which members of any recognised yacht club arriving in Malta are welcome, after paying a nominal temporary membership fee.

### History of the Lazzaretto

Before 1643, after serious plagues had swept the Islands in 1592 and 1623, a small strip of Manoel Island, then known as Bishop Island, was appropriated by Grand Master Lascaris for the construction of a *lazzaretto*, or quarantine station, to be known as the **Lazzaretto di San Rocco**. Earlier quarantine stations set up on Corradino Heights across the Grand Harbour and at the Barriera wharf below Valletta were deemed insufficient.

Many Grand Masters had a hand in maintaining the efficiency of the Lazzaretto: Nicolas Cotoner altered the buildings in 1670, Carafa initiated new works in 1683 and Vilhena made improvements when he built the Fort Manoel.

By the mid-18C, the disinfection station could accommodate 1000 travellers and their baggage at any one time. It dealt with crews, passengers, cargoes and mail off all ships arriving from the eastern Mediterranean heading for Europe. It was a time when plague would sweep through neighbouring countries, and strict control of passenger and cargo movement was necessary to prevent it spreading.

In Malta no one was exempt, no matter how exalted his rank. Ships with clean bills of health merely lay off Sa Maison for 18 days; the period of 'great quarantine' for any ship or passenger in transit from an area where bubonic plague raged was 80 days. The law was strict; the penalty for avoiding quarantine was death. Mail was disinfected by cutting vertical slits in the packaging and immersing letters in vinegar. They were then fumigated with sulphur or saltpetre. The system seems to have been effective, for the only major outbreak occurred in 1813.

Plague disappeared from Europe in 1841 and from the Near East soon afterwards. The Lazzaretto continued as an isolation hospital and during World War One took in the wounded and sick from the Dardanelles and Salonika campaigns. In 1922 it housed refugees from Smyrna, then during an outbreak of plague in Tunis in 1929 it took on its role of disinfection station again when it fumigated all incoming mail. The Lazzaretto was last used during an epidemic in 1936.

During World War Two, the British Navy took over Manoel Island as a barracks and the Lazzaretto became the base of a submarine flotilla. Its arcaded frontage on the sea is graceful but the derelict building itself needs urgent restoration.

Distinguished British travellers who spent days as enforced guests of the Lazzaretto include Benjamin Disraeli and Lord Byron. Sir Water Scott, who was here in 1831, recorded: 'It is unpleasant to be thought so very unclean and capable of poisoning a whole city.'

The word **lazzaretto** comes from Lazarus, the Biblical beggar with a pestilential disease; *quarantine* is from the Italian *quaranta*, forty—the number of days spent in isolation for the plague.

## Fort Manoel

The fort was commissioned by Grand Master Antonio Manoel de Vilhena as protection for Marsamxett Harbour on his appointment in 1722 and paid for entirely by him. The original designs were by de Tignè, a French military architect, but the Order's own architect De Mondion made considerable changes.

Much of it is lost now but it was a classic example of a fort, both elegant and functional, designed to accommodate a garrison of 500 trained men. There are fine corner bastions, imposing defensive walls and, on the centre parade ground, the Baroque **Chapel of St Anthony of Padua**, honouring de Vilhena's patron saint.

In 1800 the French force was interned in Fort Manoel until after the signing of the Treaty of Amiens, when they were crammed into British ships and returned to France. The barracks were built by the British.

## Sliema

- **Getting there**  Buses 61, 62, 63, 64, 65, 68, 70, 627, 645, 667, 671 serve Sliema. Regular ferry service to/from Valletta.
  Car parking can be difficult. Expensive pay car park is in High Street.

The main road from Manoel Island leads along the Strand to a section known to all as the **Ferries** because, although the bus terminus has always been here, two

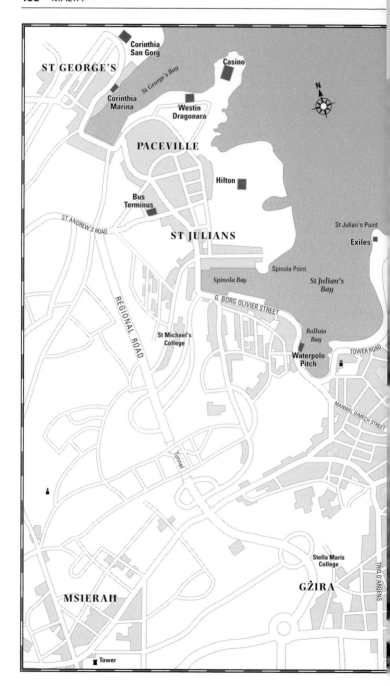

ST GEORGE'S

Corinthia
San Gorg

Casino

St George's Bay

Corinthia
Marina

Westin
Dragonara

N

PACEVILLE

Hilton

Bus
Terminus

ST ANDREW'S ROAD

ST JULIANS

St Julian's Point

Exiles

Spinola Point

Spinola Bay

St Julian's
Bay

REGIONAL ROAD

G. BORG OLIVIER STREET

St Michael's
College

Balluta
Bay

TOWER ROAD

Waterpolo
Pitch

MANWEL DIMECH STREET

Tunnel

Stella Maris
College

GŻIRA

TRIQ D'ARGENS

MSIERAH

Tower

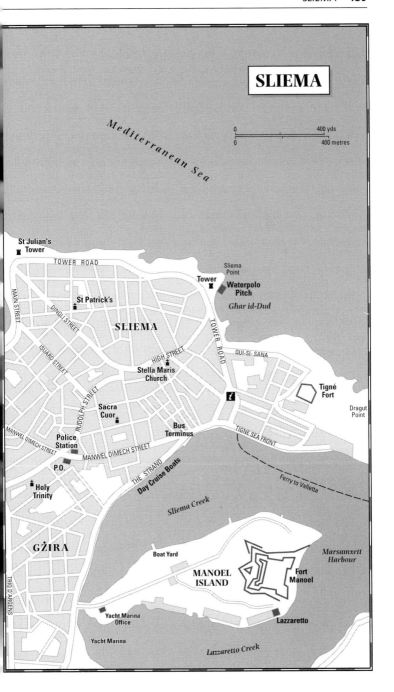

# SLIEMA

*Mediterranean Sea*

0     400 yds
0     400 metres

St Julian's
Tower

TOWER ROAD

MAIN STREET

DINGLI STREET

St Patrick's

**SLIEMA**

ISUARD STREET

RUDOLPH STREET

HIGH STREET

Stella Maris
Church

Sacra
Cuor

Police
Station

MANWEL DIMECH STREET

MANWEL DIMECH STREET

P.O.

Holy
Trinity

GŻIRA

TRIQ D'ARGENS

Bus
Terminus

THE STRAND
**Day Cruise Boats**

Sliema Creek

Boat Yard

**MANOEL
ISLAND**

Yacht Marina
Office

Yacht Marina

Lazzaretto Creek

Sliema
Point

Tower

**Waterpolo
Pitch**

*Ghar id-Dud*

TOWER ROAD

QUI-SI-SANA

Tigné
Fort

Dragut
Point

TIGNE SEA FRONT

Ferry to Valletta

Fort
Manoel

Lazzaretto

*Marsamxett
Harbour*

steam ferries used to ply from a pair of ancient wooden jetties to Valletta across the harbour. A much smaller ferry runs every 30 minutes during daylight hours from the concrete quay (opposite cafés *Oasis* and *Giorgio*).

**Boat cruises** also set out from this section. Some are workhorse toilers, others well-groomed and well-appointed yachts. There is a choice of excursions (and prices) and a variety of characters on the waterfront touting for cruise business (as well as—so be prepared—time-share). Hotels and travel agents have lists of the cruise boat schedules.

Although there were farmsteads here and fishermen used the creek, Sliema was only established in the late 19C, as Valletta's residents looked for spacious homes to escape the summer heat. It was, and still is, staunchly middle class but unfortunately, as rebuilding took place in the 1980s and 1990s, the elegant houses and villas that lined the popular promenade to St Julians were replaced by high-rise apartment blocks designed with little aesthetic consideration.

As Malta's prime residential district it has in the region of 14,000 residents, a number that increases considerably in the summer months. There are shops and department stores (mostly around the twin hills of Tower Road and Bisazza Street), language schools, hotels and cafés, as well as a coastline of smooth rock that is popular for swimming. There are a number of churches with healthy congregations; the four parish churches being Stella Maris (Our Lady of the Sea), San Girgor (St Gregory the Great), Sacra Cuor (Our Lady of the Sacred Heart) and Nazarenu (Jesus of Nazareth). The churches are uniformly architecturally uninspiring, but **Sacra Cuor** has what is considered to be Giuseppe Cali's masterpiece, the altarpiece depicting a skeletal St Jerome in his cave with bible, cross and death's head.

On Sliema's promontory is **Tignè**, with the remains of **Fort Tignè** facing Fort St Elmo to guard the entrance to Marsamxett Harbour. In British times Tignè was a large army barracks complete with family quarters. Now it is due for complete redevelopment by the consortium developing Manoel Island and will have apartment blocks and shopping complexes.

From this side of the harbour you have the finest view of Valletta, especially by night when Valletta's fortifications are floodlit.

## History of Tignè

During the Great Siege the Turkish Ottoman force established its artillery on this barren point in order to bombard Fort St Elmo. It was also here that Dragut Rais, the wizened corsair leading the Turkish force, was mortally struck by a rock thrown up by a cannon ball fired from Fort St Elmo, three days before the fort fell. This area is now known as **Dragut Point**.

It was not until 1792, 262 years after their arrival in Malta, that the Knights considered fortifying this strategic position—six years, as it transpired, before Napoleon arrived to chase them away. The fort was commissioned by Grand Master Emmanuel de Rohan and Chevalier Tignè as a formidable companion for Fort St Elmo. The two forts would secure Marsamxett Harbour and its creeks.

As fate would have it, Fort Tignè's cannons were fired in anger, but not on ships intent on invading Malta. Instead their target was the French force that had taken refuge in Valletta after evicting the Knights and now had the Maltese militia and brave locals outside the walls crying for their blood, while Britain's navy blockaded the Islands to prevent food, ammunitions and reinforcements getting through.

Sadly there is not much of the fort to see today. The British made many changes when converting Tignè into a barracks and most of the area has become derelict since their departure.

The road back to Tower Road is the **Qui-si-sana** promenade with a number of beach establishments and beach clubs. The swimming is good (off the rock shoreline into deep, clear sea). Where there are club facilities, these are basic but good too, with simple snack bar, showers and changing facilities. Although the hotels' concessions are officially for hotel guests only, lidos like the *Union Club* and *NFTS* (the student organisation) welcome day guests for a very modest fee. The Union Club is very sedate; NFTS young and rowdy.

The Tower Road promenade then leads all the way to St Julians (see below), and it too is popular with swimmers. Stretches known as Ferro Bay, Fond Ghadir and Exiles (an old water polo pitch) are where Sliema residents like to swim. Where there are no facilities, most families take picnics and containers of cold water with them, but shops are never far away. If you join the young throng at **Exiles**, you'll find two cafés on the rocks, one complete with very loud juke box.

There are few sandy beaches on the Maltese Islands, but locals enjoy swimming from rock unless they have pre-teen children. The water is clear and clean and perfect for snorkelling. It is also safe for the most part (just ensure, if you are diving in, that it is as deep at it looks). By and large, where you see Maltese in the water, the swimming is good.

By Ferro Bay is the old **Sliema Point Battery**, a fort built by the British in 1872 and now the bar and grill of *TGI Friday*. Further along is the *Torri* (the tower above the children's playground and Exiles). Converted into a simple café, this was **St Julian's Tower**, one of Grand Master De Redin's ring of defensive lookouts.

The promenade is one of Sliema's finer amenities, a pleasant place with families strolling and children learning to ride bikes or roller blades. This is where everyone comes in the cool of summer evenings to stay late gossiping.

## St Julians

- **Getting there** Buses 64, 65, 68, 70, 627, 645, 652, 667, 671 serve St Julians

Through **Balluta Bay**, dominated by the architecturally superb local example of early 1930s Art Deco, the Balluta Buildings apartment block, the road passes Neptunes water polo club with its open-air restaurant and pool. (Waterpolo is to summer what soccer is to winter, and Neptunes are one of the best teams with the noisiest supporters.)

Then you come to **Spinola Bay** around which St Julians has grown. A few fishing boats still sail out of the bay as they always did, and a very small fishing community still sells fish some morning on the slipways, where the freshwater ducks have made themselves a very pleasant seawater life.

But this is no longer a fisherman's harbour. St Julians today is the doorstep to Paceville, the entertainment area, and is where a number of the best restaurants and inexpensive cafés huddle together. Leading the restaurants is the glamourous and expensive *San Giuliano* with, not far behind, *La Dolce Vita* and *Peppino's*. For faster food there are *Caffè Raffael*, *Paparazzi* and *Pizza Hut* and for ethnic food, *Bouzouki*, *Sumatra*, *China House* and many more (for details, see

*Where to eat*, pp 26–27). The post-teen crowd like *Poco Loco*, *Saddles* and *Chains*. Parking is not easy, but somehow everyone manages although tow-zones have ruined the free-for-all traffic jams that used to occur.

As the **Portomaso** development, with the conference centre and *Malta Hilton* hotel, gathers commercial momentum, parking may (or may not) improve as streets in the development area become available. Portomaso is a purpose-built complex of offices, apartments and the new *Hilton* around a man-made creek for yachts. It opened in early 2000, and if the sea appears murky, it is because it has not yet recovered from the pollution caused by the excavations and work on the development.

There is not much more to be said about St Julians. It is a residential area that grew out of Sliema and is now where the Maltese go at weekends and the tourists every day.

### Paceville

It is difficult to see where St Julians and Paceville meet, but it is generally considered that Paceville, Malta's most crowded, busy and hectic late night district, begins at the top of **Spinola Hill** by the entrance to the Portomaso complex. It is so popular it even has its own schedule of late-night buses: nos 11, 18, 34, 49, 62, 81, 88 service most of the island, although many young late-nighters prefer to queue to share a taxi at the all-night *Wembley Garage* on Spinola Hill.

Paceville is young. A down-at-heel residential district by day, by night it is alive with neon, loud music and hordes of young people. Hamburger joints jostle with deafening bars selling cocktails with unprintable names. There are discos too. *Axis*, with latest technology and international DJs, is the most popular and has a tight door policy. The smart set arrive after midnight when the out-of-towners have gone home.

Paceville is crowded at weekends and patrolled by police as violent fights often break out in the early hours of the morning, some of them fatal. If the local newspapers are to be believed, most drugs are available here.

Through Paceville you come to **Dragonara** with the *Westin Dragonara Beach Resort* and the *Dragonara Palace Casino*.

This attractive spot used to be the summer residence of Marquis Emanuele Scicluna, a successful banker. According to locals, he made a loan to Pope Pius IX and, in papal gratitude, he was ennobled. On a tablet over the entrance gate are his words: '*Deus Nobis Haec Otia Fecit*' ('God made these leisures for us').

The family still own the land, but the leisures are of a less personal kind. Scicluna's sumptuous classical palace has been adapted to form a casino (see p 39) run by a consortium of local hoteliers. In what were the gardens and a rocky beach, the *Reef Club* lido and *Palio's* and *Compass Rose* restaurants form part of the Westin Dragonara's facilities (see also *Where to stay*, p 18). The *Reef Club* is large, well appointed and popular with families. It is also the sort of beach establishment where every woman appears to change her bikini and sarong on the hour. Day visitors pay nominal entrance fee. *Divewise* scuba diving school (☎ 336441) is also here.

### St George's Bay

Paceville merges into St George's Bay, but St George's is much calmer and restful. Away from it all on the far side of the bay are two hotels belonging to the Corinthia chain, the five-star *San Gorg* and the four-star *Marina* as well as the four-star *Bay Point*, a part of Radisson SAS.

On the near side, there is the Eden Century cinema complex with 24 screens, a bowling alley, a shopping complex and two more hotels under construction.

The bay itself has a small strip of sandy beach; there are plans to improve this and to enlarge it with imported sand.

The Regional Road leads on to Bahar-iċ-Ċagħaq and St Paul's Bay (see pp 145–147). Behind St George's Bay it passes the sturdy, attractive buildings of the former British army barracks of St Andrew's and Pembroke, which now form part of government housing developments. **Pembroke** still has the army firing ranges and these are used periodically by the AFM (Armed Forces of Malta) and by the Police for training exercises. Alongside the Pembroke ranges is one of the Islands' reverse osmosis desalination plants that convert seawater into drinking water at great expense. The Islands once had severe fresh water shortages in the summer, but plants like this one have eliminated the problem.

# The coast road to St Paul's Bay

• **Getting there** Buses 70, 68, 627, 645, 652

Travelling north from Sliema and Paceville the scenery changes dramatically for the better. An (almost) unspoiled coastline stretches before you and directly ahead, forming a horizon, are the distinctive, rugged cliff edges of the Islands of Comino and Gozo. If St Julians and Paceville are hectic, crowded and over-built, the sudden appearance of this promising vista offers images of the true Malta and the freedom to explore. Even as the government proposes more four-star hotels along the coast, this view is marked on every development plan and proposal as: *to be preserved.*

Where St Andrews ends at the four-star *Forum Hotel* next to the opulent modern villas on High Ridge, the **Coast Road** begins. To the left, hills and valleys take shape; to the right, the natural rocky coastline falls away into fluorescent blue sea. Even on one of Malta's rattling old route buses, this drive is a pleasure.

On the descent, a steep hill rises to the left, leading to **Madliena**, a pretty spot with yet more expensive villas, and should you follow it through the winding valley beyond, on the next rise is the village of **Gharghur** where young-marrieds from Sliema buy their first homes, praying one day to move to Madliena or a seaview apartment in Sliema.

**Fort Madliena** is barely visible on the crest. Built by the British in 1874, it was constructed to protect the northeast flank of the Victoria Lines, the extensive defensive wall that was built along the Great Fault that runs across Malta, coast to coast. During World War Two, the fort was a radar warning station manned by the Royal Air Force. (Tours of the fort, Sun at 10.00, 11.00 and noon.)

## The Victoria Lines

The Victoria Lines are a series of linked fortifications that stretch 12km from Fort Madliena across Malta to Fomm ir-Riħ Bay on the elevated south side of the Great Fault.

## History of the Victoria Lines

Soon after their arrival in 1800, and even more strongly in the months following the opening of the Suez Canal in 1869, the British were greatly concerned with the protection of the Grand Harbour and how it might be reached by land. In these seven decades, Malta had become their most important Mediterranean base.

While the harbour might have been considered secure because of the forts guarding its entrance, the British were concerned that newer, more powerful artillery would be able to fire from greater distances than ever before onto the harbour and its ships.

A new defensive line was needed to keep this artillery further away should the enemy land. A number of plans were proposed until a natural solution presented itself: a wall of fortifications along the Great Fault.

The fault is a natural geological feature that separates the ridges and valleys in the north of the island from the rest of Malta. Between north and south there is a wide, flat and fertile valley. On the south (Valletta) side there is an impressive almost vertical ridge which gives anyone stationed on the high ground a strategic, commanding position over an enemy approaching from the north, and as a defensive line it always presented an interesting proposition. Even the Knights considered it.

Work began in 1874 and the first three forts, Binġemma, Mosta and Madliena, quickly began to take shape. This was called the Great West Front. In 1881 it was decided that the ridge at Dwejra (overlooking the countryside outside Mosta) was still vulnerable, so a second line of defensive works, the **Dwejra Lines**, was started.

By 1895 the serious work creating a continuous infantry line linking the forts had begun. In most places the wall was (and is) no more than a couple of metres high, but from its dominating position every metre could afford adequate protection to a rifleman as he fired on the advancing enemy below.

The Front was renamed in honour of the 60th anniversary of Queen Victoria's coronation. A marble plaque reads:

*THE VICTORIA LINES*
*CONSTRUCTED DURING THE ADMINISTRATION*
*OF HIS EXCELLENCY*
*GENERAL SIR ARTHUR LYON FREEMANTLE*
*WERE SO NAMED*
*TO COMMEMORATE THE DIAMOND JUBILEE*
*OF HER MAJESTY*
*1897*

The Lines were never tested and it has often been suggested that British command decided on the construction of this line simply to give the troops something to do. In fact by World War One they were superseded by new developments in warfare.

The wall is in a sorry state in some areas but there is a move to restore the defences. There are any number of points where you can join them, and every one offers excellent views of the countryside and the north towards Gozo and Comino. *Kaċċatur* (see p 79) use them for shooting birds.

At Madliena houses are built on the Lines, but as the wall snakes westwards to Għargħur, Mosta, San Pawl ta-Tarġa and on to Binġemma there are many delightful walks in the winter and spring. A favourite is around Dwejra, where the defences' elevated position gives a magnificent view to Għajn Tuffieħa to the north and, to the south, looks across the **Chadwick Lakes**, a series of reservoirs in the Wied Tal-Qlejġ below Mtarfa that magically appear in the wet months.

If you join the Lines beyond the Binġemma Gap, the road rises again to the **Nadur Tower** (242m), where there are good examples of prehistoric cart ruts (see p 54).

## Għargħur and the coast road to Qawra

**Għargħur** has some charm although modern building masks the old streets of the village. The parish church dedicated to **St Bartholomew** took 30 years to build and is reputed to be to the designs of Tommaso Dingli. Its altarpiece is by Emmanuel Periera while other paintings are by Gaspare Formica and Giuseppe Cali. The statue of St Bartholomew is attributed to Melchiore Gafa.

On the narrow strip of road leading from Madliena is the tiny but venerated **Chapel of the Assumption** where a young maiden is said to have been miraculously saved from brink of death by prayers to Our Lady. The miracle is recorded in documents dated before 1575.

The coast road passing Madliena dips down into the hamlet of **Baħar iċ-Ċagħaq** on a rocky bay with a dull stretch of beach and roadside vans supplying refreshments ranging from cold drinks to hamburgers. Just short of the bay is the entrance to the **Splash and Fun park** for children, with waterchutes and a pool. It has a café and changing rooms. Entrance fee includes unlimited use of all facilities.

Further on is Qrejten Point promontory with **Qalet Marku Tower** standing as solitary sentinel.

---

### De Redin towers

Qalet Marku Tower is one of the ring of 13 warning towers constructed around 1658 on the coastline by Grand Master Martin de Redin. Most are in poor condition but they are being slowly restored thanks to charitable foundations and commercial business sponsorship. On sighting an enemy ship, a beacon would be lit on the tower's highest point and cannon fired. This sent a warning to the next tower in line which, in turn, would repeat the fire and cannon shot so that the countryside was warned and news ultimately reached Valletta.

---

If at this point on the road you are enveloped in a foul smell it is because this beauty spot was chosen for Malta's largest rubbish dump; the table mountain to your left is how high it has grown to date. This was once natural virgin land of considerable unspoiled natural charm covered in swathes of aloe, windblown tamarisk and flowering succulent plants. The **Magħtab** dump was designed to take only household and builders refuse, but now it takes anything, including items regarded as hazardous. Like many environmental problems locally, the government is considering the dump's long-term future.

The odour does not spoil the dramatic coastline, which remains a great pleasure. On blustery days windsurfers congregate here and the sea becomes alive with brightly coloured fast-moving sails dipping and weaving. Around the next curve on the road there is the restored **Ghallis Tower** and you enter the wide sweep of **Salina Bay** with the *Coastline Hotel* ahead of you close to salt pans and a fish farm. Sometimes in summer this little bay may be the victim of a noxious smell too but in this case it's caused by seaweed drying out by the salt pans. Across the bay is the ever-expanding resort of Qawra.

The road passes through the **Kennedy Memorial Grove** named in remembrance of President John F Kennedy in 1966. It is popular with picnickers and for scouts' summer camps. Off the track behind the grove are scanty remains of **Tal-Qadi Temple**.

## Qawra and Buġibba

- **Getting there** Buses 48, 51, 58, 70, 86, 427, 449, 652, 627

Traffic lights lead you to **Qawra** joining the Qawra Coast Road which runs along Salina Bay passing hotels, holiday apartments, restaurants, beach lidos and the rock promontory, **Qawra Point**, which is popular with swimmers. This point is a favourite spot for divers too who enjoy the superbly clear waters and occasionally recover anchors from Roman ships among other ancient trophies.

If there is a centre to Qawra, it is on this coastal road. Here too is the four-star *Suncrest Hotel*, the largest hotel on the island, with choice of restaurants and a lido. Alongside is the less expensive but nonetheless impressive ✿✿✿ *Qawra Palace*, with two pools and a lido.

While there's plenty of life to the place, Qawra is much more sedate than—and therefore, for some, preferable to—its neighbour Buġibba, just minutes away on Trunciera, the road that meets Qawra Coast Road at Qawra Point. There is a large Maltese population, but recent development in both Qawra and Buġibba has been carried out with tourists in mind.

As the road follows the coastline to enter the ever-growing seaside town of **Buġibba**, there is a fine view across the bay to St Paul's Island. On this road is the flashy *New Dolmen Hotel* (second largest hotel on Malta) with the Islands' second casino, *The Oracle,* set into its atrium to entertain anyone who cares to gamble (see *Practical Information*, p 39). An ancient dolmen incorporated into the landscaped grounds gives the hotel its name. (A dolmen is a prehistoric sepulchral chamber erected using unhewn stones to support a large flattish stone.)

Buġibba is a bustling holiday destination with apartments, timeshare blocks, two-, three- and four-star hotels, banks, money exchanges, car rental companies and all manner of inexpensive restaurants, bars, souvenir shops, places to swim and late night haunts. Life is centred around Bay Square. A jetty near Bognor Beach on Islet Promenade is used for boat cruises, including *Captain Morgan's Sea Below* glass-bottomed boat. Minutes away, the Empire complex shows recent movies.

Buġibba may not be to everyone's taste as a holiday venue—it is firmly aimed at mass-market visitors and holidaymakers on package tours. But people who like it come back as often as they can. Between January and March much of Buġibba takes the opportunity to close. Qawra is even quieter.

## St Paul's Bay

- **Getting there** Buses 43, 44, 45, 48, 49, 50, 51, 427, 449, 652, 645

Buġibba's waterfront road runs into St Paul's Bay by the small 17C **church of**

**St Paul** that marks the boundary alongside the *Gillieru*, one of Malta's longest established fish restaurants grown from just a few simple tables to very large indeed.

---

### St Paul's Bonfire

Local tradition has it that St Paul's church, often called the Church of St Paul's Bonfire, is built on the site where a bonfire was lit in the early hours of the morning to help Saints Paul and Luke and the others rescued from the shipwreck to get warm and dry. When St Paul picked up a branch to throw onto the fire, a deadly snake bit him on the hand. He shook it off into the flames and, to the amazement of the people around him, suffered no ill effects. It was, they knew, a miracle and from that moment, according to tradition, all venom was removed from snakes on the Islands. The episode naturally enhanced the saint's aura and distinction enabling him to preach and baptise the first Maltese Christians. For the record, indigenous snakes really are non-poisonous.

Less reverential tradition adds that the venom banished from the snakes fell onto the tongues of Maltese women whose tongues can be *biforcuta* (forked) and whose gossip can be spiteful. St Luke wrote about the arrival in Malta (then called *Melita*) but omits mention of snakes and gossiping women.

---

Close to the church is **Wignacourt Tower** built in 1609 by Grand Master Alof de Wignacourt to look out on the northern approach to the expansive bay. Its architect was Vittorio Cassar, son of Gerolamo who is credited with the best buildings in Valletta. It contains a tiny local museum (opening hours vary. Entrance free).

**St Paul's Bay** was for many years a quiet fishing village but by the turn of the 20C, as families became more affluent they began building 'summer residences'; St Paul's Bay was deemed popular because it was so quiet 'and not Sliema'. A few restaurants and bars opened to cater for visitors.

It is hard to believe now, but the sandy strip of Pwales Beach at the head of the bay was once used for swimming. No more. The water can be polluted in the summer months, so boats are moored there instead. In fact although there are a number of inexpensive hotels, apartments and restaurants in St Paul's Bay, visitors staying here would do well to rent a car in order to be able to see and do more and, to have a choice of places to swim. Golden Bay and Ghajn Tuffieha are (just) within walking distance on a day that is not too hot.

The far side of the bay, going towards Mistra Village, Mellieha and Gozo, is an area overlooking the water known as **Xemxija**. Here modern apartments and villas were built unhindered by aesthetics and planning permission in the late 1970s. Maltese families take up residence in summer.

### St Paul's Island

Jutting out picturesquely on the northern side of the bay is the rock formation with St Paul's Island where St Paul is believed to have been shipwrecked in AD 60. On a plinth for all to see is his statue erected in 1845. Underwater, seen by only divers or passengers in the glass-bottomed cruise boat, is a statue of Christ, dropped there with a blessing from Pope John Paul II when he visited the site in 1990.

# St Paul's Bay to Mellieħa Bay

• **Getting there**  Buses 44, 45, 48, 441, 645

Leaving St Paul's Bay on Xemxija Hill, the road joins a roundabout on the ridge with the entrance into the popular 4-star *Corinthia Mistra Village Club Hotel*, a self-contained, purpose-built mixture of hotel and self-catering apartments designed like a Maltese village and set around many pools and an amphitheatre. There are enough restaurants and facilities to keep everyone in the family happy. There is even a dive school facility.

At this point the landscape opens further, to a lush green valley and wooded hillside, as the road sweeps down to a narrow stone bridge before rising again to **Mellieħa ridge**. It is this winding hill that brings buses and most of the Islands' numerous decrepit cars to a snail's pace as they struggle to climb. (Coming down can be equally bad as a hairpin bend tests old vehicles' brakes and steering.) Much patience is required if you are driving, but on the plus side, it is scenically attractive.

Before the rise is a small sign to **Mistra Bay** and if you follow the slim track you pass under the bridge and alongside cultivated fields with vines to reach the shore. The setting is charming but regrettably the swimming off the basic strip of beach is not; it is difficult getting in and out of the water. On the far point is the **Pinto Redoubt** built in 1658 by Grand Master de Redin and adapted by Grand Master Pinto in the 18C. Today the tiny fort is an untidy mess and used as a fish farm; its pens are in the sea below. In rough weather fishermen with their rods gather here in large numbers. The rough sea helps the fish (*awrat*: gilthead bream) to escape their pens and the catches can be plentiful.

On the ridge above is the charming **Selmun Palace** with an unappealing addition of massive modern building that has become the 4-star *Grand Hotel Mercure Selmun Palace*.

The sturdy castle was built by Domenico Cachia in the early 18C on a plan inspired by Verdala Castle outside Rabat. The land on which it stands was once the property of the *Monte di Redenzione degli Schiavi*, a charitable foundation established in 1607 under the patronage of the Grand Master to pay the ransom for Christian slaves held captive on the Barbary coast. Above the entrance is the escutcheon of *Monte di Redenzione*. Naturally the chapel adjoining the palace is dedicated to Our Lady of Ransom.

• Follow the twisting road behind the hotel and eventually you come to an excellent place to swim. It is troublesome to get to, and as a result is relatively quiet and unspoiled. The trek may not be for the frail.

At the roundabout on the top of the hill, the Mellieħa by-pass takes a wide arc, sweeping across the countryside and down through more dramatic landscape to Ghadira beach and the road leading to the ferry quay at Ċirkewwa. The entrance to **Popeye Village** is on this road, overlooking **Anchor Bay**. The Village was built as the set for the 1980 Robin Williams movie *Popeye* and has been preserved as a tourist attraction with the addition of an amusement park. It is a good outing for children.

## Mellieħa

From the roundabout on the ridge the main road heads into Mellieħa, a picturesque hilltop town which straddles a long ridge. From certain vantage points there are fine views over the large attractive Mellieħa Bay with Malta's finest and largest sandy beach, Ghadira. On the outskirts of the town are Mellieħa Heights and Santa Maria Estate, two upmarket building developments where villas with gracious names enjoy the views.

Because of its dominating position there have been settlements here for many centuries. Mellieħa was made a parish in 1436 but within 100 years it had to be abandoned because it was a favourite target of corsairs who would sail their ships into the calm waters of the bay and seize the residents to sell them as slaves. Its flourishing industry of salt-making collapsed (the name *Mellieħa* comes from *melha*, salt), and it was not until the British navy began patrolling the sea in the early 1800s that the population grew again.

The steep main street descends to the parish church of the **Nativity of Our Lady** which stands proudly on a commanding spur. Inside is a painting of *The Shipwreck of St Paul* by Giuseppe Cali. Below is the **Sanctuary of Our Lady**, another place of great devotion since ancient times. It is hung with votive offerings of infant clothes because the water of the spring that runs here is believed to have miraculous healing powers for children's diseases. Also on this road are two restaurants of note: *The Arches* and *Giuseppe's* (see p 25).

## Ghadira and Mellieħa Bay

The road descends to Ghadira, the sandy beach that makes Mellieħa Bay so popular. There are beach establishments, cafés and restaurants, and you can rent boats, pedalos and canoes as well as take a 'banana ride' or paraglide behind a speedboat. (A banana ride is just that: six to eight people sit on a giant inflatable plastic banana and get towed at great speed around the bay and coves. Squealing is de rigueur.) There are jet skis available here too, but fortunately they are kept well away from swimmers.

Ghadira is popular and seriously crowded in the summer months, particularly at weekends. But it is good-natured and you can wade out 'for miles'. Children love it.

Cars park along the road that edges the beach. On the land side there is a marshy **nature reserve** with a small lake for migratory water fowl hidden behind dense bamboo. It is a bird sanctuary the shooters only rarely get to.

The bay is wide and shallow; since the remains of Roman wrecks are still found today, it must have flourished as a port when the draught of ships was not very deep.

In the last hours of the Great Siege, on 7 September 1565, Don Garcia de Toledo, the Spanish viceroy of Sicily, landed here with his relief force of 8000 men. In 1798 Napoleon chose the bay as one of his seven points of landing when he took the Islands and threw out the Order of St John. And in World War Two the British built a series of pillboxes and trenches around the bay to defend it against any force attempting a foothold with landing craft. When there is a wind blowing at the mouth of the bay, the sea becomes alive with windsurfers and small sailing boats holding junior regattas.

On the far side of the bay the road rises to pass the sprawling 4-star *Mellieħa Bay Hotel*, continuing to Marfa Ridge and the ferry quay for Gozo and Comino.

# Marfa Ridge to the Gozo ferry

The steep climb to Marfa Ridge above Ghadira beach is overlooked by the **Red Tower**, an impressively large traditional tower that is terracotta coloured and gives the wide sweep of the attractive bay extra distinction. Built by Grand Master Lascaris as St Agatha's Tower in 1649, its duties were to defend northern Malta as well as act as a link in the chain of warning towers that span Malta and Gozo. It is a gloomy fort, sombre even though it has faded colour. (A tenant painted it a shade of terracotta in the early 20C. The colour is set to remain.) At present awaiting restoration and a new use, it has excellent views, and the hillside around it is a popular winter walk.

On the crest of the ridge, a road in very poor condition runs eastwards along the length of the ridge to the tip where, close to the cliff edge, there is a small **statue of the Madonna**. About a kilometre away across the headland is **Aħrax Point**, Malta's most northerly point, much loved by divers who go there to explore a reef and underwater cave.

Off this bumpy road there are a number of turnings leading to minor sandy bays. Don't be put off by the central road's condition, but if you decide to stop for a walk, or if you find the hidden path in the tangle of trees where the road rises and decide to follow it down the cliff to swim on the tiniest and most charming beach on the Mellieħa Bay side of the bay (a dozen people make it crowded), make sure your car is parked in a visible position by the road and that nothing inside looks tempting. Cars are regularly broken into here. This beach has no name but it is an enchanted spot worth looking for.

The first turning on the road goes to the 3-star *Ramla Bay* holiday complex with its own sandy strip, timeshare apartments and a wide variety of water-sports. Other roads lead to **Armier Bay** (served by Bus 50) with the crowded *Beachcomber* beach establishment, and to **Little Armier** where *Ray's Lido* surprises everyone with its enjoyable inexpensive food and many beach facilities.

The last road leads to the White Tower which is apparently privately owned; it is guarded by barking dogs you would be unwise to approach. The tower over-looks a dull beach.

All along the ridge there are traces of a number of redoubts, bastions and batteries built by the Knights and the British.

## Ċirkewwa

- **Getting there**  Buses 45, 48, 452, 453, 645

The main road from the ridge winds through eucalyptus and mimosa trees that formed part of a reafforestation plan in the late 1970s, before it descends to the shore road facing Comino. To the right is the **Marfa quay** used for a regular ferry service to Comino in summer months. In the days when ferries were very much smaller this was the jetty for he main ferry service to Gozo.

The main road itself leads on to the four-star *Paradise Bay Hotel* facing **Paradise Bay**, a popular beach reached by a steep set of steps. The beach is crowded at weekends with families erecting tents and cooking.

Then you come to the terminal at **Ċirkewwa** with large car parks, café and kiosk selling snacks. The *Gozo Channel* ferries operate from here. So does the ferry belonging to the *Comino Hotel* (see *Practical Information*, p 21).

### Catching the ferry

Ferries sail to Mġarr in Gozo from the **north quay** unless the sea is rough, in which case they sail from the **south quay**. Both quays are marked and signs direct you to the correct one.

Be prepared for very long queues, especially in the summer months when an hour's wait is considered normal even though the *Gozo Channel* company run a shuttle service with two or three ferries. Two new ferries made in Malta's Dockyards may speed operations. **Tickets** are purchased in Gozo on the return half of the trip.

If the area where the cars line up before boarding is littered with rubber-clad divers and their equipment, it's because this is **Marfa Point**, considered one of the best diving sites on the Islands. Most dive schools bring their teams here.

Often people leave their cars at Ċirkewwa and walk onto the ferry. In Gozo they either use the **bus** to get to **Victoria** and enjoy a day there or they take a **taxi** at Mġarr quay and ask for a tour. The basic rules about taxis are: *Bargain first. Agree an all-inclusive price.* Not all taxi drivers are as honest as they look, but many make excellent informal guides and do their island proud.

A bus service meets the ferries and takes passengers into Victoria (also known as **Rabat**). Generally the Gozo bus service runs at odd hours that suit life in the small local community. If you opt for public transport, don't expect to see the whole island in one day. The bus schedules make this impossible.

Always check the ferries' timetable; it changes often. The *Gozo Channel* ticket office on the quay has free timetables, so does the Tourist Office.

In Mġarr harbour there are a number of good restaurants that serve excellent fish for dinner (see *Where to eat*, p 28).

# Inland towns and villages

The main road from Valletta to the north of the island runs through the centre of Malta rather than following the scenic route along the coast. It passes through densely populated, heavily built-up towns and villages before reaching the open countryside. If you are heading for the sandy beaches or for the Gozo ferry connection and using this route, be prepared for slow-moving traffic and congestion, particularly in the summer, in places like Ħamrun, Birkirkara and Mosta.

### Ħamrun

• **Getting there** Buses 80, 81, 88, 91, 99.

For most visitors there is little reason to stop in Ħamrun, although when the parish churches light up for a *festa* the population doubles. Ħamrun's churches are famed for their decoration and for the riotous times had by the crowds when their brass bands march.

Sunday mornings are for the brave as the towns youths take to the streets with the bands in a good-natured drunken haze, often with powdered dye to sprinkle on any-one suspected of being a fan of a rival band club. Ħamrun is so large and sprawling it has two parishes, the Church of St Gaejtan and the Church of the Immaculate Conception. Opposite St Gaejtan on the main road is *Café Elia* famed for its very sweet and unsophisticated pastries. These typically Maltese cakes are especially pop-ular on Sunday mornings when people queue to take some home as a family treat.

## Birkirkara

- **Getting there** Buses 40, 43, 44, 45, 47, 49, 71.

Birkirkara (sometimes written B'Kara on traffic signs) is even larger than Ħamrun, with a population in excess of 23,000 living happily in the crowded narrow streets. Most visitors drive straight through, on their way to Mosta or The Three Villages, but Birkirkara has historical roots too.

The **Basilica of St Helena** off the Birkirkara bypass is a wonderful example of Maltese Baroque, which has earned it the reputation of being the finest parish church on the island. Work was begun in 1727 by either Domenico Cachia or Salvu Borg and completed in 1745. Its rich façade is exuberant with pilasters, angels and pediments in a style no architect would attempt today. Although the interior does not live up to the wondrous exterior, there are some colourful frescoes.

While a modern, second parish church dedicated to St Joseph the Worker is not worth a detour, Birkirkara's old and decayed church dedicated to **Santa Maria** is—although it is not always open. Designed in the 1600s by Vittorio Cassar with a façade added by Tommaso Dingli, the church fell into terrible disrepair and had to be abandoned. There is a wealth of architectural detail in the exterior of the building and, after years of neglect, work is in hand to save the building. Its restoration is to be applauded.

Also in Birkirkara is an old **railway station**, one of the five stations that formed the railway line linking the cities of Valletta and Mdina.

### Malta's railway
The small railway system was established in 1883 with steam trains and car-riages from Britain. The service was a popular but not very fast means of trans-port; urchins regularly ran along keeping up with the carriages. The service reached its peak of success in the 1920s when it carried 1,500,000 passen-gers a year. It was never really financially viable however, and closed in 1931. As the rail track disappeared, so did the stations. Only two stations remain, the one in Birkirkara and the end-of-the-line station outside Mdina on the Mtarfa road. The Birkirkara Local Council hope to find sufficient sponsorship to be able to create Malta's own (small) railway museum around their station.

# The Three Villages

- **Getting there** Bus 40.

Birkirkara merges into **Balzan** which, with **Lija** and **Attard**, forms part of what is known to all as The Three Villages (not to be confused with The Three Cities of Cospicua, Senglea and Vittoriosa, see pp 159–172).

These large villages rub shoulders and were it not for local councils putting up signs, the demarcation lines would be even more blurred than they are. With the system of one-way streets introduced to clear traffic congestion, only true locals know their way around. Be prepared to get lost.

In social terms there is a certain cachet in being able to say you live in one of these villages. They are quiet, understated, with no shops or commerce to speak of (just a few chemists, grocers and stationers), no restaurants and only one hotel which, appropriately, is five-star. But the houses are old and traditional with bags of charm, and as a result house prices here rise steadily even during property slumps. Some of the patrician *palazzi*, the homes of old Maltese families, with their large gardens (and swimming pools) would command fortunes if they ever came up for sale.

## Attard

The parish **Church of the Assumption** sits at the centre of the village in the traditional manner, but the church is anything but traditional. Considered to be the last of the Renaissance-style churches built in Malta, its construction was started around 1600 when the Baroque style had already become the fashion. Its design is attributed to the young Tommaso Dingli who was born in the village or the much older, respected, Vittorio Cassar. The façade has an elegant temple front and main door columns with finely detailed stone carving. Six niches honour saints. The campanile was added in 1718.

There are a number of discreet residences and *palazzi* in the narrow streets, with the President of Malta as the most eminent resident—although where the official presidential residence, **San Anton Palace**, actually lies is a contentious subject. The Balzan council insists San Anton is in its locality; Attard says it is theirs.

### History of San Anton Palace

Grand Master Antoine de Paule, a Knight much given to ignoring his vows of poverty and chastity, enjoyed life to the full when he could and, a few years before his reign as Grand Master began, indulged himself with an elegant country house near Attard as a summer retreat. On his appointment, considering the journey from Valletta to the Grand Master's traditional summer place at Verdala Castle too arduous, he decided to make his summer home into a palace and in 1620 began enlarging it. Successive Grand Masters were happy to do as he did and continued the good work. A gracious palace took shape.

It was in this palace in 1799 that Britain's Captain Alexander Ball and Malta's new National Congress accepted the formal surrender of the French after besieging them in Valletta. Later it became the formal residence of the Governors of Malta and, since 1974, it has been the official home of Presidents of Malta.

The palace is elegantly proportioned and architecturally simple. Only the terraces at the entrance are open to the public, but many charitable events are held in the palace and offer visitors a view of the rooms used for official events and receptions. They are simply decorated but have a certain grandeur.

In the long tunnel-like rear entrance leading from St Anthony's Street is the chapel of **Our Lady of the Pillar** to which locals go to hear Mass each morning. Grand Master de Vilhena was the chapel's benefactor in 1722.

## San Anton Garden

Facing Vjal de Paule, the official entrance to the palace has a uniformed soldier at the gate, and, just within the garden walls, a long tree-lined drive to lead cars to the palace doors. Visitors to the San Anton Garden (open daily during daylight hours. Entrance free) use a gateway alongside the official entry.

On islands where few gardens are open to the public, San Anton stands out the biggest and best. But do not expect riots of colourful flowers or even an extensive arboretum. There are few flowers here, just trees like jacaranda, palm, Norfolk Island pine and towering ficus neatly confined by old, formal flagstone paths. A handful of swans and ducks live here too as do countless feral cats; there is also an aviary.

Perhaps by international standards the garden is not very exciting, but locally it is important. It is a charming place, a garden where people come for the tranquillity or bring the family for an outing. Toddlers love to feed the swans and ducks. Open-air Shakespeare performances are presented on the palace steps in the garden in August by an English-speaking amateur theatrical group, and when there are agricultural or bird shows, they are held here too.

The extraordinary Baroque **Eagle Pond** near the entrance, with its central statue of an angry eagle with two large, contented putti under its wings, is dated 1623, but the garden itself was not opened to the public until the British governor, Sir Arthur Borton, decided to do so in 1882.

On Vjal de Paule outside San Anton is the five-star *Corinthia Palace Hotel*, one of the first modern hotels in Malta to offer outdoor and indoor pools as well as a health centre. It is popular with visitors who come to Malta to see the Islands' historical roots rather than laze on a beach.

### Balzan

Of the three villages, Balzan is the quietest and most reserved, and that is how the residents like it. In traditional form, all roads lead to the **Parish Church of the Annunciation**, a charming edifice that looks larger from the outside than it is. Work was begun on the Annunziata (as locals call it) in 1669, when Maltese architecture was entering its Baroque phase. During the village *festa* on the second Sunday in July, all the silver is put on show and antique vestments are hung in the vestry for all to see.

In the narrow Three Churches Street behind the parish church is the tiny chapel of **Santu Rokku** built in 1593 with some simple and charming detail but rarely open, while St Leonard's, having been deconsecrated, is now part of a home. In front of these is a little square with a stone cross on a tall pillar which may mark the site of an earlier cemetery.

### Lija

This is considered the smartest of the Three Villages, possibly because it has more *palazzi* than the others. It certainly has the most imposing parish church, **Is-Salvatur**, the Church of the Saviour, which was designed by Giovanni Barbara in 1694. This splendid Baroque church stands in perfect isolation at the end of Vjal it-Trasfigurazzjoni (Transfiguration Avenue) with two obelisks by the parvis steps as decoration. Two incongruously small plant pots have been placed there too, presumably to lessen its bareness.

Lija is famous for its *festa* and its fireworks displays on 6 August when busloads of tourists are brought in for the evening.

Of more interest perhaps is **Tal-Mirakoli**, the church of Our Lady of Miracles, on the outskirts of Lija in Annibale Preca Street. Many make pilgrimages here. Built by Grand Master Nicolas Cotoner in 1664 on the site of an earlier church, it is a pleasing building. The altarpiece of *The Virgin and Child* is by Mattia Preti. On a wall is a 16C triptych of the Madonna, said to have miraculous powers since tears were seen flowing from the eyes of the Madonna during the great earthquake of 1743.

# Żebbuġ

• **Getting there** Bus 88

A turning off the main Rabat road that skirts Attard leads south through a valley to Żebbuġ, one of the 10 parishes recorded in 1436 (not to be confused with the much younger and smaller Żebbuġ in Gozo).

Żebbuġ means olives and was probably first used to refer to a settlement here in Roman times, when olive groves would have been flourishing and edible oil an industry. Centuries later, when Britain believed Malta could produce cotton to rival that grown in Egypt, trees were uprooted across the Islands to create space for it to be planted. Although cotton never became a commercial reality because the Islands could not produce enough and the quality was not high, Żebbuġ became known for its cotton fabric. Local industry used it for sails, and as recently as 1910 it was apparently not uncommon to see horse-drawn carts delivering sails to the Marsa creek in the Grand Harbour. That was before the steam age took over. Alas, neither olives nor cotton are abundant any more.

Żebbuġ gives the impression of being a wealthy village because, like the Three Villages, it has many narrow streets with houses 300 years old. It has produced a number of important sons, being the birthplace of Dun Mikiel Xerri and Bishop Francis Xavier Caruana, heroes of the revolt against the French in 1799, as well as of Dun Karm, the revered national poet and Antonio Sciortino, an important sculptor. Mikiel Anton Vassalli who wrote the first grammar book on the Maltese language, *Malti*, has a monument honouring him on a roundabout by **De Rohan Arch** (1777) once the formal entrance to the village.

---

### Grand Master de Rohan Polduc

Emanuel de Rohan Polduc, was a popular French Knight elected Grand Master in 1775. As fate would have it, although he would rule for 22 years, he was the penultimate Grand Master in the Order's reign and it would be his actions that would precipitate their departure.

When de Rohan took over aged 57, he inherited an Order that had changed dramatically. The Knights no longer took their vows seriously and the Order itself was almost bankrupt. However, he set to work with enthusiasm, revising taxes, banning many of the more brutal forms of torture in prison and permitting women to enter court. He also completed the Bibliotheca in Valletta and created 10 additional Maltese titles. He was regarded by the Maltese as benevolent and generous. But his generosity was the undoing of the Order.

In 1791, to fund King Louis XVI's attempted flight from Paris as the

French Revolution took hold, he sold much of the Order's silver. When Napoleon arrived in 1798 he remembered the royalist gesture well. So when the Order pleaded neutrality and allegiance only to the Holy Church to gain permission to remain in a Malta that had now been declared French soil, Napoleon reminded them of their gift to France's executed king. The Order was despatched, homeless again.

Work on the parish **church of St Philip** at the centre of the village was begun in 1599 and took nearly 60 years to complete. The final embellishment was carried out by Tommaso Dingli, the ebullient Maltese architect credited with the Renaissance flourishes seen in the churches of the Assumption in Attard, and the Santa Maria in Birkirkara. Its interior is equally impressive.

Outside Żebbuġ, close to the roundabout for the village of Siġġiewi, is the area known as **Tal Hlas** with a tiny, charming church once isolated in fields. The original church dated from 1500 but was flattened in the 1693 earthquake. It was rebuilt by Lorenzo Gafa. Its elevated atrium with a pair of porticoed loggias on either side was added in 1699 to give additional shelter to the congregation. Like many rural churches it has grilles over the windows on either side of the door. These gave protection to the priest and to the church's treasures during the pirate raids that were common at the time.

On the main road too is **Qormi**, a large sprawling town with car showrooms, the Löwenbräu and Coca Cola factories and spiralling narrow streets. It used to be known as *Casal Fornaro* because of its many bakeries which are still regarded as some of the best providers of Malta's superb bread. Its parish church dedicated to **St George** was begun in 1584 and has a tall façade with prominent towers; the dome was added later. During the plague of 1813 Qormi's population was decimated.

# Mosta to Bur Marrad

## Mosta

● **Getting there** Buses 43, 44, 45, 47, 49, 50, 53, 65, 88, 157, 427.

Mosta's Parish Church of the Assumption, the distinctively domed church you see at the centre of the island from almost every vantage point, is known to locals as Santa Marija Assunta, to an older generation as the Rotunda and, to everyone else, as the **Mosta Dome**.

### History of the Mosta Dome

Begun in 1833 when Mosta was still a village and not the urban sprawl it has become, the church had a bedevilled start. In the three years it took for the foundation stone to be laid and blessed, first the money collected for the building fund was diverted to help stem a cholera epidemic, then the church's French architect, Georges Grognet de Vasse, was involved in a public quarrel with the Académie Française for insisting that Malta was the northern tip of Atlantis. Finally the archbishop refused to bless the church himself, sending a deputy to carry out the duties because he, like many others, disliked the fact that the church was round rather than in the traditional Latin form of a crucifix. It was like a mosque, he said.

The church took nearly 28 years to complete, and its dome was constructed without the use of scaffolding because it was built over and around a church already standing there. Mosta once claimed it had the third largest unsupported dome in Europe, but its position has been relegated to fourth since the upstart parishioners in Xewkija on Gozo impertinently built their own larger rotunda in the 1950s.

*Mosta Dome*

Because of its unsupported dome, Mosta Dome has often been compared with the Pantheon in Rome, which may have provided the architect with inspiration. However, unlike the Pantheon with its tomb-like interior, Mosta Dome is big and light with the brightly coloured interior of the dome lit up by 16 windows and a lantern light and with a floor made of two different marbles laid in geometric pattern. The murals were painted by Giuseppe Cali early in the 20C.

In the sacristy is a large Luftwaffe bomb that came though the dome as the congregation prepared for Mass on 9 April 1942. Miraculously it did not explode and the congregation of more than 300 fled. On display among the souvenirs, the defused bomb is, they say, a warming sign of God's protection.

Another good sign not far away on Main Street is that of the **Lord Nelson**. A casual but highly rated restaurant, it was converted from one of the village bars and has developed a club-like atmosphere because regulars are very regular (see *Where to eat*, p 26).

## Naxxar

● **Getting there**  Buses 54, 55, 56, 65.

The boundary between Naxxar and Mosta is confused but Naxxar sits on the high ground northeast of Mosta. Once it was only a small community but since young-marrieds made its cottage-like houses desirable places to live, the streets have become lined with smart marque cars and large off-roaders. New buildings are going up at a rapid pace. At its centre is the Baroque parish church of the **Nativity of Our Lady** and across the road on Victory Square, behind a plain frontage, is **Palazzo Parisio**, an opulently decorated 19C *palazzo* with an elegantly formal garden. Once the home of the Marquess who owned Dragonara where the casino flourishes, the gilded *palazzo* is open to visitors and may be hired for special events, like wedding receptions and grand parties. (Guided tours Tues, Thur, Fri: 09.00–13.00. ☎ 412461.)

Not far from Palazzo Parisio in what once formed part of its extensive gardens are the **Trade Fair** grounds, where every month international or domestic trade fairs take place. Large crowds attend every night and all neighbourhood roads become traffic congested.

Further along, but within walking distance, is **San Pawl tat-Targa** (literally, St Paul of the Step), perched on the edge of the Victoria Lines (see p 143). Tradition has it that St Paul often preached homilies here that could be heard as far away as Gozo. Costly modern villas line the main road. A modest late-17C church dedicated to **St Paul** stands where the saint was reputed to stand to deliver his homilies.

Behind the church is **Gauci Tower** built privately in 1548 by Cikko Gauci who obtained permission to build the private tower from the Grand Master after members of his family had been snatched by corsairs and sold into slavery. Across the road is **Torri tal-Kaptan** (the Captain's Tower). Built in 1558 for the Captain of the Maltese cavalry, it was used as a watchtower facing north over the bays of St Paul's and Salina. In the tower are the coats of arms of Grand Masters La Valette and Hompesch. It is now a family home.

## Bur Marrad, Wardija and San Pawl Milqi

• **Getting there**  Bus 43.

Set among low-lying arable fields, **Bur Marrad** qualifies as a village although it is no more than two small sections of road with ribbon developments of houses, a plain, modern parish church dedicated to the Immaculate Heart of Mary and a cut-price supermarket alongside crossroads that lead to a cluster of houses on the hillside at Wardija.

This hamlet, **Wardija**, is considered among the smartest countryside areas to live, and land for modern villas on this hillside is priced accordingly. There are a few old houses and many new ones erected by the newly wealthy. It is an attractive spot developed with a fair amount of aesthetic feeling and popular with walkers in the spring.

In the centre of Bur Marrad, on the one-way section of road coming from Mosta, a narrow road leads up the slopes of the Ġebel Ghawzara knoll to the little church of **San Pawl Milqi** (*milqi* means 'welcomed'), where Publius, the island's Roman governor, had a country estate and cared for Paul, Luke and other survivors of the saints' shipwreck in AD 60—or so tradition relates. Malta is a country where tradition has much to tell.

There are signs that a farming community lived here around the 2C BC but it was abandoned three centuries later when the settlement was decimated by fire. It was not until the 4C AD that settlers returned. Records prove a church was built here in 1488 although the present one went up around 1620.

In the late 1960s a team of Italian archaeologists uncovered remains of the previous settlements and found relics which prove the area was used for the production of olive oil in Roman times. A well-head inscribed with symbols reading

'Paulus' and engravings depicting a man and two ships endorse the belief that St Paul and St Luke were here.

The church is in a sad state, much of it caused by neglect and much by vandalism. But it is now the target of a restoration group so the prospects of this historically important site being revived are good. Occasionally it is open to visitors—or so the sign says. Be prepared to be disappointed.

# The southeast

The area south of the Grand Harbour, from the Three Cities to St Thomas Bay, is an area steeped in history encompassing Neolithic temples and the roots of the Order of St John of Jerusalem. Here too is Marsascala, the fishermen's village that has been transformed into a casual but thriving resort.

## THE THREE CITIES

Vittoriosa, Cospicua and Senglea are towns rather than cities. The honorific title '**The Three Cities**' was bestowed on the three towns of the **Cottonera** district, not in deference to their brave history in the Great Siege of 1565 as is sometimes suggested, but by Napoleon's commander, General Vaubois. He hoped that by elevating their status in 1798, the recalcitrant residents would comply with the new French legislation being introduced.

Regrettably, there is less to be seen in the three historic towns than you might expect. Much of what had not already been allowed to fall into decay over the years was destroyed by German and Italian aircraft as they bombed the dockyard creeks around which the towns lie. It has been estimated that in one month alone, in April 1942, more than 3156 tons of bombs fell on the Cottonera.

Important buildings were lost, and after the war they were replaced by buildings hastily constructed to offer homes to the thousands that had been evacuated. The whole district was totally rebuilt and as a result the little that remains of historical or architectural interest is often masked by postwar building and development.

However, the Cottonera district is scheduled for renewed restoration and revitalisation. It was in danger of becoming an impoverished district through governmental neglect. With the development of the **Cottonera yacht marina** complex capable of taking large boats, and with hotels, shops and restaurants along Vittoriosa's waterfront as a part of its facilities, life will change rapidly. For some it will bring a new kind of entrepreneurial prosperity. Historic buildings are to be given appropriate attention too.

When the Order of St John of Jerusalem and Rhodes arrived in 1530, Vittoriosa was il Borgo, known to its residents as Birgu, Senglea was L'Isla and Cospicua was Bormla. Strangely enough more than four centuries later—long after the Knights made the changes—the original names are still used by the

Maltese, especially when talking in *Malti*. This probably says something about the Maltese psyche and powers of survival: no matter how many foreign influences have been brought to bear, the Maltese have always steadfastly remained themselves.

Fortunately for visitors, traffic signs use the names Vittoriosa, Senglea and Cospicua. They were created after the Great Siege in honour of the citizens' bravery and fortitude. *Vittoriosa* translates from the Italian as Victorious, *Cospicua* as Remarkable/Conspicuous, while *Senglea* is dedicated to Grand Master Claude de la Sengle, La Valette's predecessor, who founded the village by changing what were private hunting grounds into building plots.

## History of the Three Cities

In 1530, after Emperor Charles V had formally presented Malta to the Knights of St John, they settled in the area in the great harbour known in Italian as *Il Borgo* (The Village), which the locals corrupted phonetically to 'Birgu'. The island of Malta had a population calculated to be about 12,000 and although a number lived around Mdina, most lived and worked around Birgu. (See also pp 86 and 165.)

When the fleet arrived under the command of Grand Master Philippe Villiers de L'Isle Adam, they moored in Galley Creek (*Porto delle Galere*— today's **Dockyard Creek**) and set to, turning Birgu into a suitable base. On its tip was the small, nondescript Fort St Angelo which, they recorded scathingly, 'was armed with two guns, two falconets and a few old mortars'. If the fleet was to be protected, and if Malta was to be made a fit home, there was a considerable amount of work to be done.

The Knights believed that it was only a matter of time before the Turkish force renewed its attack, intent on chasing the Christian Order out of the Mediterranean and expanding the Ottoman empire further, and while they built the houses that would match the importance of their stature, work was begun in earnest on fortifying Birgu. This was in spite of recommendations made by Antonio Ferramolino, an Italian military engineer sent by the Emperor to oversee the defences. To be truly impregnable, he advocated ignoring *Il Borgo* and building an entirely new fortified city on the far side of the harbour, on the high ground of **Mount Sceberras**. He was overruled but his advice and knowledge of war tactics would be proved sound: the fortified city of Valletta would rise as he suggested after the Great Siege had taken its toll on Birgu and its inhabitants. Unfortunately, Ferramolino never saw the city, as he died before it was built.

As Fort St Angelo was being strengthened, the smaller Fort St Michael was established on the landward side overlooking the sheltered creek of L'Isla (French Creek) where the L'Isla (Senglea) promontory joins Bormla (Cospicua). Bastions and deep ditches were created to protect the area from attack by land, and a massive chain, known as the Great Chain, was forged in Venice to be drawn across the mouth of Galley Creek just below the surface of the water, to prevent enemy ships from entering. In the four years before the Turks stormed the island, the Knights built the finest defences of the day, able to withstand infantry assault and mortars.

Even after the Order had moved to the new city of Valletta, they still regarded the sheltered creeks as of great importance for the safety of their fleet and continued to build and rebuild the defences around Birgu. In 1638, 73 years after the Great Siege, the **Margherita Lines** of bastions were commissioned to give Cospicua added protection.

In 1641 the Turks descended again to swiftly ravage Gozo and make a brief landing in Malta, and did so yet again in 1645. Further precautions were demanded. These attacks, the Knights believed, were signs that it was only a matter of time before the Turks returned in force to wreak revenge for the disgrace of the failure of the Great Siege.

In 1670 the **Cottonera Lines** were begun under the instructions, and at the expense, of Grand Master Nicolas Cotoner. They took ten years to complete but in their semi-circular ring of eight bastions and two demi-bastions around the land perimeter of Senglea, Cospicua and Vittoriosa, they were capable of sheltering 40,000 people with their livestock. Lack of funds prevented construction of the ravelins to protect each curtain—Cotoner's defences had left him almost penniless.

These impressive bastions stretched inland in a sweeping arc from French Creek to Kalkara Creek and are still evident today. Leading into **Zabbar** (see p 173) is an impressive gate that once formed part of these lines, the **Cottonera Gate**. Designed by Romano Carapecchia in 1675, it has Grand Master Nicolas Cotoner's bust superbly ornamented with carvings in its upper structure.

During the Knights' long tenure considerable sums would be spent on this district. Later the British would add their own embellishments.

## Cospicua

• **Getting there** Buses 1, 2, 4, 6.

Because No. 1 Dock (built in 1848) is in the creek centred on Cospicua, the town took the brunt of the bombing in the World War Two as enemy aircraft raids attempted to reduce the dockyards' repair facilities to rubble and sink any ships berthed there. With peace declared, Cospicua was hastily rebuilt; every previous resident had to be rehoused.

Only a few of the original buildings escaped total destruction, among them the historic Church of the **Immaculate Conception**, built in 1584 and enlarged in 1637, that sits above rising flights of steps commanding the town and dock.

Today Cospicua is crowded with an extraordinary number of narrow streets and alleys rising with steps from the road that follows the creek. There are the vestiges of a commercial centre around the dockyard gates and a flourishing Tuesday street market in the ditch on the road to Zabbar. The area is in need of revitalisation and plans are in hand to close No.1 Dock and make it part of the new Cottonera yacht marina. An old warship may be brought deep into this creek as a floating museum.

But explore the winding streets and you come across wonderful examples of Malta's traditional skills when building with limestone. On the road leading to Senglea, ready for its own restoration, is the Church of St Paul, built in 1741.

Dom Mintoff, Malta's illustrious but fiery politician who became an internationally recognised name, was born in Cospicua in 1916.

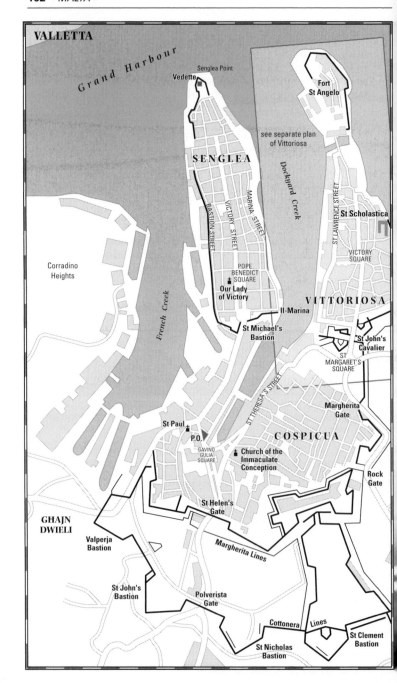

VALLETTA

*Grand Harbour*

Vedette

Senglea Point

Fort
St Angelo

see separate plan
of Vittoriosa

SENGLEA

*Dockyard Creek*

Corradino
Heights

ST LAWRENCE STREET

St Scholastica

VICTORY
SQUARE

MARINA STREET

VICTORY STREET

BASTION STREET

POPE
BENEDICT
SQUARE

Our Lady
of Victory

VITTORIOSA

Il-Marina

*French Creek*

St Michael's
Bastion

St John's
Cavalier

ST
MARGARET'S
SQUARE

ST THERESA'S STREET

Margherita
Gate

St Paul

P.O.

GAVINO
GULIA
SQUARE

Church of the
Immaculate
Conception

COSPICUA

Rock
Gate

St Helen's
Gate

GHAJN
DWIELI

Valperja
Bastion

Margherita Lines

St John's
Bastion

Polverista
Gate

Cottonera Lines

St Clement
Bastion

St Nicholas
Bastion

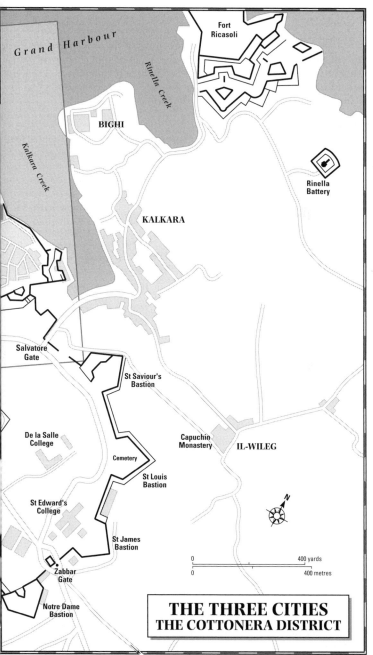

Grand Harbour

Rinella Creek

Fort Ricasoli

BIGHI

Kalkara Creek

Rinella Battery

KALKARA

Salvatore Gate

St Saviour's Bastion

De la Salle College

Capuchin Monastery

IL-WILEG

Cemetery

St Louis Bastion

St Edward's College

N

St James Bastion

Zabbar Gate

0        400 yards
0        400 metres

Notre Dame Bastion

# THE THREE CITIES
## THE COTTONERA DISTRICT

ZABBAR

# Senglea

- **Getting there**  Bus 3.

The village of L'Isla was given its new name, Senglea, as a mark of respect for Grand Master Claude de la Sengle who fortified the promontory in 1554 and increased the size of its community by the simple method of distributing free building plots to any family prepared to build a house and live there.

## The Turkish assault of 1565

De la Sengle's defences were created ten years before the Turks mounted their massive attack after the fall of St Elmo. They turned all their might against Birgu and L'Isla which, with Galley Creek between, were fortified as one entity. To ensure rapid communication between the two and to facilitate the movement of troops in an emergency, a bridge of boats spanned the creek.

When the first attacks came near Fort St Michael they were fierce. On 5 August the Turks were engaged by Maltese swimmers on the improvised palisades and, days later, Hassem, viceroy of Algiers and Dragut's son-in-law, led a land assault while his lieutenant attacked from the water with a fleet they had dragged over the land near Marsa from Marsamxett harbour thus avoiding the guns of St Elmo. More than 8000 Turks were lost in the assaults as they came under fire from Fort St Michael. A squadron attempting to land janissaries near the Great Chain was blown out of the water by Fort St Angelo's guns. L'Isla was besieged but held out.

As the days progressed, the Turks turned their attention to Birgu. If Birgu fell, so would the Knights. With their land forces they mined the walls and used siege towers to mount the bastions. But to no avail. The defences remained secure and at no time did the Knights consider withdrawing with the Order's sacred relics and archives into the safety of Fort St Angelo.

Unfortunately Fort St Michael from which the Knights and Maltese defenders fought so bravely was demolished in 1922 when the British wanted to expand the docks in French Creek. Its stones were used in the building of a government school.

Today, on the far side of French Creek is **China Dock**, built with help from the Government of China. It is the largest dock in Malta and capable of taking ships up to 300,000 tonnes.

Despite the wartime destruction that rendered it mostly uninhabitable, Senglea has regained a picturesque charm. In fact during Malta's boom period in the early 1970s it had all the makings of becoming an artists' colony, when foreign painters, writers and sculptors moved in. Now, with just a sprinkling of (mostly Italian) émigrés, it has returned to familiar local life.

Senglea's appeal stems from its excellent views over the Grand Harbour, Vittoriosa and Fort St Angelo. From the tiny garden at the end of **Victory Street** on Senglea Point, with its stone *gardjola* sentry post overlooking the harbour, they are panoramic. This *gardjola* (known also by the French word *vedette*) is a re-creation built around the remains of the original. On its sides in high relief sculpture are the symbols of watchful vigilance: an eye, an ear and a crane. It was below the *gardjola* that the Great Chain stretched across the mouth of Galley Creek to Fort St Angelo.

Circling Senglea's water's edge is a pleasant **promenade** that heads towards Cospicua. In the cool of a summer's evening, the still waters in the creek dotted with brightly coloured boats take on the appearance of a tranquil lagoon. Families gather until late, keeping the cafés busy while children rush about playing.

Follow the promenade and you come to a short tunnel cut through the bastions for traffic. This is **il-Maċina** where a wooden crane once jutted out over the water for careening ships (that is, turning them over to one side to clean or repair them) and to hoist masts and heavy structures from galleys and ships berthed alongside.

The parish church, **Our Lady of Victory**, was built in 1743 but destroyed in 1941 during a particularly heavy air raid when the target was the formidable but already damaged aircraft carrier HMS *Illustrious* berthed in Dockyard Creek awaiting repair. The carrier was forced to limp away to the USA via the Suez Canal for repair as soon as the raid was over; the church was completely rebuilt in 1957. In front of it is a monument to those who died in the conflict.

The church has two statues of which everyone in Senglea is proud: *Christ the Redeemer* (said to have miraculous powers and therefore highly venerated) and *Our Lady of Victories* (known to the locals as *Maria Bambina* and paraded on Senglea's big day, 8 September, which is also a national holiday, Victory Day).

# Vittoriosa

- **Getting there**  Bus 6.

In medieval times, as *Il Borgo del Castello*, Birgu was the principal centre of population on Grand Harbour. During the Norman period when Malta came under the Kingdom of Sicily, the king's representative, the Governor, lived here. Until 1436 it shared with Mdina the ecclesiastical division of the island into two parishes. When the Knights arrived they made it their residence and, as they had done in Rhodes and would do later in Valletta, they set about building suitable offices and accommodation.

Even after sustaining a considerable amount of damage in World War Two Vittoriosa remains an interesting place to see. The streets are redolent with history and it is an area destined for revival with both the government and local council working with enthusiasm. One unusual project is the opening of the **wartime shelters** that were dug like rabbit warrens into the rock below Vittoriosa. When the air raid warning sounded, families moved there en masse with food and bedding. Many of the tunnels have rooms where families lived in times of long bombardment.

*Seafront view of Vittoriosa*

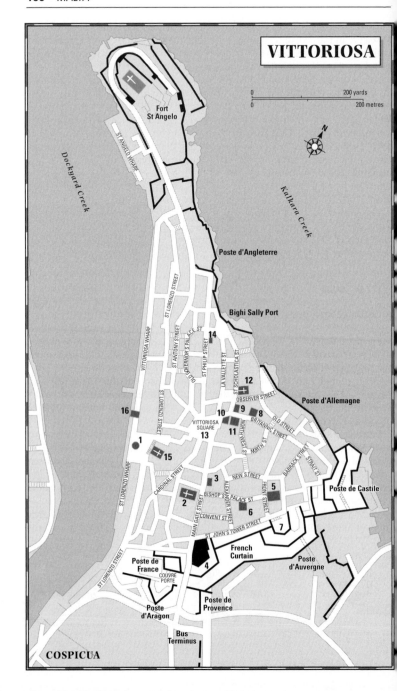

# VITTORIOSA

0            200 yards
0            200 metres

Fort
St Angelo

*Dockyard Creek*

*Kalkara Creek*

ST ANGELO WHARF

Poste d'Angleterre

Bighi Sally Port

ST LORENZO STREET

VITTORIOSA WHARF

ST ANTONY STREET

OLD GOVERNOR'S PALACE ST

ST PHILIP STREET

LA VALLETTE ST

ST SCHOLASTICA ST

**14**

**12**

OBSERVER STREET

Poste d'Allemagne

ST LORENZO STREET

**16**

**10**

**9**

**8**

BRITANNIC STREET

OLD STREET

VITTORIOSA SQUARE

**11**

NORTH WEST ST

NORTH ST

BARRACK STREET

STRAIT ST

**13**

**1**

**15**

CARDINAL STREET

**3**

NEW STREET

ALEXANDER STREET

**5**

FRONT STREET

Poste de Castile

ST LORENZO WHARF

**2**

BISHOP'S PALACE ST

**6**

CONVENT STREET

MAIN GATE STREET

ST JOHN'S TOWER STREET

**7**

French
Curtain

Poste de
France

COUVRE
PORTE

**4**

Poste
d'Auvergne

Poste de
Provence

Poste
d'Aragon

Bus
Terminus

**COSPICUA**

The most interesting way to see Vittoriosa is on foot. Park by the bus terminus at the top of the hill leading from Cospicua or on the waterfront alongside the unfortunately proportioned **Freedom Monument** (No. 1) with its dwarf representation of Maltese bidding farewell to a British sailor when HMS *London* sailed away, ending 180 years of British rule.

On the road rising from Cospicua there are three small gates known as the **Advanced Gate** (built in 1722) with attractive sculptured trophies of arms, the **Couvre Porte** (1723) and the **Main Gate** (1727), close to the stone bridge over the dry moat. At the top of the rise, cross the bridge and ahead of you, left, on Triq il-Mina l-Kbira, is the Dominican Priory with its **Annunciation Church** (No. 2). The original church built in 1528 and enlarged in 1639 was destroyed in the war. This one, more serviceable than dramatic, was built in 1960. Walk on, and on the right is one of Vittoriosa's most important buildings, the **Inquisitor's Palace** (No. 3). This, fortunately, survived the bombing.

## The Inquisitor's Palace

- **Open** 1 Oct–15 June, Mon–Sat 08.15–17.00, Sun 08.15–16.15; 16 June– 30 Sept, daily 07.45–14.00. Entrance fee.

Before 1574 the palace was much smaller and used as the law courts, the *Castellania*. But with the arrival of the Inquisitor in Malta, it was enlarged to house the court, prison, office and his residence. As the Pope's Apostolic delegate, the Inquisitor was expected to be accommodated in appropriate style. However, although in Spain his role was the suppression of heresy and the protection of the Roman Catholic faith, in Malta his duty was to keep a benevolent eye on Christianity and to ensure that only the most virtuous of Christians joined the Order of St John. In many instances he was more powerful than the Grand Master.

Until Napoleon abolished the office in 1798, 63 Inquisitors served in Malta. Two went on to become Pope and 25 became cardinals.

The exterior of the palace is uninspiring but although it is not an ornamented *palazzo* such as you might see in Valletta or Mdina, its interior sheds an interesting light on the history of the Catholic faith. The Inquisitors were men of standing and the building reflects this, although in its restoration and re-creation there is not much furnishing of merit and what little there is belonged to other buildings. But the timber ceilings are notable, as are the murals, and there is an exceptional vaulted colonnade in the 15C *Chiaramonte* style (like the Siculo-Norman Chiaramonte Palace in Palermo, Sicily) surrounding the lower left courtyard. Among the coats of arms of the various Inquisitors carved in wood are those of the two who became Pope: Fabio Chigi (Alexander VII: 1655–67) and Antonio Pignatelli (Innocent XII: 1676–89).

Beneath the palace are the prisons with the prisoners' cell leading directly into the Judgement Room. Its door was made deliberately low so that each prisoner had to bow to the presiding Inquisitor on entering.

Retrace your steps. Turn left at St John's Watchtower (No. 4) into Triq it-Torri ta' San Ġwann to follow the **French Curtain** that forms part of the city's bastion facing inland. On your right is the first **Armoury** of the Knights (No. 5), erected in 1542, since when it has served as a warehouse, hospital and military quarters.

Climb the external stairs for a fine view of **Kalkara Creek** with its traditional Maltese boats bobbing in the water.

In Triq il-Palazz ta' L-Isqof, the narrow street now running parallel, is **Bishop Cubelles Palace** (No. 6) built in 1542 and enlarged in 1615 by Bishop Cagliares. Until recently it was used as a school.

Press on past St James Watchtower (No. 7) and follow the narrow Triq id-Dejqa to Triq Hilda Tabone; turn left. You pass Triq it-Tramuntana where No. 11 is neglected house with *Chiaramonte* Siculo-Norman details on its first floor. On Triq Hilda Tabone at No. 24 you come to the Auberge de France (No.8) which, with the Auberge d'Auvergne (No. 9) at No. 17, the Auberge d' Allemagne (No. 10) and the Auberge d'Angleterre (No. 11) in Triq il-Majjistral, formed part of *Il Collachio*, the small area where the Knights' inns were situated. The **Auberge de France**, in a good state of repair, is earmarked for the offices of an environmental commission set up by the Council of Europe. In Triq Santa Skolastika the convent of the Benedictine nuns occupies the **first Hospital of the Knights**. Their church dedicated to **Santa Skolastika** (No. 12), has an altarpiece by Mattia Preti.

Entering **Misrah ir-Rebha** (Victory Square) (No. 13), you are faced with two statues. The green-toned one is known as the *Victory Monument* and was erected in 1705 to commemorate the Turks' defeat in the Great Siege. (Look at the railings which depict a sword and cross pinning down the Turkish crescent.) The white statue is of *St Lawrence*, Vittoriosa's patron saint, whose feast day is celebrated on 10 August with fireworks and marching bands. It was erected in 1880. Also on the *pjazza*, with an attractive wooden balcony, is the decorative premises of the San Lawrenz Band Club.

From the *pjazza*, Triq San Filippu leads to the church of **St Philip** (No. 14) built in 1651, enlarged with embellishments in 1779, damaged in 1940 and restored in 1949. But instead, cut down the narrow church close to Triq San Lawrenz running to the waterfront and the magnificent parish **Collegiate Church of St Lawrence** (No. 15).

### The Church of St Lawrence (San Lawrenz)

This was the original conventual church of the Order of St John (from 1530 to 1571) and contains many relics. It is believed to have been built to replace a smaller church erected here when Mdina and Birgu were the Islands' two parishes.

It was in San Lawrenz that Grand Master de la Valette heard Mass with the assembled Knights and residents of Birgu on 17 May 1565, the eve of the Great Siege, and where they gathered again, tattered but unbowed, to give thanks and celebrate the lifting of the siege on 8 September. Pope John Paul II gave thanks here too in 1990 when he visited to celebrate the church's 900th anniversary.

The church was rebuilt around 1680 by Lorenzo Gafa (1630–1710), leader of the Maltese Baroque architects, whose other notable works are the cathedrals of Mdina and Victoria as well as the parish churches of Siġġiewi and Żejtun. The towers are later additions (one in the 18C, the other in the 1930s). Gafa's signature dome was demolished in 1942 but, like much of the façade that was ruined in the raids, has been sympathetically rebuilt. It remains a stirring church in a picturesque corner.

The church's treasury contains relics brought from Rhodes including a silver processional cross used in the Crusades and carried round the streets during the *festa* celebrations on 10 August.

In the three tiny squares outside the north door is the 18C **Oratory of**

**St Joseph**, now a charming museum with both military and ecclesiastical items. The most cherished perhaps are the hat and sword worn by Grand Master Jean Parisot de la Valette during the victory ceremonies in 1565. Among the relics and books is a Latin bible printed in Venice in 1598 and used by the Inquisitors, and a pack of cards that were in play in 1609. During the Great Siege this area was the garrison burial ground.

Outside the church, through the arch alongside the Freedom Monument, is the entrance to the proposed Cottonera Marina and Fort St Angelo. The wharf has the remains of a number of buildings built by the Order of St John and later used by the British forces. Among the old buildings awaiting restoration are the Palace of the Captain of the Galleys and the House of the General of the Galleys. They are focal points of the new yacht marina development taking place.

On the wharf is the site of the **Naval Bakery** which was reconstructed by the British forces to its present form from an earlier Knights' building.

## The Maritime Museum

- **Open** 1 Oct–15 June, Mon–Sat 08.15–17.00, Sun 08.15–16.15; 16 June–30 Sept, daily 07.45–14.00. Entrance fee.

In 1841 William Scamp, the British Admiralty's architect, designed and built the Navy's bakery on the site of the Knights' arsenal (1578) and it continued to supply bread to the Mediterranean fleet for more than 100 years. It closed following the shrinking needs of the British fleet and lay empty until 1992 when it was decided to turn the building into a maritime museum.

As a museum it is seriously underfunded and relies on bequests to increase the numbers of items and objects on display. But it is a charming museum none the less: the building is fascinating and its exhibits are equally interesting and elegantly presented.

A narrow entrance decorated with simple line drawings of the ships of the Order of St John leads to a staircase and the first floor. Here paintings, models, instruments and diverse objects take you through maritime history as it affected the Maltese Islands.

There are Roman anchors found in Maltese waters, as well as outstanding displays that include uniforms, navigational books and instruments throughout the ages, selections of brass and copper weights and measures used over the centuries, cannons, and even oddities like fenders wrought from woven cane. Among the ship models are the ceremonial barge of Grand Master Adrien de Wignacourt, an impressive 2.5m model of one of the Order's 18C ships-of-the-line, and one of a lateen-rigged ferry that plied between Malta and Gozo. A fine painting shows the galleys of the Order in 1644 off Alexandria in mortal engagement with ships of the Ottoman fleet.

## Fort St Angelo

Across the narrow bridge further along the wharf is the entrance to Fort St Angelo.

The history of Fort St Angelo is as old and glorious as that of Malta and Gozo and as such it is regarded as a symbolic reminder of the Islands' past.

In 1999, after much acrimony, the upper part including the Magisterial Palace and Chapel of St Anne, was given to the Sovereign Military Hospitaller Order of St John (see p 59) on a 99-year lease to use as a base from which to carry out charitable works. The Order had wanted to return to Malta from its base in Rome on a permanent basis, and asked for Fort St Angelo by rights. In spite of some subtle courtship, to safeguard the national heritage, St Angelo was awarded to it only on lease. (A favourable one, as it happens. The lease declares the property extraterritorial and therefore not subject to Maltese taxation or laws.) This gave the Order the foothold it sought in addition to its presence in St John's Cavalier, Valletta.

At present most of the important upper part of Fort St Angelo is officially closed to visitors but the Sovereign Military Order of St John has promised to open it on certain days when restoration work is completed. The rest of the fort is still worth seeing.

Fort St Angelo is one of Malta's most interesting sites, both historically and architecturally. Under British rule as a naval headquarters it was maintained in excellent condition, but then until the arrival of the Order to take over the most important sections, it lay neglected, desperately awaiting restoration.

• **Open** June–Sept, Sat 10.00–13.00; Oct–May, Sat 10.00–14.00. Entrance ticket also covers Fort St Elmo.

## History of Fort St Angelo

In Phoenician times a temple is believed to have stood on this site until the Romans replaced it with one honouring their goddess Juno. When the Aghlabid Arabs took over around 870 they saw the position's strategic advantages and established its first fortress. When the Normans arrived to take the Islands in the name of Christianity in 1090, they further strengthened the walls to form a citadel. At its centre a small chapel was dedicated to the Blessed Virgin.

By 1430 the plateau had developed to such an extent that within the walls there was a thriving community, and a rich family called De Nava who owned it built themselves a grand house and a small chapel dedicated to St Anne. Both still exist.

When the Order arrived, Grand Master De L'Isle Adam took over the De Nava house and set about converting the citadel into a fortress. The walls were strengthened and a moat was dug to separate St Angelo from Birgu. The De Nava home became the Magisterial Palace and the Chapel of St Anne was given new life.

During the Great Siege, St Angelo was the pivot around which battles were fought, and after the fall of St Elmo it bore the brunt of the Turkish attack. It was from here that Grand Master La Valette waged his campaign with such brilliant success. His force consisted of 600 Knights and a few thousand men-at-arms.

Four of the 16C Grand Masters were originally buried in the crypt of St Anne before being interred in the crypt of St John's Co-Cathedral, Valletta: Villiers de L'Isle Adam, Del Ponte, De Homedes and De la Sengle. Grand Master La Valette died aged 75 at prayer in the chapel in August 1568 after a good day's boar hunting in Buskett, but he was buried in Valletta.

The Grand Master's office and residence moved to Valletta in 1571 and St Angelo became a fearsome prison. One especially terrifying punishment was the *Oubliette*, a hollowed-out pit dug 4m deep in the rock. Knights and other miscreants were imprisoned here in the dark, airless tomb without a time limit until they were either expelled from the Order or executed.

In 1581, Grand Master Jean l'Evêque de la Cassière was among St Angelo's unwilling guests. But he lived there in some comfort.

A monastic knight, De la Cassière was known both for his fearlessness and bravery and his deep religious conviction. But he was already in his seventies when elected Grand Master in 1572 and his zealous devotion to his vows led him into confrontation with his Knights, who he knew were taking their vows lightly and paying only scant attention to the rules of the Order. They spent their evenings carousing and gambling rather than in contemplation. He tried to stop the womanising and gambling but met with little success, so sought help from the pontiff in Rome. In response, in 1574 Pope Gregory XIII despatched the Inquisitor. If the Grand Master could not control the Knights, the Inquisitor would.

By 1581, exhausted by the righteousness of the old, deaf Grand Master, the Knights rebelled and in their coup escorted him to Fort St Angelo, placing him under what in today's terms would be considered house arrest. For comfort and companionship he was permitted to take with him an entourage of four Knights, four priests and more than 20 servants.

When Pope Gregory discovered what had happened, he summoned the Grand Master and the leaders of the coup to Rome where he instantly found the Grand Master innocent of all the charges laid before him. However, before De la Cassière could resume his office, the old Knight died and it was his body in a coffin that returned to Malta. He was buried in St John's Co-Cathedral (which he had financed), but without his heart. That was interred in Rome.

The fort continued to undergo changes over the years but the defence works created by military engineer Don Carlos de Gruenenberg in 1689 gave it the outline we see today.

Under British rule Fort St Angelo became the headquarters of the commandant of the garrison until the Admiralty took it over in 1906, and it became a naval barracks known as HMS *Egmont*. In 1933, as headquarters of the Commander-in-Chief Mediterranean Fleet, it was renamed HMS *St Angelo*, and in 1935 the Chapel of St Anne, which had been used as a store since 1798, was rededicated as the ship's chapel. Further buildings were erected to house the extensive naval station and submarine base. The slaves' quarters that were tunnels in the rock were enlarged and used as munitions magazines. Fort St Angelo took 69 direct hits from enemy aircraft during World War Two.

# Kalkara

**Kalkara Creek** on the eastern side of Fort St Angelo is a small, pretty harbour where many traditional boats are repaired or wintered. It has all the potential for making an excellent yacht marina.

There is a small village and occasionally craftsmen are found on the slipway building the traditional Maltese fishing boat, the *luzzu*, or the water-taxi that used to ferry passengers across Marsamxett and the Grand Harbour, the *dghajsa*. With the disappearance of the British Navy and the creation of quays where cruise ships could berth rather than sit at anchor in the harbour, the *dghajsa* sadly lost its role. Being rowed across the harbour in a *dghajsa* was considered an excellent way to get to or from Valletta.

Overlooking Kalkara Creek is **Bighi**, a large patrician villa with extensive grounds that was developed by Britain in the 19C into an impressively large hospital run by the Royal Navy. It closed with the departure of British forces and was converted into government housing and a school.

Villa Bighi was originally built in 1650 as the summer residence for the Order's Prior, Fra Giovanni Bighi. He died of the plague in 1676 and the villa stood abandoned until the plague struck again in 1813 when it became a fever hospital. Then, in 1830, the construction of the naval hospital alongside the villa was begun. It cost £20,000 and took two years to complete. When redevelopment plans are completed the villa and hospital will be the Malta Council of Science and Technology, a Restoration Laboratory and a new Museum of Science and Technology. The Restoration Laboratory is being established by the *Istituto Centrale di Restauro* in Italy where Maltese students currently study restoration.

Beyond, alongside the breakwater, is **Fort Ricasoli,** built in 1670 to face Fort St Elmo and guard the entrance to the Grand Harbour. In the days of the Knights 2000 soldiers lived within its walls. Like every strategic position around the harbour it was damaged during World War Two and since the departure of the British Navy has lain idle except for a small facility cleansing the holds of oil tankers. The fort has also been used as a film set.

Follow the coastline and you come to Fort Rinella.

## Fort Rinella

• **Open** Oct–June, 10.00–16.00; July–Sept 09.30–13.00. Entrance free; donations appreciated. Bus 4 or 627, then a short walk.

The fort is a 19C coastal battery built by the British Royal Engineers between 1878 and 1886 with, as its main armament, a single 100-ton gun that was so huge no other fort in Malta could take it. In fact Fort Rinella was built to accommodate it.

Designed and built by Sir William Armstrong in Newcastle, England, the gun was the largest, rifled, muzzle-loading gun ever produced. It had an overall weight of 152 tons with a barrel measuring 32 feet. It could fire a one-ton shell more than three miles to pierce ship's armour up to 21 inches thick. It was in service until 1906 when 100-ton guns were taken out of service.

The fort is managed by *Fondazzjoni Wirt Artna*, the national heritage foundation that also restored it. On a number of days each month there are historical re-enactments conjuring up the times of Queen Victoria when the fort was fully manned.

Of unusual interest too are the unique open-air **Mediterranean Film Studios** at Rinella (reached by bus 4 or 627) where many sea or water-action scenes have been shot for major international movies. In the height of summer it is not unusual from the elevated ground outside to see enemy submarines, tall icebergs or pirate galleons floating on its enormous outdoor pools ready for action.

The studios have two superb water tanks overlooking the sea, both positioned in such a way as to give the cameras the natural sky as their backdrop. One tank is for deep-water photography where scenes can be shot under water in controlled conditions.

Also part of the Studios is the **Rinella Movie Theme Park**, a small amusement park complex designed for children. A favourite attraction is walking through a corridor on board the *Titanic* as it sinks.

# Żabbar

- **Getting there** Buses18, 19, 20, 21, 22.

Outside the bastion walls that surround the Three Cities is Żabbar, a sprawling town which grew in the 17C as the danger of corsair raids from the south began to recede. It was in the fields here that the Ottoman force was established during the siege confining the Knights to Vittoriosa and Senglea.

It is not a particularly attractive town although it does have a number of elegant 19C houses. Marking its entrance on the road from Fgura is the ceremonial **Hompesch Arch** erected to commemorate the day Grand Master Ferdinand von Hompesch agreed to elevate the village's status to that of a town. For a while it was known as *Città Hompesch*. At the centre is the wonderfully florid parish church, the **Sanctuary of Our Lady of Graces**, known to all as *tal-Grazzja*.

Until 1616 a chapel dedicated to St Jacob acted as the religious focus, but when Żabbar was elevated to parish status *tal-Grazzja* was chosen as parish church because it had already become a destination for pilgrims asking for intercession from Our Lady, especially those seeking help for their children. The church was designed by Tommaso Dingli and the first stone laid on 10 May 1641 with construction finally completed in 1696. The gilding and ornamentation took another 59 years and were not finished until 1737.

Then the church underwent much change as improvements to match the parish taste were carried out. The bell-towers, for example, were added between 1738 and 1742. Side aisles were added later and so was a new façade. Even the dome we see today is not as Dingli had imagined it; it was erected in 1928 to replace one that fell into ruin.

But while purists disagree, visitors are impressed by the church's exuberance. The interior does not disappoint either, because it too is a vision of opulence, especially during the *festa* on the first weekend after 8 September, when all manner of silver, decoration, hangings and flowers festoon the church. The titular painting is the work of Maltese artist Alessio Erardi in 1715 with Our Lady's (genuine, solid) gold crown inset into the picture in 1952. The statue of the saint, which has been venerated since 1797, is the work of Mariano Gerada and has been paraded through the streets during the *festa* since then.

---

### Two 'miracles'

According to church lore, the tiny Żabbar sanctuary played an important role in the Great Siege. A white dove, the spirit of Mary, was seen hovering over the chapel before it took off to fly over Vittoriosa, appearing to the people of that town and filling them with faith and courage. And there's more. On 14 October 1975 at 13.10 hours, a Royal Air Force Vulcan bomber exploded over the centre of Żabbar showering fuel and debris onto the main road, Sanctuary Street. Houses and cars burned but only one resident was killed (though three members of the crew died in the aerial explosion and several pedestrians were burned). The unfortunate woman killed on the ground was struck by a live electric cable that had been severed in the blast. That more were not killed is regarded as a miracle.

The church remains a place of pilgrimage. On the first Sunday in Lent faithful from all over the island gather for *Ħadd in-Nies* (People's Sunday) and a blessing. In a custom started in 1951, on the eve of the patron saint's feast day cyclists and motorcyclists ride in pilgrimage for Apostolic Benediction. They come in two groups, one from Rabat, the other from Mosta, passing through as many villages and towns as possible en route, horns blowing, bells ringing.

Of considerable charm is the small **Sanctuary Museum** alongside the church (open on Sunday mornings and by arrangement with the parish priest). Among its relics and traces of the Order of St John, the museum has a delightful collection of ex-voto paintings featuring miraculous escapes from rough seas or pirates achieved by invoking the help of Our Lady of Graces.

# Marsascala

• **Getting there**  Buses 19, 20, 22.

Until the 1930s Marsascala on the coast outside Żabbar was simply an attractive bay used by fishermen, with just a small number of holiday homes used in the summer by residents of the Three Cities. Their facilities were basic, but so was the village.

Today, pretty and small though it remains, there are a number of good restaurants (fresh fish and pasta the specialities) and cafés for the crowds to pour into after they stroll the promenade.

Marsascala has become a holiday venue in its own right but it is still simple, with one 4-star hotel and a selection of 2-star hotels and guesthouses and a lazy way of life. Swimming is from Marsascala's natural rocky coastline or, a short walk away, from cream-coloured rocks in picturesque **St Thomas' Bay**.

In the winter months, with most visitors gone, Marsascala seems to doze. Only cafés facing the sun and a cinema complex gather patrons. The fish restaurants do well too (see *Where to eat*, p 25).

In was in this bay in 1614 that a small Turkish force came ashore in what appeared to be another invasion. Numbers vary, but some reports estimated a force with as many men as 50,000. They were defeated by the Order when they reached Żejtun. To prevent this occurring again, in 1615 **Fort St Thomas** was erected on the headland of the bay to watch for seaborne approaches. (It is close to the *Corinthia Jerma* hotel and masked by modern building.) During World War Two the fort was where British soldiers were sent when on detention.

Marsascala also has the unique **Mamo Tower** built privately in the 17C in the shape of a St Andrew's Cross with a central room. When the dry moat was cut the builders discovered a Punic tomb of the 3C BC.

Although the Knights gave considerable attention to this bay, a more modern defensive system was called for during the British period, and in 1886 Żonqor Battery, above Marsascala on the Żabbar Road, was built to provide covering artillery fire. There is, surprisingly, no record of its being armed at that time. Perhaps British attention was concentrated on Marsaxlokk Bay and Marsaxlokk (see p 184).

On many signposts Marsascala is written as M'scala.

# Going west

Although the western coastline of the island is edged with sheer and spectacular cliffs that offer little more than wonderful views, energising springtime walks or leisurely drives, three of the island's four sand beaches are here too, all close to each other. Because of its rough terrain, and because development has been contained within the flatter, eastern side of Malta around St Julians and Buġibba, this region is relatively unspoiled, creating a sense of being the 'real' Malta.

## To the beaches

Ghadira in Mellieħa Bay may be Malta's largest sandy beach catering for everyone's needs (see p 149), but the picturesque settings of Golden Bay and, in particular, Ghajn Tuffieħa make these beaches much more attractive. The fact that Ghajn Tuffieħa is marginally less accessible than its neighbour adds further to its exclusivity and charm.

To get to them, the easy route is the 6km of road from St Paul's Bay through the long, flat, ever-fertile **Pwalles Valley** where toiling farmers keep the fields so well irrigated that they produce rich crops throughout the year. Not worth a detour, unless you are deeply concerned about modern architecture, is the hamlet of **Manikata** on the far ridge(reached by bus 47). The pink-washed, flat-topped and boldly modern parish church of **San Guzep** (St Joseph) so visible from the road below is the work of Richard England, an eminent, internationally respected Maltese architect (in spite of his name). His work has an uncompromising hard edge, given to abundant use of concrete and patches of bright colour. Paid for by village subscription, Manikata's church is an excellent example of his style.

You can approach the beaches from Mosta too, on a scenic route passing through rugged countryside to the hamlet of Żebbieħ. Here, barely visible signposts direct you left to Mġarr, and, right, to Ghajn Tuffieħa and Golden Bay by way of the Roman Baths.

### Żebbieħ

The village of Żebbieħ is an odd, faceless cluster of modern houses on the road in front of a yet-to-be-completed modern parish church (money is in short supply). However, if archaeology is your passion, look for a tiny sign on the corner wall of a house facing the open space in front of the church. It points to the **Skorba temples** that, together with Ġgantija in Gozo, are considered to be the oldest free-standing structures in the world.

For the uninitiated there is not much to see but archaeologist David Trump, who has spent many years in Malta and Gozo studying, excavating and carbon dating the more important sites, believes Skorba was a **prehistoric village** with a small community husbanding livestock and crops. The site was excavated between 1961 and 1963 and evidence suggests there were two hut settlements here, the newer built on top of the older; the first community used grey pottery, the second red. The settlements were sacked or decayed before being used as a

Copper Age burial ground. Carbon dating places them at around 3600 BC. The scanty remains of the temple show that it was in the trefoil style as at Tarxien.

To gain access, try Mġarr police station for the key, or apply to the Museum of Archaeology, Valletta.

### The Roman Baths

- **Open** Most days except public holidays, 10.30–16.30. To ensure the gates are open, call the (unpaid) custodian of the keys, Karmen ☎ 576127. She will let you in. Admission is free but it is customary to tip 10 cents or more per person.

About 3km out of Żebbieħ as you head towards the beaches, the Roman Baths are in the dip of the valley, poorly signposted and easy to miss. They were excavated in 1929 and restored in 1961 with a grant from UNESCO, but are now sorely in need of sponsorship to make more of their abandoned site and protect from the elements what little remains, including some interesting geometric mosaic.

There is not much to see in this open-air setting in terms of splendour, but the baths and their communal lavatory do indicate how sophisticated the Romans were, and how focal baths were to social mores. In Roman times these baths would have been generously supplied with water and considered luxuriously appointed in their pastoral setting. They had a changing room, a large horse-shoe-shaped communal lavatory capable of seating nine at a time in open plan, a steam room heated by a furnace (like a sauna), a heated pool and a swimming pool. What is remarkable is the way the plumbing worked. The lavatories, for example, were seated over a duct of constant running water to flush them continuously, while another duct provided running water for bodily cleanliness.

Proceed down the hill to the junction planted with oleander trees. The western bays are to the left (for St Paul's Bay go right).

# The western bays

### Għajn Tuffieħa and Golden Bay

- **Getting there** Bus 47 51 52 652.

**Għajn Tuffieħa**, (pronounced: *eye-n toof ee har*) is the first bay you come to on this headland. It is more dramatically attractive than Golden Bay and many would consider its setting stunning, so do not be put off by the derelict concrete hotel perched on the rim or the ragged car park (tip: 20 cents but only to the attendant wearing a battered official cap). This bay is spectacular.

Getting onto the sands is either down a seemingly endless set of steps or a rough track. Either way, coming back up again is no easy task in the heat of the day.

Depending on government permits, sometimes there is a small café; sometimes in a good year the proprietor may have umbrellas and pedalos too. Most people take a picnic. It is a beach children love, but watch for submerged rocks below the waterline; rough winter seas move both the sand and the boulders.

The slopes of the bay are covered in puny tamarisks struggling to survive drought and the damage caused by family barbecues, but as barbecues and tented camps are now banned, the hillside should recover. A charitable foundation is attempting to replant the slopes with indigenous plants in order to restore their beauty and control erosion. In wet months the clay surfaces often give way in mini-landslides.

At the far side of the bay there is a sheltered cove favoured by naturists, while a grey clay slope cuts Ghajn Tuffieha's bay off from a smaller beach on the other side and a flat white rock beloved of male naturists, who are sometimes joined by a few topless tourists finding themselves there by mistake. (It is important to remember: topless and nude bathing is not permitted by law.) The climb down this clay wall to the far side can be treacherous: in summer it dries out causing many an accident, and in winter—when the slope is a favourite walk even though it can turn slippery and muddy—it is not unknown for a helicopter rescue to be mounted by the Armed Forces of Malta for a hiker with a broken leg.

• By the car park at the tip of the headland that separates the two bays is **Lascaris watchtower** built by the Knights. If the **red flag** is flying from its mast, swimmers should keep close to the shoreline. On these rare occasions a dangerous undertow further out can exhaust even the fittest swimmer.

**Golden Bay**, or Ramla tal-Mixquqa as survey maps identify it, was known in British times as Military Bay, and the **Hal Ferh Tourist Village** alongside it today was the Army Rest Camp where families would take holidays. (Hal Ferh has riding stables ☎ 573882.) The hillside is dotted with pleasant stone buildings that formed the residential quarters of this military base and there are some remains of the navy's firing range. During World War Two, Royal Navy canoeists trained in the bay ready for the invasion of Sicily. Plans are in hand to make some of this land suitable for tents and scout camps.

The bay is dominated by the *Golden Sands Hotel* designed by architect Dom Mintoff in his professional role before becoming prime minister and thorn in the side of the British.

The beach is easy to get to. There is a bus terminus and car park at the top of the hill and yet more parking on the hill down to the beach. The sand is well kept and there are facilities for renting pedalos, canoes and, regrettably, jet skis that disturb the peace of this tranquil setting. Children can have fun on banana rides visiting neighbouring bays. The café copes well with demand.

## Mġarr

• **Getting there** Bus 47.

From Żebbieh the road going due west heads into the quiet, rural village of Mġarr (pronounced: *im jar*). Hidden behind houses opposite the government school is the site of **Ta'Ħaġrat** with its cluttered patch of stones said to be a temple. The site is fenced off, but should you want to visit, the keys are at the police station on the square by Mġarr's imposing parish church.

Dedicated to **Santa Maria**, the tall church has the pleasantly naive appearance of a village church emulating one in town. Its small dome perched high above the edifice has led to its being unkindly compared to an egg in an eggcup. As in most rural communities, the church was built by donations from the indigent parishioners who, in this instance in the 1930s, had so little money that they would bring produce from their fields for the parish priest to sell on the open market in order to set up a building fund. Their *festa* on 15 August draws crowds from neighbouring rural communities, who arrive in battered Land Rovers, 1960s Austins and racy new Japanese cars.

Alongside the church are two village bars known for their ways with *fenek*, rabbit—Malta's favourite food. At weekends *Charles il-Barri* and *Sunny Bar* are crowded. Diners who come from all points on the island are a mixture of families with babies in prams and stag parties, gathering for a *fenkata* where everyone has spaghetti with rabbit sauce followed by fried rabbit with chips or rabbit stew. Lots of village red wine is drunk too, usually mixed with Seven Up to ease its flow. It's a Maltese tradition.

Behind the church the road leads to Gnejna passing **Palazzo Zammitello**, a 19th-century patrician weekend home done up like a castle but now turned into a wedding hall.

Down a very steep winding road and through arable fields mostly planted with vines is the west's third beach.

## Ġnejna

- **Getting there**  Bus 47 to Mġarr then an arduous 4km walk.

Ġnejna's beach is less popular than its neighbours. This is possibly because the road used to be impassable but more likely because it is smaller and has coarser sand. Edging the shoreline heading out to sea on one side is a seedy but picturesque clutter of tumbledown, tiered boathouses used as weekend retreats, and further around the point for the adventurous there are some pleasant spots for swimming. Bird trappers have made this wild landscape their own.

In Ġnejna beach's favour is the fact that it is never very crowded, not even in the peak holiday months. Its facilities are good, and the kiosk on the beach offers a good line in cold drinks and fry-ups while the neighbouring shack has umbrellas, beach beds and a variety of boats for hire. As public conveniences go, the facility by the car park (where it is customary to tip the car park attendant 25 cents or more on arrival) should get an award for its cleanliness.

Overlooking the bay is **Lippia Tower**, one of four watchtowers built in 1637 by the French Grand Master Jean Paul de Lascaris Castellar. In 1565 the Turkish fleet took on water here while waiting for a favourable wind to take them on to Marsaxlokk Bay to disembark the land force that would set the Great Siege in motion.

## Mġarr to Rabat

Outside Mġarr where the hill begins its descent into Ġnejna's valley, a minor road leads to Rabat through winding lanes and the cluster of houses at L'Iscorvit. A narrow turning goes to the cliff edge at **Fomm ir-Riħ** where there is a fiercely dramatic bay and rock-strewn shore. Although a house has been erected with garden gates over the pathway intending to bar anyone from reaching the beach, it is still possible to do so using rougher tracks. (There are no private beaches in Malta and although beach establishments are licensed along the foreshore, in common with many countries all land bordering the sea in Malta and Gozo is considered public property. Access here, therefore, is 'difficult'.)

The road to Rabat is interesting especially if you are looking for stunning walks and exploring. It leads across the Victoria Lines (see p 143) where Fort Binġemma was built to match the forts of Mosta and Madliena, and where there are Cart Ruts (see p 54), empty Punic tombs, and squatters who have made old army buildings into their weekend retreats. At the top of the hill, turn right to **Kunċizjoni** if you want the finest views looking back over Fomm ir-Riħ. This is a particular favourite for Malta's Sunday afternoon drivers.

Further on is a string of houses called **Baħrija** where stalls are sometimes set out on Sunday mornings selling poultry and you can chance your luck for a few cents on simple funfair games.

The signs still say Rabat when you come to a slim bridge. Right leads to the strangely mysterious and abundantly fertile valley of **Mtaħleb** overlooking the sea and fed by a number of springs. Simple signs read *Keep Out*; this farming-community reveres its privacy but you can still venture in. Nowhere else in Malta ever looks so richly fertile.

To your left a short distance further on is the road to Ghemieri with Ghemieri Palace, a private residence, and signs now also direct you to **Chadwick Lakes**, a stretch of valley that has been given a series of shallow dams to catch the winter's rainfall in a series of small pools. When the water dries out, the bed is covered in today's detritus, including plastic bottles and the occasional refrigerator.

As the road rises you reach Rabat and you are not far from Dingli Cliffs (see p 132) with Malta's highest point.

# The southwest

Dingli Cliffs signal the start of this section of rugged coastline. A walker's delight, it is an interesting area to explore especially if you venture down the cliffs—where there are obvious tracks. There are no beaches, just sheer drops into inky blue and deep sea. There are also cave dwellings, traces of ancient settlement and underground chapels. The largest village is Siġġiewi.

## *Siġġiewi*

• **Getting there** Bus 89.

The village is reached either from Rabat or, on better roads, from Żebbuġ. It is the major village in the southwest and is sprawlingly attractive with a delightful Baroque church. Smart young families with babies are moving here, so real estate prices are steadily rising.

Siġġiewi is an agricultural centre with 6000 inhabitants amid fertile fields and with a parish church of great distinction. Designed by Lorenzo Gafa and erected between 1675 and 1693, **St Nicholas** is perhaps the most spectacularly classical Baroque church on the Islands. It is not all Gafa's work; its arcaded west-facing portico was added in 1864, when the dome was being proudly elevated on a high drum between the two bell towers to impress and awe visitors to the village and to allow a flood of light to illuminate the interior. Lavishing his praise on its exterior, Quentin Hughes, Professor of Architecture at the University of Malta wrote: 'The treatment of the façade is truly dynamic. Like a ship in full sail, thrusting its bow forward, it is set trailing its two campanile in the wash.'

Among the splendid decorations inside is an altarpiece of *St Nicholas* said to be the unfinished last work of Mattia Preti.

About 2.5km out of the village travelling west the road suddenly widens and loses its potholes. This is **Girgenti** with the **Inquisitor's Summer Palace**, a beautiful house on a narrow ridge to the side of the hill. It was built after 1625 by the Inquisitor, Horatus Visconti, as his summer residence. The elegant building is only one room deep, with all seven rooms interconnecting. Near the gate is the small family chapel of St Charles Borromeo (added in 1760).

For many years the palace lay abandoned and open to vandals. It has now been restored and is used by the prime minister as a summer residence, hence the strip of excellent tarmac outside. Regrettably it is not open to visitors. Beneath its formal terrace are deep caves where the Inquisitor's staff are said to have lived, now a favourite spot for potholers.

Road signs now point to Għar Lapsi, and visible from almost any point is the hill of **Tas-Salib** (meaning 'Of the Cross') with **Laferla Cross** making its Christian statement. Should you make the climb so beloved of pilgrims to its base, there are good views of the surrounding countryside.

A turning goes to **Fawwara**, a charming spot perched below the cliffs, between the cross and the sea, with the Annunciation Chapel on the road and an underground chapel cut into the rocks. It is a wonderful place for walks—if bird shooters and trappers are not in residence.

The Għar Lapsi road passes through **Tal-Providenza** where there is a large charity-supported residential home run by the Church for the handicapped, and takes a scenic, winding trail down to an inlet on the shore. The constant rumbling, rushing noise you hear is a reverse osmosis desalination plant turning the salty Med into drinking water. Its gush of water shooting back into the sea contains all the salt.

## Għar Lapsi

- **Getting there**  Bus 94.

Its name, pronounced *arr-lapsy*, translates as Cave of the Ascension and refers to a tiny sheltered cove that has been used for centuries by handfuls of fishermen. There are fewer today than there were, but numbers are made up by sub-aqua fans who come to brave this coast's dark, forbidding but clear, deep sea where 'Big White' fish are sometimes sighted. A narrow stretch of rock passes for a small beach and there is ample car parking space outside *Rita*'s modest roadside restaurant famed for fish soup and fish and chips served at very modest prices. Għar Lapsi is popular on Sundays for hikers and picnickers.

# Travelling south

The south of the island, that is the true south rather than the area often referred to as south around Żabbar and Marsascala, was largely ignored in the development years of the 1960s and 1970s and only now is it receiving the kind of attention it deserves. There are industrial estates to bring employment, the Malta Freeport (see p 78) to add to the economy by flourishing as a transshipment port for bulk goods arriving from far distant countries, and—to give this starkly beautiful region something more environmentally friendly—a nature reserve is designated for a wild tract of unspoiled land alongside pretty bays where the sea is deep and clear and pleasure craft gather at weekends.

All roads heading south bypass the town of **Marsa** and the Marsa Sports Ground where athletics events take place and where the *Marsa Sports Club* offers tennis, golf, squash and polo (temporary members welcome). The island's only racecourse is here; it comes to life on Sunday afternoons in the cooler months with some of the finest-looking Arab horses ever seen taking part in the programme of trotting races. Although there are official booths to back your fancies, it is said that serious amounts of money (even apartment blocks) change hands in private bets.

By the nearby industrial estate you catch a glimpse of the onion-topped columns of the Turkish Cemetery which has, somewhat surprisingly, the Jewish Cemetery concealed at its rear. Where the road forks to Paola (left) and Tarxien (straight on), on the hillside to your right is **Santa Maria Addolorata Cemetery**, the Islands' largest Christian (but mostly Catholic) cemetery. Dominating the dramatic burial ground with its family mausoleums, simple tombs and florid statuary, is Addolorata's attractive Victorian Gothic chapel where funeral Mass is said *praesente cadavere* (the deceased being present in a coffin).

These cemeteries and Ta'Braxxia Anglican Cemetery at Pietà were designed by Emanuele Luigi Galizia (1830–1906) who was superintendent of public works between 1880 and 1888. His other claims to fame are Our Lady of Lourdes church in Mġarr, Gozo, and his own Moorish-style house called 'Alhambra' in Rudolph Street, Sliema. Alhambra has a conservation order placed on it to prevent it being demolished and developed into an apartment block. It also contains frescoes by Guzè Cali.

## Paola and Tarxien

- **Getting there** Buses 1, 2, 3, 4, 18, 19, 27, 427, 627 go to Paola. Buses 8, 11, 27, 29, 30, 427, 627 serve Tarxien.

The road to Paola rises to a roundabout with a mosque to the right (funded by Colonel Ghadafi and the Libyan Jamahirija), and as you turn into the town, you follow the walls of Corradino Correctional Facility (i.e. Malta's prison), home to a select crowd. *Rahal i-Ġdid* (New Town) as the Maltese know Paola, was 'new' in the 17C, but the name has stuck. It was founded in 1626 by Grand Master Antoine de Paule to house the over-crowded population of the Three Cities, but because it was outside the cities' fortifications few families made the move until much later.

At its centre is the imposing though unattractive church of **Kristu Re** begun in 1924 to the designs of Giuseppe Damato who went on impressively to design Xewkija's domed church in Gozo (see p 207). Apart from its selection of tiny silver-domed side chapels (seen best from the square at the rear), Kristu Re's exterior is dull. The much smaller original parish church of **Santa Ubaldesca** not far from the prison is marginally more interesting. It was begun in the year the town was established.

The only reason to visit Paola is an important one: to see the Hypogeum and the Tarxien Temples, two of the most important archaeological sites on the Maltese Islands, in the back streets where Paola appears to join Tarxien. (See also *Ancient Malta and The Neolithic Temples*.) There have been settlements around Tarxien since the days of the early temple-builders around 3000 BC.

The **Hal Saflieni Hypogeum** (to give it its full title) has its entrance just south of Paola Square, in Triq iċ-Ċimiterju (Cemetery Street). This subterranean site was essentially a vast burial ground although it was almost certainly also used for ceremonial events. The Hypogeum was closed for several years for major restoration and for the preservation work needed to combat the damage caused by the 'carbon dioxide emissions' generated by visitors. Now admittance to this UNESCO World Heritage Site is limited to groups of no more than ten at a time (booking essential, ☎ 825579).

The Hypogeum is often considered Malta's finest archaeological monument, and perhaps because it is underground, not only is it easy to comprehend, it is also fascinating.

The **Tarxien Temples** in Triq it-Templji Neolitiċi (Old Temples Street) are in the residential quarter behind Paola's parish church and are archaeologically impressive even though they are hemmed in by modern stone buildings. What you see is all that remains of a much larger settlement.

Excavated between 1914 and 1919, the four temples form the largest and most developed of the prehistoric sites on the Islands. Although perhaps without the immediate appeal of the temples of Haġar Qim outside Żurrieq or Ġgantija on Gozo, these are the temples to see if you care about archaeology. Some of their more important features have been removed to the Museum of Archaeology in Valletta and been replaced by replicas.

The village of **Tarxien** itself has a certain amount of old charm with houses that date back a number of centuries hidden in its narrow, twisting streets. At the centre is the 17C parish church of The Annunciation of Our Lady.

## Żejtun

- **Getting there** Buses 2,6 27, 29, 30.

The main road south to Marsaxlokk from Tarxien and Paola passes Bulebel Industrial Estate (left) and leads on to the small crossroads (again left) into Zejtun.

A picturesque old agricultural village, Żejtun was recognised as a parish before 1436 when it had a flourishing population. In May 1565, when the Ottoman Turkish force invaded, Grand Master la Valette ordered all the villagers and their livestock to be evacuated to Birgu (Vittoriosa) and it was here, in Żejtun, that the first cavalry skirmishes of the Great Siege took place. Two young Knights, one Portuguese and the other French, were captured and under torture before being put to death told lies about the position and strength of the defending force. Their lies led to the Turks making wrong strategic decisions as they waged war.

In 1614, long after the Great Siege, Żejtun was pillaged in a Turkish raid that the Knights believed presaged the return of the Ottoman force. This time, however, the Knights' cavalry quickly forced the Turks, who numbered more than 5000, to retreat to their ships waiting at Marsascala. It was the last time they would attack.

Dominating Żejtun is the stolidly impressive parish church dedicated to **St Catherine** begun in 1692 by Lorenzo Gafa, the noted Maltese Baroque architect responsible for the cathedrals in Mdina and Victoria, as well as the parish churches of Siġġiewi and Vittoriosa. It is an excellent example of his work with massive cornices and buttresses, single Doric and Ionic pilasters and two bell towers ornamented with Corinthian pilasters. The whole effect is topped off with an octagonal dome.

As impressive in its simple serenity is the old parish church of **San Girgor** (St Gregory), built in 1436 and rebuilt in 1492 with its charming low dome added a few years later. This dome is considered the earliest in Malta. (Open for Mass on Sat at 18.00; Sun at 07.30 and 11.00. For visits contact the parish priest ☎ 882050.)

When the Order of St John arrived in Malta they embellished many old churches, and to San Girgor they added the large but unfinished transept with corner pillars that detracts from the original simplicity. The façade was given a Renaissance portal in the mid-16C.

Two particular details add to the mysterious quality of the small church. The first is that the main door of the church is off-centre. This was done because the devil only walks in straight lines and therefore could not disturb a service if he happened to walk in. The second is that a small spiral staircase in the vestry leads to two narrow passages concealed in the church's thick walls. Only discovered in 1969, they contained the bones of nearly 80 people, assumed to be villagers, who hid here in a Turkish raid in 1547 and died in the hideout suffocated by the smoke caused when the interior of the church was set alight.

For many years the church was used as a store; during Britain's rule it became briefly a hospital and later, in World War Two, soldiers' quarters. When the Royal Engineers then used it as a store, they whitewashed over the precious frescoes.

Back on the main arterial road, you go through the ribbon development of houses and showrooms at Bir id-Deheb to a major junction. To the left is Marsaxlokk; straight on is Birżebbuġa and the Malta Freeport; right takes you to the village of Għaxaq. Head for Marsaxlokk (sometimes abbreviated on signposts to 'M'xlokk').

## *Marsaxlokk*

- **Buses** 27, 427, 627.

**Marsaxlokk Bay** is a deep, wide expanse that for many years slumbered, a bay where tankers and freighters waited until a berth was found for them in the more important Grand Harbour. But as the Islands developed in the 1980s, space had

*The waterfront at Marsaxlokk*

to be found for Malta's new, large electricity generating power station and for the new Freeport that would bring added prosperity to the nation. Marsaxlokk Bay was given the dubious honour of having both.

In spite of this visual scarring, because the bay is so large, **Marsaxlokk** itself has remained a picturesque village where fishermen repair their nets alongside the traditional fishing boats that still land their catches in this sheltered spot. It is the largest fishing village on the island.

On the waterfront there are countless cafés and restaurants (whose quality varies season to season) and an open-air market that caters for tourists during the week with handicrafts and lace tablecloths imported from the Far East, and for the locals on Sunday mornings when it turns itself into a fish and vegetable market. On *San Girgor*, the feast day of St Gregory on 7 April, crowds throng this waterfront in a giant day out. The road is closed to traffic, and for those not basking in the sun there is folk singing, tombola, a selection of funfair stalls, pony rides and trips on a traditionally painted *luzzu* or *frejgatina* fishing boat.

Marsaxlokk Bay has been involved in many historical events. The Turkish Admiral Piali before the Great Siege and Napoleon on his way to Egypt both disembarked their forces here, and it was also the venue chosen for The Malta Summit, the momentous meeting on board a naval ship in 1989 between US President George Bush and Soviet leader Mikhail Gorbachev destined to end the Cold War. That the meeting was a success says something for the stamina of the world leaders. That winter weekend the seas were whipped up in a fierce *grigal*, the violent seasonal storms that blow in from the northeast, and not one stretch of the bay saw calm waters.

## History of Marsaxlokk Bay

For most of the year the large crescent-shaped bay is sheltered and because its shoreline slopes gently to the water's edge, it makes an excellent landing for fishermen, traders and, of course, anyone planning to invade the island.

On 19 May 1565, Admiral Piali anchored his fleet of 181 galleys here, bringing with him 35,000 men from Mustapha Pasha's army on the first day of what would become the Great Siege. However, as his spies had warned him about the infamous winter *grigal* that could wreck ships, even though it was summer Piali moved his fleet into Marsamxett Harbour rather than anchor at sea to blockade the Grand Harbour. This meant that while the rest of his land force encircled Birgu (Vittoriosa), Mustapha Pasha would also have to take Fort St Elmo by land if he wanted to subdue the fort and take it out of commission. By 23 June when the fort did fall, the Turks had lost 8000 men.

In 1614 a smaller Turkish force of 60 ships returned but were frightened off by the guns of **Fort St Lucian** (established in the bay in 1610) and landed at Marsascala instead. On that occasion they advanced only as far as Żejtun before being forced to withdraw by a squadron of cavalry. Fort St Lucian is now the government-run marine biology station.

On 10 June 1798 it was one of five places Napoleon Bonaparte chose to disembark his force under cover of darkness ready to take Malta from the Order of St John. They landed unimpeded.

Months later, this was where Horatio Nelson's fleet took on supplies and carried out repairs while blockading the French force Napoleon had left behind in Valletta.

## Delimara

- **Getting there**  Bus to Marsaxlokk, then a long walk.

If you follow the easterly road out of Marsaxlokk to Delimara on the left of the bay, you come to the promontory that is home to the power station. At the junction at the top of the hill, behind plain stone walls facing the attractive complex that is a Carmelite monastery, is the protected site of **Tas Silġ**. Here between 1963 and 1972 Italian excavators painstakingly uncovered a Punico-Roman temple. Vases dedicated to the goddesses Tanit and Hera, and a Punic inscription to Astarte (Juno to the Romans) carved in stone, suggest that this is the celebrated **Temple of Juno** that the Roman orator Cicero recorded as plundered by Verres, the Roman governor of Sicily and Malta between 73 and 70 BC. The site has remained untouched since the excavation to give future generations the opportunity of uncovering history.

Follow the road to Delimara Point into the narrow twisting dip in the arable fields until you come to a fork where trees start. The left leads to **Island Bay** (or Xrobb il-Għaġin), a breathtakingly attractive bay. Follow the bumpy track and just past the tiny chapel of St Paul (there are Neolithic traces behind it) a small stretch of cream-coloured rock lies before you. It is reached by a perilous descent on the cliff edge but offers some excellent swimming—everyone likes to swim to the island—and in the height of summer smart boats anchor here. This side of the bay is protected terrain and the virgin ground will remain a natural, undeveloped area inhabited only by chameleons, snakes, rodents and migratory birds. During summer, seawater is dried out in shallow pans cut into the shoreline just outside the bay ready to be gathered as fresh sea salt. Across the sweep of the bay is a smaller inlet, il-Ħofra ż-Żghira, a miniature version of Island Bay.

What you may not notice as you drive through the trees before reaching the chapel is a narrow entrance and metal bridge crossing a dry moat that lead to **Tas Silġ Battery**, built by the British in the late 1880s. Turned to compassionate use, this is currently the *Island Sanctuary*, a home for unwanted dogs that survives on charity.

Back on the road by the clump of trees, the right fork heads past the towering chimney of the power station where, on the left, a small track leads to a car park (a farmer's field; tip 20 cents) and down to the shoreline to **Peter's Pool**, another excellent place to swim off cream-coloured rock. Further along the point, with its own car park, is the attractive bay of **Delimara** much favoured by families for swimming and picnicking. Lots of steps or a climb here too.

At the tip of the promontory is **Fort Delimara** built in 1881 (no admittance) and the south coast's lighthouse. It used to be an attractive spot but is changed since an ugly shanty town took root. It is also a spot favoured for *kaċċa* (see p 79) and the kind of *kaċċatur* who make visitors unwelcome.

To go in the opposite direction out of Marsaxlokk, follow the road out running alongside the open market. It leads past an inlet where boats are repaired and past Fort St Lucian and the Islands' gas cylinder supply depot to St George's Bay and Birżebbuġa.

In fact, to get to Birżebbuġa and the Freeport you do not need to take the scenic route via Marsaxlokk. You can go straight ahead at the Bir id-Deheb junction (see p 183) following the signs. In signwriters' shorthand, Birżebbuġa often appears on signs as 'B'buga'.

This road takes you along the valley of Wied Dalam with the fascinating caves of **Għar Dalam** (the Cave of Darkness) where bones of animals living on Malta during the Ice Age have been found.

## Għar Dalam

- **Open**  1 Oct–15 June, Mon–Sat 08.15–17.00, Sun 08.15–16.15; 16 June–30 Sept, daily 07.45–14.00. **Buses** 11, 12, 13.

The site was first studied in 1865, and although it became an air raid shelter in World War Two, it remained untouched until 7 April 1980 when, in the dark of night, irreplaceable relics were stolen in a burglary staged presumably to satisfy a private collector. Four tusks belonging to dwarf elephants and the skull of a Neolithic person, assumed to be a child, were among the haul.

### History of the cave

> The cave's history spans the Pleistocene era, the Ice Age, when the world was subjected to torrential rain and freezing temperatures. It was then that Malta's valleys were formed. At that time it is assumed the island was joined to Sicily, and as the ice melted and the world warmed up, animals travelled south only to find themselves trapped eventually on Malta, as the Mediterranean developed into an inland sea with the water pouring in from new rivers swollen by melted ice. There were elephants, hippopotamus, deer and bears, and as these creatures adapted to the cramped island space they evolved, becoming smaller and smaller, requiring less food and water in order to increase their chances of survival. Dwarf species developed.

The floor of the cave consisted of five layers. At the bottom was a metre of sterile clay with, above that, a metre of bones, tusks and teeth, mostly of dwarf elephants and hippopotamus. The remains go back more than 180,000 years when the animals began to become extinct. Above this was red earth nearly 2m deep in which were bones and antlers of deer, while the top layer had traces of human life in the Neolithic and Bronze Ages. It is thought the bones found their way into the caves because the valley overlooked by the Għar Dalam had a fast-moving river that washed the carcasses in.

Restored skeletons of animals of some of the species are on show in the **museum**, together with bones from some 7000 animals.

Across the valley are the remains of a Bronze Age village, **Borg in-Nadur**. Important though the site is as representative of a period that spanned 2500 to 700 BC, there is not much to see.

## Birżebbuġa to Għar Ħasan

Now you come to seedy **Birżebbuġa** with a distant skyline made of a forest of towering cranes that load and unload the giant container ships at Malta Freeport.

Once a fishing port, Birżebbuġa (served by buses 11, 12, 13) now has an air of having seen better days although it is apparently affluent and the local council is trying hard to restore colour and beauty. For example, **Pretty Bay** (almost a misnomer) is a wide expanse of cream sand at the centre of the town alongside the bus terminus. It is being carefully nurtured and cream-coloured sand is imported if the winter seas steal some. A handful of palm trees have been planted to give it glamour. The bay, however, is incongruous in this plain town. Even the modern parish church dedicated to Birżebbuġa's patron saint, St Peter in Chains, seems forlorn.

If you follow the road out of Birżebbuġa from the bus terminus, you come to the short stretch of **Kalafrana** waterfront (bus 12) where today the Malta Freeport (see p 78) proudly stands. Here between the two World Wars, the seaplanes of Imperial Airways would land their cosseted passengers as they pioneered routes around the world. Later it became the base of Britain's Royal Air Force, with four-engined Sunderland bombers and Swordfish seaplanes attempting to take off in all weathers.

Kalafrana was bombed unmercifully during the war but, by a sweet turn of events, when Italy signed the Armistice on 8 September 1943, most of the 76 ships of the Italian Navy that surrendered were anchored in Marsaxlokk Bay, under the gaze of the Fleet Air Arm's depleted force.

Follow the signs again and a connecting road heads past Fort Benghisa (closed to visitors) to Għar Ħasan, a large cave on a cliff face hanging over the sea.

**Għar Ħasan** is said to have been used by one Ħasan, a Saracen hiding to avoid expulsion in 1120. He is reputed to have regularly seduced nubile young Maltese girls and then lowered them down the cliff face into waiting Saracen boats to be sold into slavery rather than to enjoy the romantic future they had been promised. Of course he fell in love with one of the girls and they lived romantically with their fine view of the sea until discovered by Christian soldiers, when they leaped hand-in-hand to their deaths.

Għar Ħasan is permanently open to the elements, but there is not much to see. Entrance is by a narrow path cut along the face of the cliff with just a rusting railing to keep you from the sea 130m below. As you need a torch to explore the littered caves, young boys loiter there to rent you one for 25 cents.

Head back to the crossroads and the sign to Żurrieq. To your left behind commercial development you can see the traces of Ħal Far Airfield, one of the RAF bases in World War Two.

## Żurrieq

• **Buses** 32, 34, 38, 138.

Żurrieq is the largest village on the south of the island and, because of the nearness of the Blue Grotto at Wied iż-Żurrieq just 3km away, and the Neolithic temples of Ħaġar Qim and Mnajdra 2km further along the cliff road, it figures prominently on any tourist route, although few venture into the village itself. In fact, there is little reason to. So, to encourage visitors to see more of the area, the five neighbouring villages of Żurrieq, Safi, Kirkop, Mqabba and Qrendi are promoting themselves as a tour. It is an area rich in historical remains, dolmens, Roman towers and temples. But the sites are isolated and you have to look hard to find them.

At the centre of the village, the church of **St Catherine of Alexandria** dates back to 1632. Designed by the incumbent parish priest, Dun Matteolo Saliba, it took more than 25 years to complete. It is a fine church and highly decorated. Mattia Preti, the Italian Baroque artist who turned the vault of St John's Co-Cathedral into the spectacle we see today (see box on p 92), lived for a while in the village and completed six superb paintings for the church including a magnificent *St Catherine and the Angels* behind the altar and, in the nave, *St Andrew* labouring under the weight of the cross. Two statues in the church of which the villagers are especially proud are carried in the *festa* on the first Sunday in September. One is *St Catherine* by Mariano Gerada and the other *Our Lady of Mount Carmel* by Salvu Psaila.

In Mattia Preti Square a few metres from the church is the **Armoury**, or **Armeria**, of the Knights (now a private house; no admission). It was built at the end of the 1600s and in use until the late 1700s, when it was sold as a family residence. Only the eight semi-circular worn steps and balcony indicate that it might once have been an important building.

Dotted around Żurrieq in areas known as **Ta'Gawħar**, **Tal-Baqqari** and **Tat-Torrijt** are three Roman towers dated to the 3C AD. Even older is the remaining part of a Punic building in the courtyard of the parish priest's residence.

There are a number of small chapels with long historical roots. One in the hamlet of **Bubaqra** that forms part of the village, is dedicated to **Our Lady**. It was once two adjacent chapels dedicated to St Rocque and St Sebastian, but after the great plague of 1676 they were rebuilt as one structure. Then in the 1960s the chapel was expanded to accommodate the growing community. A votive painting of *St Rocque* (dated 1599) is by Giovanni Battista Riccio. In Bubaqra too is the Żurrieq cemetery with a small chapel dedicated to **St Leo**, in which a painting dating back to 1604 is said to have been rescued from a small chapel (founded in 1343) on the rock island of **Filfla** (visible all along this coast). The parish priest used to venture there to say Mass for fishermen until the outbreak of World War Two. After that, the island became a target for the ships of the Royal Navy and the Royal Air Force, and what remains is now a bird sanctuary. Visitors are not allowed ashore; there are many unexploded shells.

## Ħal Millieri

• **Buses** as for Żurrieq.

The most interesting site in the area is Ħal Millieri on the road into Żurrieq that skirts Malta International Airport. It is worth a quick detour to see this forgotten spot few people seem to get to. Look for the almost invisible sign on the right and you come across all that remains of the 15C settlement; two low, chapel-like churches and a stone cross that says you are on the village square.

Ħal Millieri was once a hamlet, but as its residents moved into flourishing Żurrieq the settlement fell into disrepair.

There are two small churches. The bigger one, with an old Roman olive-crusher once used as the parish's baptismal font standing in front, is dedicated to **St John the Evangelist**. The smaller one, truly enchanting in its garden setting, is the **Church of the Annunciation** dating from around 1430. Until the late 1960s when the charm of Ħal Millieri was rediscovered and a fund was established for its restoration, this little church was a stable for a farmer's donkey. For a while it was vandalised, but now if you go through the unassuming door you find a number of simple Christian frescoes that give the place a uniquely charged atmosphere.

Ħal Millieri has become Żurrieq Local Council's project, so the whole site is due for sympathetic restoration. Opening hours vary.

## Wied iż-Żurrieq

● **Buses** 38, 138.

For most visitors, this tiny, well-signposted, attractive fiord set among the sheer cliffs is a must-see, especially if the weather is calm and they want to visit the Blue Grotto.

Wied iż-Żurrieq consists of a small string of simple houses, souvenir shops and cafés selling cold drinks, fried fish and light snacks, all hovering above boathouses and a narrow fissure in the rocks where fishing boats tie up. A steep slipway allows the boats to be brought ashore for maintanence and reapplication of all the colours traditional Maltese fishing boats wear. The Eye of Osiris (see p 79) is repainted here too, as is the name of the patron saint invariably found on each boat.

On the narrow concrete jetty, boatmen gather waiting to transport passengers to the **Blue Grotto** and the caves formed under the cliffs. It is a pleasant excursion lasting about 25 minutes. The Grotto itself is small but attractive, its colours seen best before midday when they are enhanced by the angle of the morning light.

Whatever you do, bargain first before getting into a boat. Although there are set rates (Lm1.75 per adult and Lm1 per child), fares can vary according to how wealthy you look.

## Ħagar Qim and Mnajdra

● **Buses** 38, 138.

Ħagar Qim (meaning 'Standing Stones') and Mnajdra are Malta's most important Neolithic temples, erected high on the cliffs near Wied iż-Żurrieq around 3600 BC, a millennium before the creation of Stonehenge in England and the earliest pyramids in Egypt.

Both temples were built with a fine view of the great rock, Filfla, rising from the sea ahead. Perhaps the Neolithic people believed the rock had mystical powers. Ħagar Qim, like its companion Mnajdra lower down the hillside in a magical, sheltered position, was built and added to throughout the Temple Period. (See *Ancient Malta* pp 50–56 and *The Neolithic Temples* p 189 for background and details.)

From Mnajdra, looking left along the coast, you see one of the Knights' watchtowers. Nearby is a monument erected to Sir Walter Congreve, the Islands' Governor between 1924 and 1927, whose favourite spot this was. He was buried at sea close to Filfla in a lead-lined wooden coffin.

The villages clustered in the rural landscape around Żurrieq all have their points of interest and considerable amounts of simple charm. There are many interesting walks too but the villages would not normally feature on a visitor's route or itinerary.

## Safi

● **Bus** 34.

The village joins Żurrieq by the petrol station on the main road from the airport. Set back from the main thoroughfare, Safi's cluster of narrow streets, many edged with tall swaying palms, surround the original village square and the charming **Church of St Paul**.

When Safi became a parish in 1598 there were five churches in the village, but St Paul, already on the register of churches in 1436, was selected as the parish church. Over the centuries parts were demolished and then rebuilt to a much larger scale as money became available. The churches of St Agatha and the Virgin Mary were demolished for their stone, and in 1725 the 41 families that made up the parish did the work themselves. The titular painting, *The Conversion of St Paul*, was painted by Stefano Erardi, c 1693.

Safi's simple *festa* on the last Sunday in August draws crowds from all the nearby villages.

### Kirkop

• **Bus** 34.

Sited unfortunately close to the airport's busy runways, Kirkop has nonetheless grown in recent years as affluence has reached it. The original 16C parish church (rebuilt in the 18C) was dedicated to **St Leonard** at a time when his fame was better known. A French abbot who lived in the 5C, Léonard de Noblat was the patron saint of anyone falling into the hands of corsairs. Since until as late as the 18C Saracen corsairs regularly raided the Islands, intent on taking as slaves all who crossed their path, the saint's intercession was important.

On display, set into one of the side altars of the church, are the bones of St Benedict, which were donated to the parish in 1790 by Pope Pius VI. If its dome looks more recent, this is because a bomb hit it in 1942 and the church was severely damaged.

### Mqabba

• **Buses** 35, 38, 138.

The countryside around Mqabba (pronounced: *im ub ba*) is the area where much of Malta's cream-coloured limestone, used for building the island's distinctive stone houses, is hewn out of the ground. The village is surrounded by the deep quarries you see on landing or taking off at Malta's airport. The quarries are fascinating: a hot, sun-baked world with a fine layer of dust, and with man and machine way below cutting perfectly formed building blocks with back-breaking effort.

Mqabba's parish church of the **Assumption of our Lady** was completed in 1689. Its location alongside the runways of Luqa, the Islands' original airfield, means it was severely damaged during World War Two. Older, but still retaining many of its original medieval architectural features, is the 16C **Chapel of St Basil**, separated from the younger **Chapel of St Michael** by the village cemetery.

### Qrendi

• **Buses** 35, 38, 138.

Although most visitors take the scenic route via Żurrieq and Wied iż-Żurrieq to the Neolithic temples, Qrendi is nearer to them, just a short distance from Mqabba. It is a distinctive village and provides a pleasant alternative route to Ħagar Qim and Mnajdra.

From the direction of Mqabba you first come to the church of **St Catherine tat-Torba** with its odd façade seemingly fashioned from plain blocks of stone projecting from a recessed front in order to give it a structured pattern. The façade is older than it looks; it was added in 1625 to an older nave.

As you enter the long, narrow village, the parish **church of St Mary** is to the right. It is an imposing edifice with steps leading up to huge carved wooden doors and said to be partly the work of Malta's great architect Lorenzo Gafa who took over responsibility for the half-finished building in 1685. The village *festa* is on 15 August, the same day as that of the neighbouring village—and therefore rival—Mqabba. Naturally each year brings some form of band club rivalry and friction.

A short walk away, surrounded by homes erected in the 16C, is the **Cavalier Tower**, whose claim to fame is to be Malta's only tower on an octagonal plan. The villagers used to take shelter there in times of danger, and from its flat roof above the tower's three storeys, they would rain down rocks and boiling pitch.

If you now take the signposted turning towards Wied iż-Żurrieq you come to St Matthew's Chapel and the well-signposted **Il-Maqluba**. In Maltese this means 'turned upside down' and it refers to a deep hole, a vertical fault about 50m deep and 70m across, caused by the collapse of the roof of an underground cavern. Peering down it looks eerily unpleasant and few locals would venture down onto its threatening floor, not so much because of the dense tangled vegetation that grows there or the promise of whip snakes and worse, but because of its legend.

---

### Il-Maqluba

The inhabitants of Il Maqluba, it seems, were a bad lot and so displeased God that he tore away the ground beneath their feet and sent them hurtling down towards hell. A deep hole was formed. The place, legend says, is cursed.

An alternative version of this tale has a touch of humour. The devil did not want them either; their sins were too heinous even for him. So when they came hurtling down he caught them and with his great might threw them, sinners and the ground on which they stood, into the air. They descended, upside down, into the sea and the island of Filfla was born.

---

## Gudja

- **Bus** 8.

Gudja's claim to fame today is that the spacious, efficient Malta International Airport terminal is on its doorstep. Once people would say Luqa Airport to refer to the airport hub. Now it is Gudja (pronounced: *goo dya*).

The village dates back to the 14C and the street plan cannot have changed much. It is said to have been the birthplace of Gerolamo Cassar (1520–86), architect of many of Valletta's finest buildings including the Grand Master's Palace and St John's Co-Cathedral. The nearby village of Għaxaq also claims this honour but Gudja's local council, emphasising their case, have named a street near the church after him. It is in Maltese: *Triq Glormu Cassar*.

On the road midway between Gudja and the neighbouring town of Luqa, is the church of **St Mary ta'Bir Miftuh**, a 15C medieval parish church. Its shape is similar to Hal Millieri's charming Church of the Annunciation (see p 188) which dates from around 1430, but this one was built some years later and is larger with interesting detail. Much was added over the centuries. Its interior has remains of early 17C murals of the Last Judgement.

On Main Street leading out of Gudja towards the airport, is **Palazzo D'Aurel**, (1770) known originally as Palazzo Dorell or Villa Bettina, one of Malta's finest 18C country palaces. The noble Bettina Muscati Dorell is said to have entertained in turn both Napoleon Bonaparte and Horatio Nelson here (Nelson was accompanied by Sir William and Lady Hamilton).

Bettina Muscati married the Marquis Dorell, a Frenchman, and became Lady-in-waiting to Queen Carolina, Marie Antoinette's sister, the wife of the King of Naples and the Two Sicilies. When Bettina lost the queen's affection she retired to Malta. Today the *palazzo* with its recently Frenchified name remains the home of a Maltese noble family so is not open to viewing. In the gardens is a collection of animals carved in stone and a round tower believed to date from the Byzantine period.

## Luqa

• **Buses** 32, 34, 35, 36, 138.

It would be a shame not to mention Luqa, which gave its name to the Islands' airport that saw so much heroic action in World War Two, when planes took off day and night on raids to Sicily and North Africa. It suffered unmercifully as the enemy bombed the area trying to reduce it to rubble. In the conflict Luqa, the village that had grown from an agricultural centre established in 1634 to a strategic target, was severely damaged. But, like the parish church of **St Andrew** (begun in 1650), Luqa has risen again, restored and affluent.

# Neolithic temples

Around 3600 BC, a millennium before the creation of Stonehenge in England and the earliest pyramids in Egypt, Malta experienced the start of an extraordinary building boom which was to continue for nearly 1000 years. Vast stone temples rose all over the Islands in astonishing profusion. There is nothing remotely like them anywhere else in the world and together they are now designated a UNESCO World Heritage Site. (See also *Ancient Malta*, p 51.)

The structures have been called temples because there are many indications that religious ceremonies were carried out inside them and religious terms are now used to describe their architecture and contents. All rounded chambers and alcoves are called *apses*, large stone blocks and ledges are *altars*, holes in threshold steps are thought to have been for *libation* (pouring of wine or other liquid in honour of a god) and those low down in walls are linked with *oracles*, especially if there is a hidden room behind them. Holes and V-shaped notches in doorways are thought to have been for wooden bars, leather-hinged doors or curtains.

**Religious rites** Hoards of charred animal bones, a long flint knife hidden in a secret altar niche and fire-reddened hearths are pretty solid evidence that at least part of the rituals involved animal sacrifices. There are other indications that the religion involved fertility in its widest sense, and possibly birth, death and rebirth.

**Deities** So many carved stone statues of grossly overweight figures, of indeterminate sex, have been found in the temples there can be little doubt that they represent the chief deity. But there are also carved phalluses, a snake, animal friezes and simpler stones representing male and female fertility which may mean that there were also minor cults.

**Structure** Most of the major temples have the same basic plan of two large oval chambers with a corridor running through the centre of them and an apse at the far end. In most of the early temples this final apse is quite large. Later it is usually little more than an altar niche. All are enclosed in vast encircling walls built of massive stones, which were altered and extended when more temples were added to the same site.

The oldest of these monumental 'overcoats' were made of rough blocks of huge dimension with far smaller, rough stones used for the temples themselves. But by the end of this great period of creativity, both exterior and interior walls were made of massive slabs cut with far greater precision. The largest stone, at **Ħaġar Qim,** is 7m. long and estimated to weigh 20 tons. No mortar was used and the only tools available were made of stone, bone, flint and the volcanic glass, obsidian.

Malta is blessed with two types of limestone. For the later temples, the hard type, *coralline*, was used (except at Ħaġar Qim) only for the protective overcoats. The softer, golden *globigerina* provided the ideal material for the temples themselves and for their intricately carved screens and altars.

**Decoration** The earliest carved decoration was a simple, but effective series of pitted dots. Later, animal friezes and intricately carved spirals became the vogue. (Until radiocarbon dating proved otherwise the decorative spiral had been thought to be a much later Greek invention.) Red ochre, perhaps then the ritual colour of death, was liberally used on interior walls.

As the religious rituals developed over the centuries, the temples became more secretive places, possibly the sole preserve of the priests. Apses were screened off and large forecourts were built outside for the congregation.

**Ġgantija** on Gozo and **Mnajdra**, near Ħaġar Qim, Malta, are the best preserved of the temples: the walls can be seen to be arching inward at the top, though whether they could have supported a stone roof is a matter of hot dispute. A combination of wooden beams, brushwood and clay is the most likely alternative. The entrances, set into the concave façades were made of three monumental slabs of golden stone: two uprights with a huge lintel stretched across them (known as trilithons). Sadly, few of the lintels have survived.

The great slabs were moved around on large stone ball-bearings (still to be seen on many of the sites) and then manoeuvred into holes in the ground with wooden levers and, maybe, ropes.

There are 23 known temple sites and 25 clusters of giant stones not yet thoroughly investigated. There is also the **Hypogeum**, which has an astonishing subterranean temple, carved out of the living rock in a labyrinthine burial area. This and the four best preserved surface temples are certainly worth a visit.

# Malta

### Ħaġar Qim (Standing Stones)

- **Open** 1 Oct–15 June, Mon–Sat 08.15–17.00, Sun 08.15–16.15; 16 June–30 Sept, daily 07.45–14.00. **Buses** 38 or 138.

This golden temple stands high above the cliffs near Qrendi, in the southeast of Malta, with a fine view of the great rock Fifla rising sheer from the sea. Its imposing position is only one of the many ways in which it differs from all the other complexes. It was built and added to throughout the Temple Period.

Since there was no hard, grey limestone available here, both the external and internal walls are built of the softer, golden stone and it is surprising that it has weathered as well as it has done. Uniquely, Ħaġar Qim has several entrances, chambers of unusual shape arranged in a capricious manner, an intriguing external shrine and the longest single stone. The typical trilithon main entrance is original, though some of the slabs above it are replacements.

The first temple to be built here was of the early five-apse design. Then the final apse was turned into a rear entrance and the second left apse was extended to form a passageway to the later additions.

Many of the 'fat figures' now on show at the Museum of Archaeology in Valletta were found here, buried beneath a deep step in one of the inner chambers.

*Ħaġar Qim*

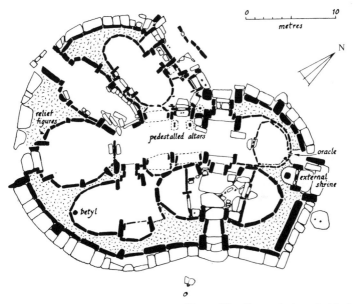

*Ḥagar Qim, the main temple block*

## What to look for

The first pair of **apses** are unusually secretive, so thoroughly walled off that they could only be entered through the small, porthole slabs.

The second right apse has some small upright stones, which could possibly have been a pen for animals awaiting a sacrificial end, and an **oracle** hole with a small room behind it only accessible from outside the temple walls.

In the extended second, left apse, there is a unique pair of small, stone **altars** set on pedestals and a copy of a small, block altar, with elegant pot plants finely carved on all four sides (the original is in the Museum of Archaeology, Valletta).

The **largest stone**, all 7m. and 20 tons of it, lies to the right of the main entrance, along the eastern wall.

The **external shrine** just beyond it may look like a haphazard assemblage of stones, but the central column and the tapered block in front of it are thought to symbolise male and female fertility.

There is one more oddity to see if you are prepared to hunt around a bit. It is almost exactly opposite the shrine, just inside the first break in the outer western wall. Here, on the left, the third stone of the inner wall seems to have been recycled. It must once have been part of a large, relief carving of two 'fat deities', though now only their massive calves remain.

There are a few other ruins tumbled around the site. The cluster of small chambers in front of the façade is known, for want of any better explanation, as the **priests' quarters**. To the north, there are the remains of what looks like an early temple but is now thought to have been built later than those in the main complex.

## Mnajdra

• Entry and buses as for Ħaġar Qim.

A paved path leads down from Ħaġar Qim to this bewitching site; your Ħaġar Qim ticket allows you to enter here too.

These three temples share the same expansive sea views as their neighbour but, tucked into a gentle hollow, they have a charm unmatched elsewhere. They are ranged around an almost circular forecourt and, as at Ħaġar Qim, are accompanied by a dishevelled cluster of 'priest's quarters'. The golden stone used for the interior walls had to be hauled all the way down from the crest of the hill above.

### What to look for

The first **Small Temple**, standing on its own, is the oldest, built very early on. It has only three apses, set out like a clover leaf, and has been extensively restored using such small stones that you can almost hear the Neolithic temple builders sneering.

The **Middle Temple**, the last to be built, was added towards the end of the Temple Period around 2500 BC and its architect appears to have been something of a rebel. Instead of the usual trilithon entrance, it had one colossal porthole slab 3m high. The stones of its first course are also much shorter than normal, though cut and placed with marvellous precision.

The largest upright in the left wall of the inner passage has a small **sketch of a temple façade** cut into it. Several models of temples have been found but this is the only known carving of one. In the inner, left apse there is a handsome porthole slab, framed by a trilithon, with an altar behind it.

The **Lower Temple** is the most atmospheric of all these great buildings, still steeped in mysterious ancient rites. Take care as you approach the small, conical stone standing on its doorstep: it may represent a deity.

In the first apse on the right the walls still rise to a height of 4m, giving some idea of what it must have been like to wander in these great buildings when they were roofed and lit only by flickering fires and lamps. Once again, there is a small room with an **oracle** hole and external entrance.

The first apse on the left contains the finest piece of original stonework still to be found in any of the temples: a superb **porthole slab**, framed by a trilithon decorated with finely pitted dots.

## Tarxien

• **Open** 1 Oct–15 June, Mon–Sat 08.15–17.00, Sun 08.15–16.15; 16 June– 30 Sept, daily 07.45–14.00. **Buses** 8, 11, 27, 29, 30, 427, 627.

This last, triumphant flourish of the temple builders' craft is now entered from an incongruous suburban side street, Triq it-Templji Neolitiċi (Old Temples Street), in **Paola**, southern Malta (see p 182). It was the only one of the great temple complexes to be completely silted over and the only one to have been professionally excavated. As a result, it retained far more of its treasures. It was discovered in 1914, when farmers complained of catching huge stones in their ploughs.

The three main temples were all built during the last phase of the temple era, the middle one being a very late intruder. There are also the scanty ruins of a small, much earlier temple. Spectacular as they are, they are still only a fragment of the Neolithic remains that once stood in this general area.

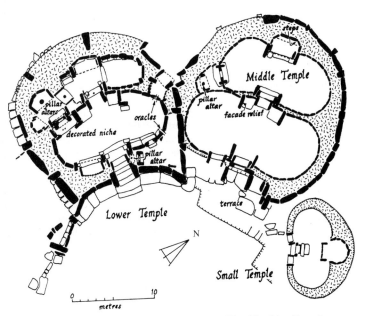

The Mnajdra Temples

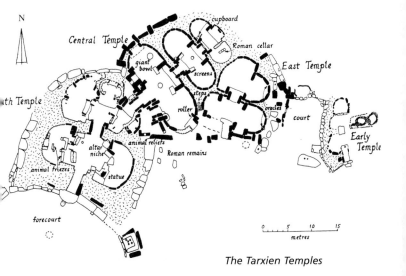

The Tarxien Temples

The carvings found here were so fine and so well preserved that most of them are now in the Museum of Archaeology, in Valletta. Those on the site were once good copies but now show signs of weathering.

## What to look for

At each end of the great, concave entrance façade there is a large slab of stone on the ground with a stone frame around it. The one on the right is the better preserved. There are several holes pierced into it and piles of small, stone balls were found nearby. There has been much speculation about the purpose of all this, ranging from libations and divinations to a gambling game for bored guards.

The lintel across the entrance to the **South Temple** is a modern replacement, carefully calculated for size. The passageway as you enter, with its finely carved horned spirals, is the most lavishly furnished and decorated of any temple area. It is paved with a huge, single block of stone.

In the **right apse** there is by far the largest of the **fat figure** statues. In its pleated skirt, it would have stood nearly 3m. high, if it had not lost its head and torso to the farmers' ploughs. From its size and position, there can be little doubt of its importance. The block to the right of it appears to be decorated with an impressionist's version of a herd of cattle. In the **left apse** there are carved friezes of sheep, goats, a plump pig and more cattle.

A mass of charred animal bones was discovered in the elaborate **porthole niche** further on, and what must surely have been the sacrificial weapon, a long, flint knife, was discovered in the secret compartment of the altar in front of it. The loose plug covering this compartment can be seen in the altar front, camouflaged by the spiral decoration.

The **final apse** appears to have been an elaborate altar raised on a platform decorated with more horned spirals. This is the largest carved slab found in any of the temples.

The break in the wall of the second left apse is modern but the changes to the right apse were made long ago to form a passage when the central temple was wedged into the complex around 2000 BC.

The **Central Temple** is the largest of the three (23m. long internally), the best built and the best preserved. It is unique in having six large apses instead of the usual four. What impresses most here is the precision fit of the wall slabs and the massive paving stones. The reddening of the walls and floor was caused by fire at the end of the Temple Period around 2500 BC, possibly fuelled by the collapse of the timber and brushwood roof.

In the middle of the court between the first two apses there is a circular stone hearth possibly for burning herbs or cooking the sacrificial animals, the flesh of which may have been shared with the worshippers outside.

In the **first left apse** there is a massive stone bowl, a hugely enlarged version of the many small pottery bowls found within the temple, and a fine pillared opening leading to a small chamber within the walls.

In the **first right apse**, where the wall has been broken through to give access to the East Temple, one of the great floor slabs has been lifted so that you can see not only the magnitude of these blocks (they were certainly no mere paving stones) but also the stone balls on which they were trundled around. Also in this apse are a couple of carvings that could be read as the epitome of male and female: a glorious humpbacked bull and a sow suckling her litter.

The deep step up to the **final chambers**, the inner sanctum, is decorated with two great spirals which, like a pair of watchful eyes, seem to warn the uninitiated to go no further. Beyond them lay the Stone Age carvers' greatest achievement: two huge **stone screens**, decorated with a magnificent array of spirals which are now in the entrance hall of the Archaeology Museum.

The **East Temple** is a bit of a let-down, except for a couple of oracle holes in both right apses and its marvellous **masonry**. The fine cutting of the upright stones here is astonishing. Their sides are slightly curved, which called for huge skill in making the perfect fit. The small, semi-circular notches at their base took the wooden levers with which they were manoevred into position.

The narrow, external staircase tucked between the Eastern and Central Temples may have been a secret route into the Central Temple's inner sanctum, or it could have been used for something more prosaic, like mending the roof.

Later, the Bronze Age invaders used the South Temple for cremating their dead and for storing the ashes in pottery urns.

## The Hypogeum

- Admittance limited to groups of no more than 10 at a time. Advance booking recommended ☎ 825579. **Buses** 8, 11, 27, 29.

This unique subterranean labyrinth of ritual rooms and burial chambers is a short walk from Tarxien. The entrance is just south of Paola Square, in Triq iċ-Ċimiterju (Cemetery Street), Paola. It has been closed for several years for much needed restoration and admittance is restricted (see above).

*Hypogeum* is an archaeologists' catch-all word for any underground chamber and gives little indication of what was discovered here in 1902, when workmen excavating water cisterns for a row of new houses broke through into this amazing warren. Chipped ever deeper into the soft rock, there are rooms exquisitely carved in imitation of the temples above ground, burial chambers, a 2m-deep pit which may have housed sacred snakes and, as a final surprise more than 10m below the surface, what appears to have been a huge granary. From the number of bones discovered, it is estimated that 7000 people were buried here. It all seems to have started with a small burial cave close to a surface temple, from which only a few stones remain.

Two intriguing, small, clay statuettes found in the Main Chamber suggest that this great room was used for more than funeral rites. They are both charmingly plump, indisputably female figures, wearing elegant, long skirts and reclining on couches. Known as 'Sleeping Ladies', and now in the Archaeological Museum, they could be a clue that people slept here, seeking cures for illnesses; or perhaps they were priestesses hoping for prophetic dreams.

### What to look for

The **Main Chamber** is stunning. This soaring, corbelled room with seductively curved walls is carved out of the living rock to represent the precision masonry of the later temples.

The **Oracle Room** has painted spirals on its ceiling and the capacity to freeze your blood. A deep voice, speaking through the oracle hole, echoes and reverberates, ricocheting through the corridors and chambers in eerie repetition.

The entrance to the chamber known as the **Holy of Holies** is a magnificent affair. Its porthole slab is set beneath a lintel with four upright supports, which are framed by a trilithon and topped with a corbel. The entire confection has been carved out of the rock face.

The renovations, carried out with the help of UNESCO, have included drying out this wonderful labyrinth, and many painted decorations unseen for years are now visible again.

# Gozo

## Ġgantija (The Giantess)

• **Open** Mon–Sat 08.30–16.30, Sun: 08.30–15.00. **Buses** 64 or 65.

The two temples here are tucked beneath the lip of the plateau, as you enter the village of **Xagħra**. They gaze out over a later, Bronze Age hilltop settlement site, to a flash of sea and Malta beyond. Both were built early in the Temple Period—though the one on the left (the South Temple) is considerably older than its companion—and share one colossal overcoat. They are the best preserved of all the temples and the easiest to decipher.

After more than 5000 years their walls still stand, unrestored, to a height of 6m. Here, more than in any of the other temples, you have the sensation of standing in a monumental building of a kind that only a great faith inspires.

### What to look for
The **South Temple**, with its massive threshold slab (the largest in any of the temples), has a spacious final apse, typical of the early period. The first left apse still has its original floor covering which is a type of cement made of crushed soft limestone and water. Until a few years ago, traces of red-painted plaster could still be found clinging to its walls.

If you squint at the side of the large stone block lying around in the right apse, you may just be able to make out traces of its carved spiral decoration.

The inner apses, larger than the first two, measure 23.5m. from end to end (the longest span in any of the temples). The left one here is particularly striking, both in height and size. The short slabs supporting the altar are modern additions. The step up to the final apse is decorated with the early pitted dot design.

There are fire-reddened hearths in the floors of both right apses and, scattered around, a range of mysterious holes to puzzle over.

The smaller final apse of the **North Temple** still has a few remnants of what was once an elaborate altar.

The **outer shell** is perhaps the most awesome feature of the whole complex. Several of its massive blocks are over 5m. long and several courses of smaller stones still teeter above them.

It is worth peering over the forecourt wall to see the massive foundations there too. Its less impressive upper courses are the result of later repairs.

# GOZO AND COMINO

# Gozo

Gozo, the second largest of the Maltese Islands, is less populated and more rural than its big sister but still has many varied attractions, from its ancient Citadel (Il-Kastell), Stone Age temples and charming small museums to its beaches and unspoiled countryside. The sun-baked, biblical, summer landscape of terraced hills and valleys turns in spring into a riotous carpet of lush crops, wild flowers and herbs, all bounded by the shimmering sea. Gozo is no longer quite the island where time stood still as it was billed a few years ago, but its pace is still pleasantly undemanding and its welcome as warm as it has always been.

In Maltese the island is called *Ghawdex* (pronounced *ow-desh*), a name that dates from the Arab occupation. 'Gozo' came later when its rulers from Aragon translated its medieval Latin name, *Gaudisium* (which also means 'joy'), into Spanish. According to tradition, it is Homer's Ogygia, where the nymph Calypso beguiled the Greek hero Odysseus for seven years. It still has the power to enchant.

## Getting there

From early morning until 23.30 car ferries make regular 25-minute crossings between Malta's northern harbour, Ċirkewwa, and Gozo's main port, Mġarr. In summer months they also run throughout the night. Winter gales occasionally cause them to be halted or rerouted. There is no ticket office in Malta: you pay at Mġarr before making the return journey. Buses from City Gate, Valletta, connect with the ferries (schedules by telephone: Ċirkewwa ☎ 580435/6; Mġarr ☎ 556114 or 561662). There is also a helicopter service between Malta International Airport and Gozo's Heliport (☎ 557905).

See also *Practical Information*, p 15 and box on p 17.

## Check list

On a quick visit to Gozo see the following:
Ġgantija Neolithic temples
Victoria: St George's Basilica, the Citadel, the Cathedral
Xewkija: the Rotunda church
Ta'Pinu national shrine
Xlendi
Marsalforn

## Transport on Gozo

There are well-signposted roads from Mġarr to the main town, Victoria (which is still generally called by its old name, Rabat), and from Victoria to the villages and main beaches. Bus routes radiate from the terminus in Triq Putirjal, the southern crossroad at the centre of Victoria. Between 06.00 and 19.00 (later in summer) there are buses at Mġarr to coincide with ferry arrivals, but they don't wait long, so it is best to head straight for them when you disembark. From the Victoria terminus, buses leave half an hour before all ferry departures between 06.00 and 19.00 (later in summer). Other services vary greatly, according to season, and it is best to check at a Tourist Office or the bus terminus. During the day there are taxi ranks at Mġarr, near the Victoria bus terminus and, sometimes, in Victoria's main square, Pjazza Indipendenza. It is wise to negotiate the fare in advance.

### Tourist Information Offices

Mġarr Harbour (☎ 553343); Pjazza Indipendenza, Victoria (☎ 558106).

## History of Gozo

Though basically sharing the same fate as Malta, the smaller and less well defended island of Gozo was plagued for far longer by pirate and Turkish raids and it never fully profited from Malta's peaks of prosperity. In 1551, the Turks ransacked its Citadel, destroyed its suburb (Victoria) and carried off thousands of its inhabitants into slavery, though many were later ransomed or found their way back home. Until 1637 all Gozitans were forbidden, under threat of severe penalties, to sleep at night outside the security of the Citadel walls. It was not until 1708 that the Turks made their last foray. Many stories are told of Gozitan farmers turning a generously blind eye to petty pilfering of their crops by lone Turks or pirates, left behind after some of these raids, and then being saved from slavery by the recipients of their charity when the next marauding fleet sailed in.

However, for a few months during Napoleon's brief conquest Gozo did have complete independence. It negotiated unilaterally with Nelson to rid it of the sniping French soldiers, trapped in the Citadel by the local militia, and declared itself the Nation of Gozo from October 1798 until the French were finally ousted from Valletta the following September. With life being rather tougher on Gozo, its people have always strived harder and have provided the country with a number of top officials out of all proportion to its size.

A lively audio-visual run through the island's history, culture and geography, '*Gozo 360°*', is shown daily at the **Citadel Cinema** in Victoria (every half hour from 10.30 to 15.00).

# Mġarr

This pretty little port, where the majority of Gozo's visitors first step ashore, combines most of the ingredients that make the island so appealing. Tiny, terraced fields march up its hillsides, and brightly painted fishing boats, protected both by Christian shrines and the pagan eye of Osiris, bob in its calm waters. The heights are also doubly guarded by a pinnacled neo-Gothic church (the Lourdes Sanctuary, built in 1888) and the sterner ramparts of **Fort Chambray**, the last great building enterprise of the Knights of Malta, and named for their last great warrior, the Norman Knight Grand Cross, Jacques de Chambray, admiral and commander of the galleys.

Disillusioned by his Order's peacetime degeneracy, Chambray spent his last years as Governor of Gozo and paid for the fort with his accumulated prize money. He had intended it to be an elegant fortified city, like Valletta, but managed no more than the walls, a chapel and barracks. It was put to the test only once, in 1798, a decade after its completion, when Napoleon's troops stormed the island. Undermanned and surrounded by three French platoons, it surrendered. It later became a British garrison and in World War One was used as a military rest camp for soldiers wounded in Gallipoli. For many years it was the island's mental hospital. Now it has become something like the walled city the old sea-dog envisaged, but with houses aimed at the tourist market.

# Victoria (Rabat)

The island's capital was given its present name and city status by Queen Victoria to mark her 1887 Diamond Jubilee. The Gozitans, however, aren't rushing to switch from the old Arabic name, Rabat, which means a suburb and exactly describes its origins: the town below the Citadel. It is liveliest in the mornings and late afternoons.

The site has been inhabited at least since the Bronze Age and was stoutly walled by the Romans. Three stone crosses (at the central crossroads, in Pjazza San Franġisk and Pjazza Santu Wistin) mark its Roman limits. In the Middle Ages both Victoria and the Citadel were bustling, tight-packed communities. A few medieval houses have survived in the Citadel and one or two in the still narrow, twisting lanes and alleys behind the main square of the lower town.

**Triq ir-Repubblika** (Republic Street), Victoria's main street, cuts through the town from east to west. Until Malta became a republic, it was called Racecourse Street and it still lives up to its old name twice a year, on the feast days of the Assumption (15 August, known locally as Santa Marija) and St George (the third weekend in July), when a great throng turns out to cheer a sweltering mass of horseflesh galloping uphill towards a prodigious display of silver cups and trophies. Santa Marija is a popular feast, and Maltese come to Gozo in their thousands to enjoy the weekend.

The public gardens, **Ġnien Rundle**, on the left at the bottom of the hill, hosts a lively agricultural show every year for Santa Marija. Next door, the island's oldest hotel, the *Duke of Edinburgh*, built in 1881, was named for Queen Victoria's son, though the present Duke and the then Princess Elizabeth did drop in for tea. (It is currently closed, awaiting redevelopment.)

The bow-windowed façade a little further up the hill belongs to the *Aurora*, one of Gozo's two band clubs and opera houses. The other, the *Astra*, is higher up on the right, opposite the post office. One is connected with the cathedral (which celebrates Santa Marija) and the other with St George's Basilica. They were originally founded to provide march music for church feasts. This led to some lively rivalry (which is what usually gets things going in Gozo) and they now also compete to put on the best operas twice a year.

## Pjazza Indipendenza

Pjazza Indipendenza, marble paved and ringed with ficus trees, is Victoria's heart. The Gozitans have been calling it *It-Tokk* (meeting place) for as long as they have been saying Ghawdex, and are likely to continue. In the mornings market stalls jostle café tables and greengrocers pile up their wares outside the square's rim of shops. Its war memorial commemorating Gozitans who died in World War Two was unveiled by Queen Elizabeth II in 1954.

The decorative, semi-circular building on the right, is the **Banca Giuratale** built in 1773 for Gozo's governing jurats. Along with a new hospital in Pjazza San Franġisk (now the offices of the Minister for Gozo) it was part of Grand Master Vilhena's scheme to introduce some of Malta's Baroque splendour to its long-neglected smaller sister. It was designed by Vilhena's resident military engineer, Charles François de Mondion, who turned Mdina into a Baroque city for his master. It now houses cultural and tourist offices.

Facing it, the small Church of **St James** stands on the site of several earlier churches, including a chapel razed by the Turks during their 1551 devastation.

It was recently completely rebuilt after its 1740 foundations collapsed. Its parishioners' habit of ringing the bells to drown out unwelcome political speakers in the square led to a very long wait for a building permit.

**St George's Basilica**, in a small square behind the *pjazza*, is the most lavishly decorated church on an island of lavish churches. It was built between 1672 and 1678, enlarged and given a more imposing façade in 1818 and added to again in the 1930s. The paintings of events in the life of St George on its richly gilded ceiling are the work of an Italian artist, Gian Battista Conti, who laboured on them from 1949 until 1964. The striking bronze altar canopy is a (reluctantly, no doubt) scaled-down copy of Bernini's in St Peter's in Rome. The altarpiece of *St George with white charger and felled dragon, and the Souls in Purgatory*, which hangs in the left transept, are by Mattia Preti (1613–99), the greatest artist after Caravaggio to work in Malta (see box, p 96).

Behind St George's lies the oldest part of town, **il-Borgo**, a warren of narrow streets and alleys designed to confuse invaders and deflect arrows and musket fire. Few of the houses are as old as the streets, but there are some fine stone balconies and religious niches to look out for.

## The city walls

The great, golden walls that rise above Victoria, protecting il-Kastell (the Citadel), were built by the Knights in the first years of the 17C, after years of neglect, piecemeal repairs, discarded plans and official parsimony. Medieval monarchs had added to the Arabs' original defences, but they were still no match for Turkish gunpowder when Sinam Pasha and the most feared of all corsairs, Rais Dragut, assaulted them in 1551 and slew or carried off most of the population. Only 300 or so managed to escape by clambering down ropes and hiding in the countryside. After this catastrophe it still took nearly 50 years and a substantial donation from King Philip II of Spain, before work began on the magnificent curtain walls, bastions and cavaliers that now dominate the skyline. They were designed by the Italian military engineer Giovanni Rinaldini and Malta's Vittorio Cassar, son of Gerolomo, who designed Comino's fort. The Gozitans also contributed to their cost through taxes on wine, oil and other agricultural products.

The hill on which the walls stand was the acropolis of the old Roman town, and probably of the Carthaginian one too—a Punic inscription thanks the Gozitans for helping to restore several of their temples (a quick count of the church domes visible from the ramparts today indicates that this was work very much to the Gozitans' liking). By the mid-13C, there were enough houses, chapels, hospitals and storerooms within the walls to give permanent or overnight protection to the island's 203 Christian, 155 Muslim and 8 Jewish families. After the rule that everyone should sleep here was lifted in 1637, many of the inhabitants drifted away to build houses in the lower town or closer to their fields. Sixty or so years later an earthquake reduced most of the abandoned buildings to rubble, but there is still enough left to make a visit well worth while.

## The Citadel

Having climbed It-Telgha tal-Belt (City Hill), which leads off the main square, the first, large, arched entrance you see is a modern violation. It was cut through in 1956, causing much protest, to accommodate the large statues carried shoulder high in religious processions. The unfortunate coincidence that the Minister of

Culture (later President of Malta) who sanctioned the deed was called Miss Agatha Barbara encouraged local wags to revive an old Roman pun: *Quod non fecerunt barbari, fecit Barbara* (What the Barbarians failed to do, was done by Barbara).

The old entrance, guarded by a formidable bastion, is further along. The Roman inscription in the wall of its covered passageway is the base of a statue erected by the people of Gozo to honour the son of a Roman high priest and benefactor of the island. Just beyond the passageway, on the right, is the iron-barred gate to one of the sallyports.

It has to be said, however, that the new archway has opened up a fine view of the cathedral and its square, Pjazza tal-Katidral. On the raised terrace to the left, the Law Courts (rebuilt in 1687) link up with the **Governor's Palace** (rebuilt at the beginning of the 17C but given the plump mouldings typical of the Knights' earlier buildings in Malta). On the right are the cathedral's vestry and chapter hall, both built towards the end of the 19C, after the square had been cleared of the last of its medieval houses.

The **Cathedral** replaces a smaller one irretrievably damaged in the 1693 earthquake and stands on the site of two—maybe three—earlier churches, a Roman temple to Juno and possibly a Carthaginian temple dedicated to Astarte. It was designed by the Maltese architect Lorenzo Gafa, who also designed Mdina cathedral. Money ran out before the dome was finished but the compromise solution has provided one of the cathedral's most fascinating features. In 1739 Antonio Manuele di Messina painted a *trompe l'oeil* substitute which filled the gap so successfully it has never been replaced. From the nave it is hard to believe it isn't the real thing, but try looking at it from near the main altar.

The floor, like that of St John's in Valletta, is a splendidly colourful mosaic of tombstones with marble coats of arms, prelates' hats and grinning skulls. The two cannons on the cathedral steps were cast in 1680 and bear the arms of Grand Masters Cotoner and Caraffa.

The **Cathedral Museum** (in Il-Fosos street, on the left of the cathedral. Open Mon–Sat 08.30–16.30, Sun 08.30–15.00) has marble columns from the temple of Juno, church vestments and silver, a bishop's landau and altarpieces from long-lost country chapels.

The **Folklore Museum** (in Triq Bernardo De Opuo, first left after the Cathedral Museum) has a charming display of domestic and agricultural tools and machinery in a unique group of medieval houses (open Mon–Sat 08.30–16.30, Sun 08.30–15.00). The ground floors were built in the 14C. The upper storeys, with their delicately carved, twin-arched windows divided by a slender column, were added a century later.

Further along, on the right, a plaque on the wall marks the house of the Sicilian soldier hero for whom the street is named. In the 1551 siege, choosing death rather than slavery, Bernardo de Opuo killed his wife and two daughters then polished off as many Turks as he could before being felled by a scimitar.

At the end of the street, on the left, is **Palazzo Cagliares** and its adjoining chapel built in 1625 by the Bishop of Malta, Baldassare Cagliares, and restored in the 1930s. Opposite, there is another interesting survivor, a covered passage with a trio of late medieval pointed arches. To the north of this is the only surviving section of the medieval fortifications.

The **Natural History Museum** (Triq il-Kwartier San Martin. Open as Folklore Museum), in a cluster of late 16C houses, has a piece of rock brought back from the moon as well as a fascinating survey of the island's geology, flora and fauna. The arched room on the ground floor is thought to be the Citadel's oldest surviving chapel.

The **Armoury** opposite does not open to visitors as such—you view through the iron-barred doors. It is probably more interesting for its history and architecture than for the small display of helmets, shields and lances. Two 19C hearses, one for an adult, one for a child, have found their way here too. The flying buttresses and massive central column were a way of dealing with a lack of wood for beams. Over the centuries it was used for municipal meetings, a dormitory for monks, a granary and barracks for British soldiers in World War Two.

The **Archaeology Museum** (through the small arch in Cathedral Square. Open as Folklore Museum) resides in the Citadel's last surviving private palace. It was restored in the 1930s when the design of its lavishly carved balcony was painstakingly copied from the original's shattered remains. It has exhibits from the Stone Age to the time of the Knights. The finely carved 12C tombstone of a young Muslim girl, Majmuna, is particularly moving, and the Roman draped marble statue is of exceptional quality for a small province. The first room on the right has, among other objects discovered at Ġgantija Temples, a carved snake on an upright stone which is probably an indication of a fertility cult.

Up the lane from the museum, little gift shops, tucked into rooms which once housed the cannon carriages, have a more cheerful array of local wares than the official craft display in the former prisons further along.

The **ramparts** provide a magnificent panoramic view of Gozo's haunting landscape, with its distinctive flat-topped hills, tight-packed villages and church domes. Across a glint of sea, Malta can be seen, and on a clear day even Sicily, 90km away, is visible.

# Down south

## *Xlendi*

A roller-coaster road plunges southwest from Victoria to Xlendi, the smaller of Gozo's two holiday resorts. This sparkling bay, little more than a fissure in the great cliffs that guard the island's southern approaches, has tamarisk trees, restaurants, bars, an attractive four-star hotel and souvenir shops lining its small strip of sand and gaily painted fishing boats anchored beyond. Beneath them lie the wrecks of Roman merchant ships, snared by gales and a submerged reef at the bay's entrance (still a hazard). A path on the left passes over a small bridge to its guardian **watchtower**, built in 1658.

The steps up the cliff face on the right lead to **Carolina's Cave**, where the island's Dominican nuns for many years used to swim in long dresses and suitable seclusion. In recent years the bay has been overloaded with holiday apartments, but even in the height of summer it is still surprisingly peaceful in the evenings.

On the way down from Victoria the road passes on the left, just as you leave Fontana, a cavernous **17C wash-house** adorned with coats of arms, and on the right an abundantly spring-fed valley, previously the Knights' private game reserve. Anyone caught poaching was sent off to row the galleys. On the last dip down to the sea, *La Grotta*, an open-air disco with exotically terraced gardens, pulls in the young from all over Malta in summer.

## Ta' Ċenċ

Due east of Xlendi rough rural roads (or a smoother one from Victoria) lead to the village of Sannat and the spectacular cliffs of Ta' Ċenċ. Here, a precipitous 145m above the sea, shearwaters call like banshees to their chicks on summer nights, and rare plants and Bronze Age structures survive. The cliffs are the site of the island's prime luxury hotel, also called *Ta' Ċenċ*, which regularly features on lists of the world's top hostelries. It is built around a 17C *palazzo*, the country retreat of a Knight of St John. Behind it, on the left of the ridge, two **dolmens** remains intact in the tumbled remnants of a Bronze Age burial area. Many examples of the mysterious **cart tracks** (see p 54) sweep over the plateau, though they tend to be elusive.

Further east along the coast another small inlet, **Mġarr ix-Xini**, has a minute shack of a café and splendid swimming and diving off its sandy beach and rocky ledges. Its **watchtower** was built in 1658, over 100 years too late to help the Gozitans shipped out from here by the Turks after their 1551 raid. It can be reached by a tortuous track from Sannat but is better signposted from Xewkija.

## Xewkija

This is one of Gozo's earliest villages and hard to miss since its inhabitants built the largest church on the island with by far the largest dome. Dedicated to St John the Baptist, this great enterprise—known as the **Rotunda**—is based on the design of Santa Maria della Salute in Venice. It was begun in 1951, built by voluntary labour and funded by weekly contributions from the village's 300 families, gold jewellery from the ladies, and donations from Xewkijans abroad. It was constructed around and over an 18C predecessor, which was dismantled only when the new church was in good enough shape to be used. Some of the exquisitely carved stonework from the old church, thought to have been the work of a Sicilian seeking sanctuary from trouble back home, is on display in a side chapel. Whether the dome is, as the people of Xewkija fervently believe, larger than Mosta's on Malta, or indeed of all other church domes in Europe, except for Rome's St Peter's and London's St Paul's, is still a hot issue involving complex calculations of girth and volume.

# Out west

The remains of a 19C arched aqueduct, marching alongside the road as you head west from Victoria to Gharb, represent a relative newcomer to this particularly tranquil corner of the island. Protected by cliffs and early coastal defences, small, farming communities developed earlier here than in most of the island and it is still bathed in a sleepy, rural atmosphere. Church, family and fields remain what matter most.

It is an appropriate setting for Malta's national shrine, **Ta' Pinu**, built near the spot where in 1883 a local peasant woman heard the voice of the Virgin telling her to pray in a small chapel close by. A friend confided that he too had heard the voice and together they prayed for his critically ill mother. She recovered, miracle cures multiplied, and so did the number of devotees visiting the chapel. By the 1920s, it was thought necessary to build a vast, neo-Romanesque church to accommodate them. The little chapel is still there, tucked behind the new shrine's altar. In a corridor on the right a poignant display of naive votive paintings, crutches, splints and baby clothes bears witness to many other escapes from sickness or peril.

Ta' Pinu is well marked on the Victoria to Għarb road. You will come across it too approaching through zigzagging lanes that lead to the shrine from the village of Għammar by way of Għasri, which is on sheltered ground just below the hilltop village of Żebbuġ. Since *żebbuġ* means olive in Maltese and Għasri stems from the verb to press, it seems likely that the Romans and Arabs had a thriving oil industry in these parts.

## Għarb

Għarb (the name means 'west') has a splendid array of 18C carved stone balconies and one of the island's most interesting churches. Dedicated to the Visitation, its foundation stone was laid in 1699, 20 years after the village became a parish and after the fledgling parishioners had been asked what kind of church they wanted. New rules stipulated new parish churches had to be built on high ground. (The cemetery chapel of Tas-Żejt is built on the site of the earlier chapel.) The village then was no more than a few well-trodden paths, a tiny chapel and a mere sprinkling of farmhouses, but their choice was far from parochial. They selected as their model the church of Sant' Agnese in Rome's Piazza Navona, designed by Francesco Borromini, one of the chief pioneers of the latest style, Baroque. The result, although not quite like the church in Rome, is enchanting. The main altarpiece, the *Visitation of the Madonna to St Elizabeth* by Malta's most gifted 18C painter, Francesco Zahra, was donated to the church by Grand Master Manoel de Vilhena. A new **Għarb Folklore Museum** (open Mon–Sat 09.00–16.00, Sun 09.00–noon. Entrance free) in the church square has a large and fascinating collection with some unusual extras, like a printing press and carriages, all beautifully displayed in a rambling old farmhouse that is as interesting as its contents.

## San Lawrenz and Dwejra

The main road to the neighbouring village of **San Lawrenz** passes the *Ta' Dbieġi Craft Village*, where hand-made lace, knitwear, jewellery, pottery and glass are on sale in a former British army camp recently given a facelift. The village church, dedicated to **St Lawrence** who was martyred on a gridiron, was built on the site of an ancient country chapel at the end of the 19C. The main altarpiece and the paintings of *Christ on the Cross, Our Lady of Pompeii, St Michael* and *St Joseph* are by Giuseppe Cali (1846–1930), a popular Maltese painter of Neapolitan descent. On the left of the square, a steep road winds down to Dwejra and a trio of dramatic rock formations caused by a series of geological faults.

**Dwerja**'s landscape is dramatic, summer or winter. Perhaps the most spectacular formation is the **Azure Window** (on the right), a massive, natural, stone archway with one mighty foot in the ocean. Behind it is the **Inland Sea** formed when the roof of a cave fell in and the sea poured through a cavernous breach in the cliffs. This pebble-beached crater, more modest in size than the name implies, makes an excellent, wind-free zone for early swimming, and small boats wait beside its jetty to take sightseers out through the breach to view the Azure Window from the sea and other attractions in the area.

*'Azure Window', Dwerja*

**Fungus Rock** (on the far left) guards a much larger and deeper collapsed cave. This rock was so prized by the Knights for the rare, red plant thought to be a fungus, which grew on its top, that they smoothed down its sides to prevent poaching and put a sentry on the box-and-pulley device that carried authorised gatherers to its summit. When dried and pounded the fungus was believed to be such a valuable cure for dysentery and haemorrhages that Grand Masters sent it as gifts to monarchs. Sadly, not only has the plant proved to be a parasite rather than a fungus but it is now thought to have no medicinal powers at all. The **watchtower**, built in 1651, to warn the Citadel of likely invasions and scare off pirates, was restored in 1998.

# Heading north

## *Marsalforn*

From Victoria a road heads straight to the coast and the bay of Marsalforn. Though larger than Xlendi and spreading further inland with its hotels, apartments and guest houses, it still retains much of its old fishing village charm. The undulating Marsalforn Valley is dominated by a conical hill bearing a statue of *Christ the Saviour*, his arms outstretched. Some years ago its concrete predecessor was demolished by lightning, which had the whole island holding its breath for a while. The present statue is made of fibreglass. This small resort is Gozo's chief summer playground and not only for tourists. Many Gozitans and Maltese close up their town houses and spend the hottest months here. With its rim of restaurants, cafés and small shops, and with sand, shingle or rock to swim from, Marsalforn offers plenty of choice.

Along the coast road to Qbajjar on the left of the bay, a fort (built in 1620, but sadly altered after being used recently as a restaurant) presides over the first stretch of shimmering **salt pans** that line this part of the coast. Some of these small troughs and reservoirs cut into the golden clifftops have been in use from Roman times and still produce tons of salt each year.

## Xagħra

The hilltop village of Xagħra (pronounced *shar ra*) can be reached from Marsalforn, but its prime attraction, the magnificent Stone Age temples of **Ġgantija** is easier to find when approached from the Mġarr–Victoria road. (Open Mon–Sat 08.30–16.30, Sun 08.30–15.00. Entrance fee.) These massive Neolithic structures are tucked just below the lip of the plateau at the entrance to the village. Together with their forecourt, raised on another huge wall, they cover 1000sq m and still rise to a height of 6m. (For background and details see *Ancient Malta*, p 51 and *The Neolithic Temples*, p 193.)

Ġgantija means giantess in Maltese and old folk tales attribute the temples to a huge woman who strode the island with a baby at her breast, the great stones balanced on her head and, to keep up her strength, a kilo of beans in her pocket. Gazing at the massive megaliths that encase the two temples it is easy to see why superhuman powers were thought necessary.

The Ġgantija admission ticket also gives access to the nearby windmill, **Il-Mithna ta' Kola**, built in 1725, which still has its original, wooden machinery and has recently been beautifully restored. There are ancient tools of many trades and a forge downstairs. The upper living quarters look as though the miller and his family are expected home any minute. (Open as Ġgantija.)

The main square of Xagħra is particularly attractive, with old shopfronts, tiny local bars and *Oleander*, one of the few good restaurants still providing genuine local dishes. The imposing church, dedicated to **Our Lady of Victories** in honour of Malta's Great Siege of 1565, was built in the first half of the 19C, with the dome and transept added 50 or so years later. The lavishly carved marble pulpit made in Lucca, Italy in 1955, so pleased the congregation that it led to marble facing on the church's entire interior. The large glass casket beneath the third altar in the left aisle contains bones from a Roman catacomb thought to be those of St Fortunatus, and a striking papier-mâché representation of this 3C soldier-martyr.

Signs near the church point to **Ninu's Cave** and **Xerri's Grotto**, which both have an astonishing assortment of stalagmites and stalactites in basements reached through the front doors of otherwise normal village houses. As the guides point out, there are all manner of strange formations, from giraffes and elephants' ears to what looks remarkably like streaky bacon.

A little further away in Triq Ġnien Xibla, on the road to the island's most spectacular beach, Ramla Bay, there is another village house with a surprising interior, the **Pomskizillious Museum of Toys** (open Mon–Sat 10.00–noon and 15.00–18.00. Mid-Oct to April, Sat only 10.00–13.00. Entrance fee). Its delightful collection, which includes several very fine doll's houses, is presided over by a life-size model of the 19C British artist and nonsense rhymer, Edward Lear, who provided its curious name. Having spent some time on Gozo, Lear described it as 'pomskizillious and gromphiberous, being as no words can describe its magnificence'.

## Ramla

A left turn at the end of the street takes you to **Calypso's Cave**, perched high in the cliff face next to a modern viewing platform, which looks down on the great sweep of Ramla's red-gold sands below.

It was here, according to Homer, that the fair nymph Calypso kept Odysseus in thrall for seven years after the hero of Troy washed up on the shore, clutching the last plank left from his great fleet. The cave now has none of the comforts described in the *Odyssey*, but it is said to be something of a labyrinth, dipping to sea level in places. Small boys, loitering hopefully, rent out candles to those prepared to clamber down its precarious shaft.

The remains of a luxury Roman villa are buried beneath the beach, but happily very few building permits have been handed out since then. Of the Knights' defences, all that remain are a section of a gun battery (on the left) and the wall they built across the bay, just below the surface of the sea, to scuttle Turkish galleys. Together with a now dismantled fort, they were enough to make Napoleon's men choose a precipitous, undefended gully on the other side of the headland when they invaded Gozo.

# Eastern approaches

## *Nadur*

On the left of the lushly fertile Ramla Valley a road climbs up to Nadur. This is Gozo's largest hilltop village. Its wealth, mainly due to those of its inhabitants who emigrated to Australia and North America, is evident in the size of its church, as large as many cathedrals elsewhere. This magnificent Baroque building dedicated to **St Peter and St Paul** was begun in 1760 and was still receiving major additions 150 years later. Two of its most prized treasures are on the right of the main altar. In the richly worked silver frame are relics thought to be of St Coronatus, and a papier-mâché model of this martyr dressed in silver armour. The gold-framed casket contains a copy of the chains with which St Peter was bound while confined in a Roman prison. The main altarpiece depicting Saints Peter and Paul on their way to martyrdom is from the workshop of Mattia Preti.

A sign in the square points to a new attraction, the **Kelinu Grima Maritime Museum** (open Mon–Sat, except public holidays, 09.00–16.45. Entrance fee). This astonishing collection, handsomely displayed in an old village house, is the result of one man's lifetime obsession with ships and those who manned them. Model sailing ships, naval emblems, uniforms, photographs and other paraphernalia span 300 years of maritime history. Until recently this hoard, gathered over 80 years by Kelinu Grima, was crammed into his house on the edge of the village.

Another interesting Nadur landmark is the **Kenuna Tower**, built in the 1850s on the spot where warning bonfires were lit when the Knights ruled the Islands. It has recently been topped with some very modern equipment to deal with global maritime distress signals, part of which, an eye-catching piece of golden metalwork, looks like a futuristic bird in flight.

North of the village is the island's prettiest bathing spot, **San Blas**, a miniature Ramla, with the same red-gold sand, shaded by tamarisks. However, the last stretch down, a narrow footpath plummeting between fig trees and lemon groves, is not for the faint- or weak-hearted.

A little further east, **Dahlet Qorrot** has a small sandy bay ringed with boathouses cut into its cliffs, and a fine place to walk along a wide ledge of rock on the right.

**Hondoq ir-Rummien** (the Valley of the Pomegranates, though there aren't many around any more) is reached via the neighbouring village of Qala. With its white-sand beach, the turquoise sea here rivals that of Comino's Blue Lagoon, which looks it in the eye across the strait. The now disused quarry in the cliffs here provided the stone for the crypt of Liverpool's Catholic cathedral. The tiny chapel above the bay is said to have been built for the benefit of Comino's small farming community. Mass was said here when the sea was too rough for a priest to cross over from Gozo and the farmers participated at long-range, gathered on the nearest bit of Comino's shore, a kilometre or so away.

In **Ghajnsielem**, on the main road from Mġarr to Victoria, the early 17C **St Cecilia's Tower** (near the Gozo Heliport outside Xewkija), built in 1613, stands in an area cleared in 12 days in 1943 to make an airstrip for the Allied invasion of Sicily. It is the lone survivor of the four towers that once guarded Xewkija and takes its name from the small 16C pitched-roofed chapel nearby.

Also on this road, metres away from the chapel is *Gozo Heritage*, operating from a particularly fine old farmhouse. It offers a brisk trot through 7000 years of the island's history in the company of fibreglass models, spectral voices and lighting effects. (Open Mon–Sat 09.00–16.30. Entrance fee.)

Ghajnsielem's great neo-Gothic church, with its rebel spire in an island of domes, was begun in 1922 and finished with a flourish in 1978 when the parish priest won the National lottery and donated Lm10,000 for its new altar. It is dedicated to the **Black Madonna of Loreto**.

# Comino

The island of Comino, little more than a picturesque large rock measuring 2.5sq m, sits in the channel between Malta and Gozo. It has great stark, sun-baked charm, pretty bays, a small hotel and a handful of permanent residents who rarely number more than five. It has no roads, just footpaths and one ancient off-road vehicle to do the chores. It also has the Blue Lagoon, an enchanted sheltered stretch of water that draws yachts and day cruise boats with their picnickers and swimmers.

## History of Comino

While Malta and Gozo have Neolithic temples and long illustrious histories spanning the centuries, tiny Comino (known in Maltese as Kemmuna after the cumin that once grew here), although a part of the larger picture, ˙ained relatively ignored. There are Punic traces but there were no settle- and the bays were too small to accommodate more than just a ship or ˙ne, cerainly no fleet of any stature.

˙er hand, Comino's bays were suitable for corsairs and pirates. ˙e pirates from the Barbary Coast of North Africa sheltered ˙ur forays on the rich ships trading in the Mediterranean, and it ˙ base when times were lean and a lightning descent on Gozo or northern Malta would lead to the capture of the farming community who could then be sold in the slave markets that flourished on the great sea's coastal towns to the east.

Comino's only known resident of note was a 13C eccentric Jewish sage and professed prophet from Saragossa. Known as the Spanish Messiah, **Abraham ben Samuel Abulafia** lived in caves on the island in dire poverty between 1285 and 1291, having fled Rome before the sentence of death by burning could be carried out. His crime was that of having caused the death of Pope Nicholas III. Abulafia was explaining to him his quest on earth—the creation of a new religion that united Christianity, Judaism and Islam.—when the Pope apparently had an apoplectic stroke at the mere thought of such blasphemy, and expired. It was on Comino that Abulafia wrote his *Kabbala* philosophy and his major work, the *Book of the Sign*.

In 1416, in an effort to rid the channel of corsairs, the Maltese petitioned King Alfonso V of Spain for help and in response he instituted a wine tax to raise money locally to pay for a fortified watchtower. However, he spent the money elsewhere and it was not until 1618, after the arrival of the Order of St John, that Grand Master Alof de Wignacourt gave instructions for St Mary's Tower to be built. The Grand Master hoped that this significant, generous gesture of installing a military presence would lay the foundation for the colonisation of the island. But although for a brief spell a community of nearly 200 formed, Comino remained steadfastly a game reserve with wild boar and hares. An edict published in 1695 declared that any trespasser found with gun, net, dog or ferret would be sentenced to three years as a galley slave on one of the Order's ships.

In 1800, after the British had answered Malta's call for help in chasing out the French, 2000 French prisoners-of-war were interned here in a tented camp until their repatriation. Then in World War One the British built a small isolation hospital by St Mary's Tower, in an effort to prevent any contagious diseases carried by wounded servicemen being introduced to Malta. These buildings now make up Comino's 'village'. During World War Two, the British navy used the island for torpedo practice.

## *Getting there*

If you are staying at the *Comino Hotel*, your arrival is in their hands, and their own brightly painted ferry will collect you on the quay at Ċirkewwa on Malta's northern coast or on the jetty in Mġarr, Gozo, alongside the car ferries. You can use the hotel's boat too if you want to enjoy the facilities of the hotel just for the day, or if you plan simply to explore the island and picnic there. There is an all-in day rate for anyone wanting to enjoy the hotel's facilities or a modest ferry charge if you just want to get to the island and have an independent day. For timings and prices, call the *Comino Hotel*: ☎ 529821-9.

A regular ferry runs in summer months from Marfa, a short distance before you get to Ċirkewwa. This is the old Gozo ferry landing and it now offers a regular hourly service to the Blue Lagoon (Lm2 return).

A similar service often runs from Mġarr, its schedule and regularity dependent on the boat owners' enthusiasm. Enquire on the quay.

Another route to the island is on board the day-trip boats that leave from Marsalforn, Mġarr, Xlendi, Buġibba and Sliema. A number, like the red-painted *Captain Morgan* flotilla, have a bar and buffet service. All sail to the Blue Lagoon.

## The Blue Lagoon

The waters around Comino are clear and clean, perfect for any sea sport, especially diving and snorkelling. In the sheltered Blue Lagoon, with its white sand seabed, the water is a superbly inviting shade of turquoise. As a result the lagoon is very popular indeed and inclined to be overcrowded with pleasure craft, particularly at weekends. Fortunately the main swimming area is cordoned off by ropes and marker buoys, keeping out speedboats and intrusive jet skis.

If you have a boat, it is best to visit the Blue Lagoon before 11.00 when the first pleasure craft arrive or after 17.00 when they have all departed. (although in the summer months the day-trip boats often disturb the tranquillity with their late-night on-board barbecues and loud discos).

As you enter the Lagoon the small rock formation to your right is the 'island' of **Cominotto** (Kemmunet, to the Maltese). This is Comino's even tinier sister.

## Walking and diving

In the winter and spring months walking across the island can be very pleasant, especially from March onwards when the wild flowers are in their profusion and the wild thyme is covered in purple blossom. There is no longer a shop here, so you will need to take a picnic. Although much of Comino is designated as a bird sanctuary, a number of *kaċċatur* (see p 79) pay no heed to the ruling. If you see a hide, nets or a man with a gun, keep your distance.

A walk in the summer can hardly be recommended. The heat can be intense and there is no shade.

Divers have identified three good sub-aqua locations. For beginners they suggest the reef off the west part of the coast, close to the Blue Lagoon and **Għar Għana**. For intermediate divers, especially those armed with a camera, there are caves off **Ghemieri**, the headland protecting Santa Marija bay. And for the proficient, on the southwestern tip of the island at **Ras l-Irqieqa** there is a sheer dive of 40m. The currents in the channel appear to keep the waters here generously stocked with fish.

The strange rafts you see bobbing off the southern coast of the island, facing Malta, are not a wreck. They are the pens that make up a fish farm.

## St Mary's Tower

The classical square fort on the southwestern cliffs overlooking the Gozo channel was designed by Vittorio Cassar and built in 1618 on the orders of Grand Master Alof de Wignacourt to form part of the defensive chain of forts and towers stretching from the furthermost tip of Gozo to southern Malta. Its view commands the main sea crossing between the Islands and was designed for a garrison of 30 soldiers. In a neglected state today, it nonetheless manages to look imposing. By night, floodlit in a variety of soft colours, it creates a romantic image when seen from passing ferries and boats.

## The village

In fact there is no village, just the converted old isolation hospital near St Mary's Tower, now providing a number of homes and what once passed for a shop. In its heyday the central square was known as Liberty Square and two rocky paths leading out from it were Battery Street and Congreve Street.

On the track that takes you to Santa Marija Bay is the island's charming little

**chapel** dedicated to Our Lady said to date back to the 14C. Mass is often said here at weekends by a priest who comes from Qala in Gozo (although Comino comes under the Gozo parish of Ghajnsielem).

The island's police station, an attractive, whitewashed, one-man office, is above the boathouse in Santa Marija Bay. You can tell when it's open: the duty policeman (also from Gozo) flies the red and white Maltese flag. ☎ 573960.

## Santa Marija and San Niklaw bays

On the coast facing Gozo, these are the tiny island's best sandy beaches. **San Niklaw** has been taken over by the *Comino Hotel* and is currently only for residents or non-residents who use the hotel's facilities for the day. (It is best to pre-book this. Their charge varies season to season but it includes a buffet lunch as well as full use of beach and pool facilities. Ferry crossings extra.)

The four-star hotel and its outcrop of bungalow-type accommodation is popular with honeymooners looking for escape and with watersport fans. There is a dive school and tennis tuition and the hotel is comfortable in a simple manner though not particularly attractive. Since coming into Maltese ownership, standards and facilities are much improved and future plans will add yet more to its individuality.

**Santa Marija** is not a private bay; and as there are no mobile kiosks selling refreshments, it is a quiet, uncrowded beach—except at weekends when the gin-palace boats arrive. The sand is good but there are submerged rocks in the shallows that need avoiding, and sometimes seaweed may mar aesthetic qualities. Take a picnic and lots of water and use the tamarisks for shade.

# Index

If you would like more information about
Blue Guides please complete the form below
and return it to

Blue Guides
A&C Black (Publishers) Ltd
Freepost
Eaton Socon
Huntingdon
Cambridgeshire
PE19 8EZ

or fax it to us on 020 7831 8478
or email us at travel@acblack.co.uk

Name ......................................................................................

..............................................................................................

Address ..................................................................................

..............................................................................................

..............................................................................................

..............................................................................................

..............................................................................................

..............................................................................................